HIDING

IN

PLAIN SIGHT

HIDING

IN

PLAIN SIGHT

by

Ken Bowers

BONNEVILLE BOOKS™
Springville, Utah

ISBN 13: 978-1-55517-473-6

Published by Bonneville Books, an imprint of
Cedar Fort, Inc., 2373 W. 700 S., Springville, UT, 84663
Distributed by Cedar Fort, Inc., www.cedarfort.com

Typeset by Kristin Nelson
Cover design by Adam Ford
Cover design © 2000 by Lyle Mortimer

Printed in the United States of America

10 9 8 7 6 5 4 3 2 1

Printed on acid-free paper

ACKNOWLEDGMENTS

I wish to give thanks to Dr. Clarence Waterfall for his help on the technical aspects of the book, as well as Suzie Chapman, Karen Madrid, along with John Sampson for his encouragement and legal advice.

Let me acknowledge my father who gave me the spark to know about secret combinations. His desire to know the truth was instilled in me early and has never left. I also wish to thank Joseph O. Stradling for his spiritual advice and Dr. W. Cleon Skousen for his encouragement.

Perhaps most of all, I wish to thank the men who we call the Founding Fathers for their inspiration that brought forth this nation dedicated to the principle of human liberty. In the history of the world, there have been few men as selfless as these.

DEDICATION

This book is lovingly dedicated to Amy, Laura, Michael, Paul, Alyson and Kurt.

My heroes.

Hiding In Plain Sight

In the intelligence community, it is taught that the best way to hide something is to place it in open view. As an example of (this), when Germany wanted to hide its prize new Messerschmidt fighter plane in 1938, the aircraft was put on display at the Paris Air Show. While secret agents and spies were collecting information from hollow tree trunks and from behind loose bricks in a wall, the information they sought was staring them right in the face.

Dr. John Coleman

Conspirator's Hierarchy: The Story of the Committee of 300

Table of Contents

More alarming than the ride of Paul Revere...This eye-opening book takes "Conspiracy" ...into the realm of well-documented information.

—Richard L. Wilde,

National Chairman of the Principles and Issues Committee,

Independent American Party

"Hiding in Plain Sight" finally puts many of the missing pieces of the puzzle together. Ken Bowers has simply and precisely elevated the awareness of different secret groups and forces that control the world's economies, agendas and our very future. A must-read for protecting and educating all Americans.

— C.E. Cornell, international businessman

Preface

The opinions and views expressed herein belong solely to the author. As you read this book, you will notice that there are no footnotes. I enjoy reading. While reading, I check out the references that come from the footnotes. It is always a pet peeve to have to either look at the end of the chapter or the end of the book to check out a footnote reference, while keeping a finger on the page being read, then afterwards re-establishing the flow of the text in my mind, only to go to the next footnote two sentences later and repeat the process. To obviate that inconvenience, all references will automatically be included at the end of the quotation allowing the reader to continue without interruption. From time to time I also add bold type to quoted passages I wish to emphasize.

The material presented in this book comes from a lifetime of study on the subject of conspiracy, the Constitution, liberty and related subjects. However, an important point should be made here. That is, some conclusions may be incorrect. That arises from the fact that it is extremely difficult to uncover the truth about secret combinations. They have a great deal of cunning in covering their tracks. It is an arduous task to pry out bits of evidence here and there. I have attempted to make sure of at least two independent sources for most of my conclusions. But, as I stated, due to the inherent difficulties of uncovering the truth, there may be some inaccuracies.

Please do not therefore come to the conclusion that the premise is wrong just because some items may be inaccurate. The basic premise of this book is that there exists an all-encompassing secret conspiracy that exerts effective but not total control (which will be explained later), over all nations, kindreds, tongues and people. The conspiracy has been prophesied throughout history and is here in full force today. A corollary to this premise is that this combination is able to hide in plain sight by deceiving most people into thinking that there is no combination.

This book will not try to fill in every single detail about this great combination. Much of the subject matter discussed herein is already found in other publications. After making a particular claim and furnishing relevant proof, the reader will be pointed to one or more references to reinforce that claim. My approach is to give a general overview of the conspiracy and let the reader fill in the details via his or her own study. To motivate you, dear reader, to research the subject and find the truth for yourself is my object. That would give me the greatest pleasure.

It may be hard to believe but the war in Heaven over man's free agency is still going on. In fact, it never stopped and is being waged today right before our eyes. We are involved in it, even if we don't think we are or don't want to be. We will be judged by God on how well we fought to establish the cause of liberty. The war will increase in intensity in the future until Christ comes again to establish a thousand year millennial reign of peace. It will be a severe test. May we, with God's help, be ready for it.

Introduction

Don't you wish that all mankind dwelt in peace? Wouldn't it be great to be able to trust all people, confident that everyone esteems his neighbor as himself? How wonderful it would be to see a world built on love and kindness, forbearance and charity. Or that we could put all locksmiths, police departments, criminal courts, armies and soup kitchens out of business. Through the Scriptures, we know that Christ will come again to establish His kingdom of universal peace and we long for it. The righteous of all ages pray for it.

However, between now and that time will be the tribulations of the last days. They have been prophesied by countless men who were moved upon by the Holy Ghost, both ancient and modern. This period of time, some of which we have already passed through, will not be a happy time. It is and will be a time where Satan reigns, evil will flourish and the saints will have to patiently endure it. It therefore behooves us to be prepared for it. To be forewarned is one way to be prepared. That is the reason for this book.

Please consider the following quotation:

Satan is making war against all the wisdom that has come to men through their ages of experience. He is seeking to overturn and destroy the very foundations upon which society, government, and religion rest. He aims to have men adopt theories and practices which induced their forefathers, over the ages, to adopt and try, only to be discarded by them when found unsound, impractical, and ruinous. **He plans to destroy freedom—economic, political, and religious, and to set up in place thereof the greatest, most widespread, and most complete tyranny that has ever oppressed men. He is working under such perfect disguise that many do not recognize either him or his methods.** There is no crime he would not commit, no debauchery he would not set up, no plague he would not send, no heart he would not break, no life he would not take, no soul he would not destroy. **He comes as a thief in the night; he is a wolf in sheep's clothing. Without their knowing it, the people are being**

urged down paths that lead only to destruction. Satan never before had so firm a grip on this generation as he has now.

First Presidency Heber J. Grant, J. Reuben Clark Jr., David O. McKay,
"The Message of the First Presidency to the Church,"
Conference Report, October 1942, (14).

According to the above quotation, Satan will try to destroy economic, political and religious freedom. In our day he has established three kinds of secret combinations to accomplish that task. They are: economic combinations, political combinations and religious combinations that all work together. This book is written in the attempt to explain them and their purposes.

In order to be forewarned of the coming times, it will be necessary to broach the spiritually depressing subject of evil. Once a friend asked the question: "Why study something evil like secret combinations? Isn't it much better to dwell on the positive than on the negative?" The answer lies in a quotation from Ezra Taft Benson:

I am not here to tickle your ears, to entertain you; I will talk to you frankly and honestly. The message I bring is not a happy one, but it is the truth. And time is always on the side of truth. As the German Philosopher Goethe said, "Truth must be repeated again and again, because error is constantly being preached round about." ...As a people, we love sweetness and light. Especially sweetness. Ralph Waldo Emerson said that "Every mind must make a choice between truth and repose." **Those who will learn nothing from history are condemned to repeat it.** This we are doing in the Americas today. George Washington stated, "Truth shall ultimately prevail, where there are pains taken to bring it to light..."

"Stand Up For Freedom",
Talk by Ezra Taft Benson,
1965

So we must learn the lessons of history or we are doomed to repeat it. Unfortunately, history is often slanted to one side and what we learn in school is not necessarily accurate. That is because the very nature of evil demands that it try to cover itself with respectability and taint the truth with a whitewash. Human history has often been subjected to 'revision'.

Therefore, much of what you read here may put history and current events in a different light. As a matter of fact, the contents of this book may be starkly different from what you have heard. Please do not let that discourage you. The pursuit of truth is worth it.

As you read, let the Holy Ghost be your guide. Pray about it and He will reveal the truth of what is said here and of all things.

Punch and Judy

Do you remember the Punch and Judy shows? They are too old for today's kids to recall but they were very popular with grandparents, especially in Europe. Actually, they have been around for centuries as entertainment to delight children of all ages. The proprietors set up a small stage on a sidewalk or in a park and put on a puppet show featuring, of course, the Punch and Judy hand puppets. No matter what the script, the puppets sooner or later wind up hitting or battling each other which gives the kids a scare and stimulates their imaginations. They related to children of all ages and were very popular.

Unknown to the kids, the puppets were an innocent deception. Each of the two hand puppets were controlled by an invisible person under the stage, one puppet per hand. To the kids however, the puppets, the stage and story seemed real. But no matter what it seemed to be, it was all fiction. The puppets weren't real, neither the script; and the outcome was carefully orchestrated.

Suppose now that the basic idea behind that puppet show could be found in real life. That for instance, people, organizations and even governments were really controlled this way. To illustrate the point, let's pretend that Punch and Judy had different names. For instance, let's call Punch "Communism" and Judy "The Free World." Incredible! Or how about this–Punch is "Israel" and Judy is "The Arab World." Or, Punch is the "Democratic Party" and Judy the "Republican Party." And to a certain extent, all these labels apply! I realize how hard it is to hear something so far from normal everyday thinking. The common reaction is to say "It can't be true."

Something so extraordinary as the above is hard to accept. As a matter of fact, the idea of a world-wide conspiracy is still hard for me to believe after studying it for almost forty years. But let us examine the evidence slowly and deliberately. As it comes together piece by piece, you will find that there is more to the conspiracy scenario than meets the eye.

To return to the Punch and Judy idea, this is indeed a radical concept–that there is a 'person' that controls many world events, history and even governments from the shadows. He creates revolutions and hatred on a global scale. This 'person' is Satan, who works through a combination of secret and not-so-secret organizations here on earth to bring into fruition his goal which is a one-world government.

An important point must be made at this time. There is, indeed, a conspiracy that controls world governments from behind the scenes. But it is effective control, not total control. Remember that concept for it is very important. The majority of the world doesn't believe in a world-wide conspiracy. Many scoff at the idea that we are being controlled when it appears that we dominate our own destiny to a large extent.

If there were a great conspiracy that ruled the world, some say, the world would look more like Stalinist Russia or the book 1984 by George Orwell. Since most people vote, live their lives as they wish, freely worship as they please, travel where they want and engage in whatever business or profession that suits them, this conspiracy–if it exists–is not very powerful. Don't we freely debate the issues, presenting both sides evenly through our 'free press'? Aren't people able to express whatever opinion they want? Most importantly, the very fact that this book is being published and sold proves there is no conspiracy for if there were, this book would be banned and I would be shot. The world just doesn't look like it should if there were such a conspiracy.

But the above is an example of total control. Effective control is more subtle. **The conspiracy controls the overall direction in which humanity is moving, not our everyday activities**. In other words, they try to gradually manipulate humanity in the direction of a one-world government. To show an example of how we're moving in a gradual direction that is already laid out for us, let's examine the gun control issue. Fifty years ago gun control in America was non-existent. Anybody could own almost whatever kind of gun they wanted, as many as they wanted and nobody thought anything about it. Today it's a question of how many and what kind of guns will the population be allowed to own and under what circumstances. A few years down the road, if things go the conspirators way, the issue will be if anyone at all will own any guns under any conditions.

That kind of manipulation is called 'gradual habituation' and the conspirators do it all the time. Gradual habituation is so piecemeal that many think it is merely the natural evolution of public opinion. But the evidence demonstrates that a perspective favorable to the conspiracy is first created by them. Then slowly and inexorably it is placed before us again and again until we are conditioned to gradually habituate our thought processes to accept the end result they want all along. In this case, it is a gun-free society. They want that because a populace with no means of self-defense is easily conquered. Gradual habituation is perhaps what President Grant was talking about when he said:

...Without their knowing it, the people are being urged down paths that lead only to destruction. (See the quotation at the beginning of the Introduction).

Another example of effective control is the publication of this book itself! For the time being, the conspirators couldn't care less that this book is published exposing their scheme to the world. That's because they already influence much of the very public opinion this book tries to reach. The conspirators diffuse anti-conspiracy efforts by their domination of the media and the public opinion the media tries to influence. Years ago rich businessmen purchased the major (but not all) news media. After acquiring the media, they slowly cultivated the public into the belief that a global conspiracy was 'fringe element' thinking.

Manipulation of public opinion on this issue is so profound and complete that when anyone tries to bring the truth about the conspiracy to light, negative labels carefully cultivated over the years such as kook, right wing extremist and nut automatically spring into action. This name calling has the effect of turning the public off to positive evidence of their machinations. There are many books, tapes, videos and other presentation media that provide clear substantiation of a conspiracy, but few people bother with them because most have been conditioned to reject anything that smells of a global conspiracy. Therefore, any effort to bring the truth to light swims against the current of a strong media pressure that is subtle, effective and very powerful. That means that it is hard but not impossible to reach the public with the truth.

Gradual habituation and manipulation of public opinion are but two examples of effective control. Effective control does not guarantee that the conspiracy will win every battle but they accept occasional defeats so long as the overall direction stays the same, which is the road towards one-world government.

Although it's hard to conceive of a conspiracy that would have to be vast and pervasive in order to be so all powerful as I'm suggesting, it is nevertheless true, as President Benson stated in General Conference, October, 1988:

> Secret combinations lusting for power, gain, and glory are flourishing. A secret combination that seeks to overthrow the freedom of all lands, nations and countries is increasing its evil influence and **control over America and the entire world**.

> *Ensign*, Nov. 1988, (86).

The evidence suggests that many people in powerful positions throughout the world, be it in finance, politics, religion, media, foundations, labor, capital, entertainment, etc. are in secret agreement to bring about a one-world government even though in public they sound like they all have different opinions about the future. To illustrate that idea, read the next two quotations, one from the leader of the Free World, the other from a former leader of the Communist World. This will be your introduction to a Punch and Judy show right before your very eyes.

> What is at stake is more than one small country, it is a big idea—a **new world order**...to achieve to universal aspirations of mankind...based upon shared principles and the rule of law...The illumination of a thousand points of light...The winds of change are with us now.

> President George Bush
> In his State of the Union Address
> during the Gulf War.

> We are beginning to see practical support. And this is a very significant sign of the movement towards a new era, a new age...We see both in our country and elsewhere...ghosts of the old thinking...When we rid ourselves of their presence, we will be better able to move toward a new world order...relying on the relevant mechanisms of the United Nations.

> Former Soviet President Gorbachev,
> At the Middle East Peace Talks in Madrid, 1991.

These men are supposed to be opponents politically (democracy vs. communism), economically (capitalism vs. socialism), and religiously (judeo-Christian vs. atheism). It is almost impossible for two cultures and political systems to be more different and yet these leaders are both promoting the same idea, a new world order. Whatever the New World Order is, why are they both promoting it? What kind of political differences would they have to espouse in order to get them to reach opposite conclusions for the future of the world? What about all the political, economic and religious opposition they supposedly represent?

Perhaps the whole capitalism vs. socialism, democracy vs. communism argument is just a smokescreen. Perhaps it is a Punch and Judy show. On the surface it seems that the Free World and Communism have been in opposition to each other for years, but when one digs a little deeper another view emerges. You will see this scenario happen again and again. It's much like the scene in the Wizard of Oz when the terrifying image of the Wizard tells Dorothy not to pay any attention to the man behind the curtain. We are supposed to think that the image is more important than reality.

We need to become aware of this conspiracy and warn others. The Doctrine and Covenants tells us plainly that it is our duty to do so (DC 123:13-15). Some brave people throughout history have taken great pains to bring the truth to light. They displayed great courage swimming against the current of popular opinion. Some have even been killed.

We should cultivate a deep appreciation of our founding fathers, whose single-minded dedication to the ideal of liberty gave us the freedoms we now enjoy. Many of them paid dearly for that dedication in property and lives during the Revolutionary War. They redeemed the land by shedding their blood. Let their unselfish sacrifices laid upon the altar of liberty always be cherished.

Finally, may God bless this our native land, a promised land, a choice land, whose Constitution now hangs by a thread as prophesied by Brother Joseph.

Chapter One

Wherefore, O ye Gentiles, **it is wisdom in God that these things should be shown unto you,** that thereby ye may repent of your sins, **and suffer not that these murderous combinations shall get above you,** which are built up to get power and gain—
Ether 8:23

There is NO Conspiracy, so There!

The Book of Mormon teaches us many things. It not only teaches about things that have been but also about things that will come to pass. The foreknowledge of what will come to pass is represented in the Book in two ways. 1—Through prophecy. It has been said that direct prophecy makes up almost one-third of the Book of Mormon. 2—Through historical simile. That is, the Lord made sure that certain historical events of the Nephites and Lamanites were included in the Book because He knew that something similar to what happened to the Nephites in the past would happen to the Latter-day Saints in our day. In other words, historical simile. These particular events were included as a guide for us to follow, that is, by following in a similar manner what the righteous did in those days to solve their problems, we will be able to extricate ourselves from comparable problems in our day. It is true to some extent that history repeats itself.

Perhaps the desire to help us with our problems today is what prompted Moroni to pen these poignant words:

Condemn me not because of mine imperfection, neither my father, because of his imperfection, neither them who have written before him; but rather give thanks unto God that he hath made manifest unto you our imperfections, that ye may learn to be more wise than we have been. (Mor. 9:31)

Hopefully, we who inherited the Book of Mormon will learn to be wiser than they. We know that they tried to warn us about conditions in the latter days on many occasions. Here are a few examples: Moroni warned us about the false doctrine of infant baptism in Moroni 8. Nephi warned about false sectarian doctrines of churches in our day in 2Nephi 28. In the same chapter, verse 28 he warned about the complacency and apathy of members of the church in our day when they say: "All is well in Zion, yea, Zion prospereth, all is well." These and other warnings come to us today because these prophets and others throughout the Book of Mormon saw our day. They loved us and cared about what we have gone through and will go through.

For that reason Moroni gave us the warning found at the heading of this chapter and which comes from Ether 8:23. The warning is quite specific and plain, about as plain as words can be. Let's go over those words and digest them bit by bit.

"Wherefore, O ye **Gentiles**..."

That means us. In other places in the Book of Mormon, we gentiles are referred to as the agents through whom the Book of Mormon will come to the Lamanites, their descendants. For instance, read 3Nephi 21:2-7. So the use of the word gentile in Ether 8:23 is indeed referring to the people of our day, both members and non-members.

"...it is wisdom in God that **these things** should be shown unto you,"

What things? The things that Ether 8 is talking about. And what is Ether chapter 8 talking about? Secret combinations in the days of the Jaredites. The whole chapter deals with, and only with, secret combinations. That is borne out by the next sentence:

"...that thereby ye may repent of your sins, and suffer not that these murderous combinations shall get above you..."

So it is wisdom in God that He show us gentiles of the last days about evil secret combinations. Now why would God want to show us ugly stuff like that? Shouldn't we concentrate only on the good? Or, as Elder Benson said, "sweetness and light, especially sweetness." The answer to that is that while we should concentrate on the good things of the Gospel, we should also know about evil.

Why? Because we don't have to go out of our way in life to know evil, it will manifest itself to us without our consent. When the author was pursuing a degree at Phoenix College in Phoenix, Arizona, people would approach him from time to time and either ask for drugs or offer to sell him drugs. Drugs were so prevalent that anyone was susceptible to being approached about it at any time. Surely many of the readers can relate numerous stories of their own to substantiate the truth about evil seeking us out without our consent. That is because God has **allowed** Satan to tempt us to see if we will obey God of our own volition or not. And Satan, wanting our destruction, will try his best to see that we are tempted as much as he can tempt us.

The reason God allows us to be tempted is found in DC 29:39:
And it must needs be that the devil should tempt the children of men, or they could not be agents unto themselves; for if they never should have bitter they could not know the sweet—

That **does not mean** that we have a right to give in to temptation, just because it is allowed to be shown us. Nor does it mean that we should seek evil out to know about it. As was mentioned earlier, we don't have to seek evil out, it will come to us. But it is important to be tempted since it is a necessary step to godhood. But one good thing about knowing about evil is that we can prepare and avoid it if we know about it. Otherwise, it is possible for us to be deceived into supporting evil without knowing it to be evil. God will not help us if we do not prepare beforehand to know what evil is and how it tries to deceive us. Which brings us to the theme of this chapter.

Despite the repeated warnings from prophets ancient and modern as to the reality of secret combinations in the last days, most people, including (unfortunately) many members of the Church, do not believe in them. One good brother said to me, "There is no conspiracy because this nation was founded by God and He would never let some evil conspiracy take us over."

What he said is both true and false. It is true that the Constitution was ordained of God. The Doctrine and Covenants bears ample witness to that. (D&C 98:5,6; 101:77,80.) But it is not true that God will always defend this nation. He will *not* uphold any nation in sin, and the Book of Mormon states unequivocally that if the United States of America, in these last days, ripens in iniquity, we will be destroyed. (Ether 2:9-12.)

The truth is that there have been secret combinations since the beginning of time. There were secret combinations in the days of Adam and Eve (Moses 5:51). There were secret combinations among the Jaredites (Ether 8). After that, secret combinations destroyed the nation of the Nephites (Helaman 2:13,14; 7:4,5). Throughout history, Satan has *always* set up secret combinations in all ages to counteract God's Kingdom or influence on the earth. *That is the way Satan operates.* And you can take that statement to the bank. If you still doubt it, please re—read the statement of President Benson in the Introduction. And yet, denial of the truth keeps cropping up time and time again. "There is nothing wrong with our government. They really look our for us. And there certainly is NO conspiracy, so there!"

Today, when one mentions the word "conspiracy," most people automatically think of a Communist conspiracy or the mafia or maybe even the KKK but not in an all pervasive, controlling, binding conspiracy that has an enormous international scope. But the scriptural evidence is overwhelming. Also look at 1Nephi chapter 14.

Faced with this scriptural evidence, one would think that at least the Latter-day Saints would understand and believe the truth but the sad fact is that most don't. Many who believe in a latter-day secret combination have been ridiculed and scoffed at from time to time by people in and out of the church.

So why is it that throughout the history of the world, secret combinations have *always* been around (as proved in the scriptures) but most people think that they *cannot* and *absolutely do not* exist today? Why are people so unwilling to accept both the scriptural and modern day evidence of a conspiracy? There are many reasons for this and some of the more important ones are listed below.

Here are some ideas as to why there cannot be a conspiracy today.

1. The conspiracy premise is too simplistic.

That statement says that whatever happens in today's complex world can't be simply attributed to some all-powerful conspiracy. Most people say that the belief in a world-wide secret combination is escapist. That is, rather than deal with life's complexity, those who believe in a conspiracy simply try to blame all the world's problems on a nebulous "conspiracy" concept they can't control and due to its secretiveness, is hard to prove.

The statement that the conspiracy idea is simplistic, dodges the real issue. The real issue is not simplicity nor complexity but truth and accuracy. Deferring the issue of accuracy for later, let's now confront the question of simplicity. The answer is found in the magazine, *The New American*, "Conspiracy" issue, 1997 edition:

Occam's razor is a well-established test for reaching a conclusion based on limited information. It is named for the prominent 14th century philosopher William of Occam. Formally termed the "principle of parsimony," it suggests that the least complicated explanation for a phenomenon that fits the known facts is most likely to be the correct one. Responsible advocates of the conspiracy scenario contend that the least complicated explanation for many of the destructive trends in politics, economics, morality, and other key areas over the past two centuries is that a secretive, amoral, well-organized movement has been striving relentlessly to make it happen.

Occam's razor, or the principle of parsimony, is used by law enforcement personnel, lawyers, scientists, judges and others who try to discover the truth from information that is deliberately withheld, covered up or by its nature, just hard to expose. They use it all the time. They use it successfully and it has proven to be a valuable tool in researching the truth. But in the realm of the idea of a world wide conspiracy, debunkers conveniently overlook Occam's Razor and accuse those who believe in conspiracy as being "too simplistic." So it seems that this test can be used by anyone as the need arises, but can't be used to explain the trends we see in the world today as a conspiracy.

However, as stated before, the real issue is not simplicity but truth and accuracy. Those who disbelieve the conspiracy scenario try to convince the populace that a gigantic conspiracy is too simplistic an idea to be true; therefore, just forget about it. That, in itself, is a rhetorical device called a red herring. In debating circles and in a courts of law, a common practice is to throw the opponent off the correct scent or notion by giving them an false scent or idea to pursue. The red herring or false scent is "A world-wide conspiracy too simplistic," but the correct question to ask is, "Is the conspiracy idea true and accurate?" If the statement that there is a world wide conspiracy is true, then it doesn't matter if the conspiracy idea is simple or complex. The issue of simplicity actually becomes tangential. As I said, the real issue is truth and accuracy.

But that dredges up a conundrum for those who disbelieve conspiracy theory. If they say that a world-wide conspiracy is a lie, they would eventually have to face the inevitable evidence. Those behind the scenes know that if anyone really investigated the conspiracy idea for themselves, they too would come to the realization that there is ample evidence to show that a conspiracy does, indeed, exist. The information is out there.

The problem is that the conspirators can't cover it all up nor destroy all the evidence. They therefore deftly dance around the issue. Their behavior is actually very subtle. In avoiding the real issue of truth and accuracy, they don't call it a 'lie', they just say "It can't be true because it's too simplistic." This red herring is effective.

Please investigate for yourself and find out what many others have already discovered, that there is indeed a very powerful, subtle and pervasive combination in our day that, in the words of President Benson, "is increasing its evil influence and control over America and the entire world."

2.If there were a giant, world-wide conspiracy, our press would alert us of it. After all, we do have a "free press."

This statement is both true and false. It will be covered in greater detail in the chapter called, "All The News That's Fit to Print," but while it's true that our press is free from government control to a great extent, that does not mean that it is not controlled. To reiterate, the press was bought years ago by conspiring people who wanted to cover up their conspiracy. All mainstream media is owned by the conspirators and does their bidding. Therefore, you will never hear of the details of this conspiracy from the mainline media. Some of the people in the media are controlled by the decisions of editors and publishers while others are willing actors in this giant Punch and Judy show. However, the conspirators do not control *all* media. There are some outlets that tell the truth.

3.A gigantic, monolithic conspiracy such as you suggest cannot exist because there would be too many personality clashes, philosophical differences, ego conflicts, and infighting for it to be either secret or successful.

That statement, again, is both true and false. It is true that there are personality clashes, philosophical differences, ego conflicts and infighting. As a matter of fact, the conspirators will occasionally assassinate one another, reminiscent of the mafia. But in such cases, these political murders are covered up by the controlled press so that we don't hear about it.

The truth is that the conspiracy is both monolithic and fractionated. That is, the participants in this conspiracy are extremely united in one sense, but very much divided in another. How so?

The conspirators are completely united as far as overall strategy and goals are concerned, but there is considerable difference of opinion as to tactics to achieve those goals. There have been instances when the differences over tactics were so great that they actually came to blows in their planning meetings. But make no mistake about it—they are out to control the world. In that respect, they act as one. So as far as you and I are concerned, what difference does it make which tactics are used, if the end result (one-world government), is the same?

To support the claim of unity amidst discordance look to examples from history. The Greek city-states during the age of Athenian democracy show a history of petty infighting, bickering and warfare amongst themselves until a common foe (like Persia) threatened. When that happened, the city-states became as one and helped each other defeat the foreign invader. Then afterwards, the Greeks went right back to fighting each other again. The same can be said for the medieval Japanese shoguns. They would war with each other until China or someone else threatened them. At that time the shoguns would unite, defeat the foe, then return to their infighting.

Another example comes from the Pearl of Great Price. In J.S. History 1, Joseph Smith tells of the religious movement that started around Palmyra, New York, when he was growing up. There were many religious sects of the day, and they began a religious revival during Joseph's fifteenth year. He writes in verse 6, "For notwithstanding the great love which the converts to these different faiths expressed at the time of their conversion, and the great zeal manifested by the respective clergy, yet when the converts began to file off, some to one party and some to another, it was seen that the seemingly good feelings of both the priests and the converts were more pretended than real; for a scene of great confusion and bad feeling ensued-priest contending against priest, and convert against convert."

And yet, against the backdrop of intersectarian strife and bickering, Joseph made this profound observation after he had told one of the aforementioned ministers about the vision he had in the sacred grove: "I soon found, however, that my telling the story had excited a great deal of prejudice against me among professors of religion, and was the cause of great persecution, which continued to increase...and this was common among all the sects, **all united to persecute me**." (Verse 22.)

From the above examples we can make a major deduction. If the devil controls organizations or governments, they will be fractionated and fight against each other, for the devil is the author of contention. However, there is an exception to that rule. That is, they will unite to *fight against whatever God establishes on the earth*, whether that be His church, a government, or a people established by Him. In the case of these latter-day secret combinations, they are extremely monolithic in their goal of one-world government. They are especially desirous of destroying the Constitution of the United States and Christianity in general. That is because both the Constitution and Christianity were originally established by God. But when it comes to implementing their goals, i.e. tactics, they often clash. The conspirators are both united and fractious.

4. There exist powerful organizations that operate from behind the scenes, but these are just "good-ole-boys clubs" that evolved through natural selection, not through some overall scheme or plan. They aren't inher-

ently evil, nor are they part of a powerful world-wide conspiracy. They just look out for themselves first.

That observation was made to me by a person involved in both local and national politics. He knows all of Utah's congressional delegation personally. He has been involved in many local and national campaigns. He helped defeat the military's plan to deploy nuclear missiles in the deserts of Nevada and Utah. He has also attended meetings of one of the semi—secret organizations I will talk about later. He came away from those meetings with the impression that the organization wasn't part of a conspiracy, nor was it particularly secret, although he conceded it did wield considerable influence.

Each organization composing the overall conspiracy did not just "evolve," nor are they just a "good-ole-boys-club" but each was deliberately created with the goal in mind of controlling governments from behind the scenes. These organizations will be discussed in turn.

5.We don't have to worry about an evil conspiracy in the last days, because all we have to do is live the Gospel, go to church and listen to the Prophet.

The rebuttal to that is found in a talk given by Elder Ezra T. Benson to the BYU student body on Oct. 25, 1966:

Satan's Perverse Reasoning

Now Satan is anxious to neutralize the inspired counsel of the Prophet and hence keep the Priesthood off-balance, ineffective and inert in the fight for freedom. He does this through diverse means including the use of perverse reasoning.

For example, he will argue, "There is no need to get involved in the fight for freedom—all you need to do is live the gospel." Of course this is a contradiction, because we cannot fully live the gospel and not be involved in the fight for freedom.

We would not say to someone, "There is no need to be

baptized—all you need to do is live the gospel." That would be ridiculous because baptism is a part of the gospel.

How would you have reacted if during the War in Heaven someone had said to you, "Look, just do what's right, there is no need to get involved in the fight for free agency." Now it is obvious what the devil is trying to do, but it is sad to see many of us fall for his destructive line.

6.If there were such a conspiracy, wouldn't some have defected and helped expose the alleged plot?

The answer to that comes from The New American, Special Report, *Conspiracy for Global Control*, 1997:

Many have done exactly that. Indeed, it is truly amazing that such a large number of defectors bringing such a vast quantity of high-quality evidence over such a long period of time have been so effectively censored from the history books. We see this with Weishaupt's Illuminati, which many establishment historians still insist was apocryphal, or certainly of no significant influence. The facts show quite the opposite. In 1784-85 four professors of the Marianen Academy who had been inducted into the Illuminati— Gruengerger, Renner, Utzschneider and Cossandey—all came forward to give sworn testimony to the Bavarian Government concerning the criminal activities and plans of the Order....

Closer to our day, communists such as Whittaker Chambers and Elizabeth Bentley were instrumental in exposing the existence of at least three communist cells within the U.S. government. Included on this list was high-ranking State Department official Alger Hiss...

Both Chambers and Bentley were, in accord with the standard communist smear tactic, attacked unmercifully. (*New American*, 1997)

But there are more people than that. One of the most prominent examples is that of Carroll Quigley. He is an example not of a defector, but of one on the inside who voluntarily talked. And talk he did. He published a book called, *Tragedy and Hope* in which he bragged about the conspiracy. He spilled the beans, so to speak. And he remained a conspirator until his death in 1974. There will be more information on him and others in upcoming chapters.

Now let us look for evidences of a secret combination. And the basis of all successful secret combinations begins with money. You will learn something about financial institutions that you never heard about in your school history lessons. This may be the first of many new revelations to you.

Chapter 2

History shows that the money changers have used every form of
abuse, intrigue, deceit, and violent means possible to
maintain control over governments by controlling the money and the
issuance of it.
—President James A. Madison

The Golden Rule

Have you heard of the Golden Rule? Simply put, it goes like this:
He who has the gold makes the rules. If anyone is interested in
knowing who really runs this world (from a worldly point of view), the
main thing to know is remember the Golden Rule and follow the
money. The statement is a sweeping generalization, and is not applic-
able in all cases but in a general sense does happen to be true. Money
confers worldly power, period. Few and far between are situations to
the contrary.

That is true no matter if it is an emperor (or sovereign) who has the
money, or someone behind the throne. As a matter of fact, control
from behind the scenes tends to be the "norm" in our day of so-called
democratic nation states. That's not the way things *should* be, merely
the way things are. The person (or organization) with the money, the
majority of the time, rules the family, community, state, nation and
world.

It is true that real, spiritual power comes from living God's
commandments, but I want to emphasize that this book is intended to
show where worldly power begins. And it begins with money. We will
follow the money, so to speak, and find out where it leads. As we do,
the reader may learn that power is concentrated in organizations he or

she never heard of before. Do not be incredulous, merely because these organizations or people are unknown to you. The fact that they are relatively unknown is intentional.

Before proceeding further, we need to know that a discussion about money necessarily needs to include some discussion about the kind of economic system in which that money would function. However, a discussion about economic systems could take volumes and the intent here is only to give a brief background. A few salient points about the system within which money operates and flourishes will be mentioned.

That system is basically, with a few modifications here and there, free enterprise capitalism. The fundamental idea behind it being that people are more or less free to engage in any business enterprise they choose, within certain bounds. They are free to succeed or fail, reaping the rewards of their success. The ability to succeed *and fail* is crucial for the success of capitalism. One of the best overall treatments of free enterprise may be found in one of the oldest books on the subject. It is *An Inquiry into the Nature and Causes of the Wealth of Nations*, by Adam Smith. Published in 1776 in Scotland around the time of the signing of the Declaration of Independence in America, it is a thorough and revealing treatise on the virtues of capitalism.

He explains the Law of Supply and Demand like this: "The market price of every particular commodity is regulated by the proportion between the quantity which is actually brought to market and the demand of those who are willing to pay the natural price of the commodity, or the whole value of the rent, labour, and profit, which must be paid in order to bring it thither." In other words, the price is regulated by the supply of a good available divided by the demand of society for that good.

Bad press notwithstanding, capitalism is the best economic system in existence. And when it is allowed to flourish, people generally are better off economically. To the degree it is stifled, the general standard of living decreases. That point is illustrated by showing the difference between the economic status of Russia and America. No one can disagree that Russia's economy is very anemic while America's is very strong. The difference being, of course, that free enterprise capitalism, while taking root, is still stifled in Russia while it is basically encouraged here. There are, indeed, many virtues to capitalism.

But free enterprise capitalism has both good and evil built into it. The good side of it is that persistence and hard work are indeed rewarded. It builds self reliance. It teaches the value of work. Industry and thrift are monetarily rewarded. The Brethren have expounded on these and other positive themes over the years.

When capitalism is working as it should, it's as if God were directing it. Adam Smith, in his book *The Wealth of Nations*, called this phenomenon the "invisible hand." The "invisible hand" was a phrase invented by Smith to show how people under capitalism, and acting solely in their own self-interest, actually wind up helping society, as if God's hand were directing the results for the benefit of humanity. To illustrate that, let's make up a scenario of a tanner and a cobbler.

The tanner, acting entirely in his own self interest, tans hides for the cobbler to make shoes. But even though he is only looking out for himself, the act of selling his hides to the cobbler benefits both because the cobbler needs the leather in order to do his job. Thus, the tanner receives a profit and the cobbler gets the raw material he needs to make his shoes so that he can sell them to the tanner who needs shoes to conduct his business. Both profit. The same can be said for all others engaged in an honest endeavor. Even though all are motivated for selfish reasons, the community as a whole benefits. Goods are directed to where they're needed. Surpluses or shortages are lessened. It's as if divine providence was guiding everything in order to help raise the standard of living for all.

As evidence of that, let's read this statement:

It seemed a miracle when West Germany—a defeated and devastated country—became one of the strongest economies on the continent of Europe in less than a decade. It was the miracle of a free market. Ludwig Erhard, an economist, was the German Minister of Economics. On Sunday, the twentieth of June, 1948, he simultaneously introduced a new currency, today's Deutsche Mark, and abolished almost all controls on wages and prices. He acted on a Sunday, he was fond of saying, because the offices of the French, American and British occupation authorities were closed that day. Given their favorable attitude toward controls, he was sure that if he had acted when the offices were open, the occupation authorities would have countermanded his orders. His measures worked like a charm. Within days, the shops were full of goods. Within months the German economy was humming away.

Free to Choose
by Milton and Rose Friedman, (56)

Now, economists may not all agree on how to keep an economy running at peak efficiency, but they all know how to produce shortages. That's through wage and price controls. It happens every time.

Also, because of political and economic freedom vouchsafed by our wonderful Constitution, America is indeed the glory of the world. We have been a moral force for good, and our ability in giving all who are willing to work a just reward is known world wide. If you doubt this, just think of all the immigrants, legal and illegal, who come here because, compared to their home countries, economic conditions are much better. You never hear of Communist China patrolling its borders to keep people out, but America does. China patrols its borders to keep them in. People have been willing to risk their very lives to enjoy the economic freedom and prosperity we take for granted.

On the other hand, the bad thing about free enterprise capitalism comes from the nature of the beast itself. That is, following the dictates of capitalism bequeaths the idea that we can "own" things. Yes, the basic evil of capitalism is that we are conditioned to think that whatever we earn through our effort and skill is "ours." For instance, if Joe

Blow earns enough money to buy a house through diligence and hard work, and pay off the mortgage, it's easy for him to think the house is his. He sits back and thinks, "Well now, look at what I've accumulated here. All this is mine. I can go on and acquire more stuff and get ahead of my neighbor." Most of us tend to think in terms that whatever we earn is ours. That is the conditioning and brainwashing that comes with free enterprise capitalism. That, in turn, can create selfishness. That is, when we think that everything we have is ours, we begin to think that we can go ahead and accumulate more and store it up only for ourselves. Now let's look at what the Gospel teaches. Look in Psalms 24:1-2:

> The earth is the Lord's, and the fulness thereof; the world, and they that dwell therein. For He hath founded it upon the seas, and established it upon the floods.

The truth is established in the first phrase. <u>The earth is the Lord's</u>. It always has been and always will be. He created it. He placed all life upon the face of it. He put all gold, silver, gems, land and natural resources on the earth for us to <u>use</u>, not own. He has never given away title of anything to anybody, and all earthly title deeds are the vain imaginations of man.

The point being that since everything is the Lord's, then logically everything must be used in His way, according to His will. If people buy cars, (thinking in a worldly vein, that whatever they buy is theirs), do they not have the right to stipulate to others how their cars are used? Why then does the Lord not have the right to stipulate to us how to use His stuff? And his will for the use of earthly things is expressed in D&C 70:7-11; 14.

Therefore, when men accumulate more and more possessions, they must be cognizant of the idea that those possessions really belong to the Lord. This view places man in the role of a steward, or manager, not owner. He then becomes accountable to the Lord for how he uses the Lord's resources here on earth. Father wants us to share our bounty with our fellow man, accounting him equal to ourselves. That is the basic idea behind the Law of Consecration.

Now back to the real world. The illusion that we "own" things has bred selfishness and inequality. And those who accumulate great abundances of wealth and property can be *changed inwardly* by it:

> Let me tell you about the very rich. They are different from you and me. They possess and enjoy early, and it does something to them, makes them soft where we are hard, and cynical where we are trustful, in a way that, unless you were born rich, it is difficult to understand. They think, deep in their hearts, that they are better than we are because we had to discover the compensations and refuges of life for ourselves. Even when they enter deep into our world or sink below us, they still think that they are better than we are. They are different.
>
> F. Scott Fitzgerald
> *The Rich and the Super-Rich*
> by Ferdinand Lundberg

Perhaps that is what Christ was referring to when he said, "It is easier for a camel to go through the eye of a needle, than for a rich man to enter into the kingdom of God". (Matt.19:25).

Riches don't necessarily corrupt all men, for one only has to look at the examples of Abraham and Job. But it is true that life is full of traps that can snare the soul unless one has a correct perspective on riches. If not, one can easily be swept up in false ideas to govern one's life. The correct perspective of material possessions seems to be a concept difficult for men in general to grasp. (Luke 12:13-21).

Let us see how the accumulation of wealth has changed some people. We shall now look at a few that have done quite well indeed and see what effect their riches had on them and the rest of the world. In doing so, watch the Golden Rule in action.

The House of the Red Shield

Mayer Amschel Bauer (1743-1812) was born in Frankfurt-on-the-

Main in Germany to Moses Amschel Bauer who was an itinerant money lender. Moses had moved around Europe for a while when he decided to settle down upon the birth of his first child. He opened a counting house in 1750 and over the door leading into the shop he placed a large red shield.

Europe was different in those days from the Europe we know today. The idea of a "nation state" was beginning to take root, (like France or Germany), but conglomerations of large and small kingdoms, fiefdoms and duchies were the rule and they were in constant conflict. Political intrigue, wars, alliances and double dealing were very common. Just like today. Serfs were tied to the land of their lord for life. Many generations worked out their lives for nothing but the pleasure of their masters and had no political rights at all. There was discrimination against gypsies, Jews, beggars, and most other ethnic groups not connected with "your" particular group.

Kings asserted that they had the "divine right" to rule. That is, they were given their kingdom by God, and were only amenable to Him and not to anyone on this earth, not even the Pope. Many declared that they were gods themselves and that whatever edict they decreed had to be obeyed with no questions asked.

Religious intolerance was supreme. Anyone not a member of the Roman Catholic Church was intensely persecuted. Protestants and Catholics fought each other and both groups persecuted Jews as "Christ killers." Unfortunately, the Jews had little or no official influence to counteract it.

It was into this background of religious intolerance and bigotry that Mayer was born, his family being Jewish. At an early age, Mayer demonstrated an immense intellectual ability. Moses taught him all he knew about money lending and goldsmithing and the son learned rapidly and well. Originally, Mayer was to be trained as a Rabbi, but Moses died while he was still a youth, and those plans were discarded.

A few years later, Mayer Amschel went to work as a clerk for a bank owned by the Oppenheimers in Hannover. His abilities were quickly realized and he rapidly advanced to the position of junior partner.

Shortly after that he returned to Frankfurt and purchased the business his father established back in 1750. The big red shield was still hanging over the door. Mayer knew its significance, it being a symbol of the red flag which was an emblem of revolutionary Jews in Eastern Europe. Mayer Amschel Bauer changed his last name to Rothschild (Red Shield), and the House of the Red Shield, the first truly international banking dynasty, came into being.

At this point it should be noted that although the Rothschilds are of Jewish ancestry, it does *not* follow that the secret combinations of the last days are a Jewish-Zionist plot against the world. There are many other people involved that are not Jewish. The conspirators backgrounds cut across all religious, political and ideological lines. This particular part of the conspiracy happened to begin with Jews. They still participate to this day, but the majority of the conspirators are non-Jews, and that must be acknowledged.

One of the charges that the media brings against those who believe in this conspiracy is that they are "anti-semitic race mongers" if they say that Jews are "in" on it. That way the media turns the minds of the public against those who say, rightfully, that international Jewish banking families are indeed part of the conspiracy. To try to stay away from that appellation by pretending that the Rothschilds, Warburgs and other Jewish families do not participate is to shun the truth.

To continue, Mayer Amschel Rothschild became acquainted with Prince William of Hanau and became his financier. That was the beginning of contacts between the House of Rothschild and heads of state, but not the last. The basic modus operandi of Mayer Amschel was to lend money to governments at a certain interest rate and thus gain influence and power over them.

Mayer Amschel married Gutele Schnaper in 1770 and had five sons and daughters. The names of the sons were Amschel, Salomon, Nathan, Kalmann (Karl) and Jacob (James). These young men, when they came of age, started central banks in London (Nathan), Berlin

(Amschel), Vienna (Salomon), Paris (James), and Naples (Karl) with their fathers financial aid and through considerable scheming and utter ruthlessness. They began to control these governments from behind the scenes through the act of money lending. All the central banks of all the industrialized countries throughout the world are either descended from, or were taken over by the Rothscilds and/or business colleagues. All central banks in the world are private lending institutions (including our own, which will be discussed later), that are lenders of last resort to governments.

For further details about the family or its history from that point on, please feel free to read three different reference books that will shed more light on this international banking family. 1. *Tragedy and Hope* by Carroll Quigley, Macmillian Co., 1966, 2. *The Rothschilds* by Frederic Morton, Fawcett Crest, 1961, and 3. *Jewish Encyclopedia*, 1905 edition. As before stated, this book is an over view of the history of all the organizations that make up this secret combination, and will mention only the highlights. To try to be more specific would take volumes, and these books can fill in many details for the reader. Therefore, what has already been printed will suffice.

Before moving on, however, please read the following quotation to help explain the subtle, often overlooked power that money lending has on governments:

> The power of investment bankers over governments rests on a number of factors, of which the most significant, perhaps, is the need of governments to issue short-term treasury bills as well as long-term government bonds. Just as businessmen go to commercial banks for current capital advances to smooth over the discrepancies between their irregular and intermittent incomes and their periodic and persistent outgoes (such as monthly rents, annual mortgage payments, and weekly wages), so a government has to go to merchant bankers (i.e. international bankers) to tide over the shallow places caused by irregular tax receipts. As experts in government bonds, the international bankers not only handled

the necessary advances but **provided advice to government officials and, on many occasions, placed their own members in official posts for varied periods to deal with special problems**. This is so widely accepted even today that in 1961 a Republican investment banker became Secretary of the Treasury in a Democratic Administration in Washington without significant comment from any direction.

Naturally, the influence of bankers over governments during the age of financial capitalism (roughly 1850-1931) was not something about which anyone talked freely, but it has been admitted frequently enough by those on the inside, especially in England. In 1852 Gladstone, chancellor of the Exchequer, declared, "The hinge of the whole situation was this: the government itself was not to be a substantive power in matters of Finance, but was to leave the Money Power supreme and unquestioned". On September 26, 1921, The Financial Times wrote, **"Half a dozen men at the top of the Big Five Banks could upset the whole fabric of government finance by refraining from renewing Treasury Bills"**.

In 1924 Sir Drummond Fraser, vice president of the Institute of Bankers stated, **"The governor of the Bank of England** (i.e., an international banker) **must be the autocrat who dictates the terms upon which alone the Government can obtain borrowed money"**.

In addition to their power over government based on government financing and personal influence, bankers could steer governments in ways they wished them to go by other pressures. Since most government officials felt ignorant of finance, they sought advice from bankers whom they considered to be experts in the field. The history of the last century shows, ...that the advice given to governments by bankers, like **the advice they gave to industrialists, was consistently good for bankers, but was often** disastrous for governments, businessmen, and the people generally. Such advice could be enforced if necessary by manipulation of exchanges, gold flows, discount rates, and even levels of business activity.

Tragedy and Hope by Carroll Quigley, (61)

As an example of how this is done, let it be related how they managed to acquire the finances of the government of France. After Napoleon's crushing defeat at Waterloo, the French struggled to get back on their feet financially. In 1817, they negotiated a substantial loan from the prestigious French banking house of Ouvrard, and from the well-known Baring Brothers bankers of London. The Rothschilds were left out.

In 1818, the government needed another loan. As the bonds of 1817 were increasing in value, it appeared that they would retain the services of the aforementioned bankers. The Rothschilds tried everything they knew to influence the French to give them that business, but to no avail. Even so, the French couldn't have known that the Rothschilds had an unprecedented cunning in the manipulation of money, but they were about to find out.

On November 15, 1818, out of the clear blue sky, the French government bonds began to fail after a year of steady appreciation. Every day it got worse, then other government securities began to fail too. King Louis XVIII was desperate. The government began to worry about the fate of the country. The only ones who didn't seem too concerned were James and Karl Rothschild. They smiled, but said nothing.

Slowly it occurred to the government that maybe the Rothschilds were somehow responsible for the fall of the bonds. Was it possible that they manipulated the market? Did they engineer the panic?

As a matter of fact, in October, the Rothschilds, through their agents and unlimited reserves, bought up huge quantities of French government bonds freshly issued by their rivals, the Ouvrards and Baring Brothers, causing the bonds to increase in value. Then on

November 5th , they dumped them all on the open market all over Europe, causing a panic.

Of course, the government knew nothing of this for certain, and suddenly, the Rothschilds, who were recently frozen out of French finances, became the center of attention. They became the lender of choice, and, of course, locked out all rival lenders from that day on. The Rothschilds had gained control of France. They truly practiced the golden rule, and according to the historical accounts, they were utterly ruthless in who they used and destroyed. They continue to do so to this day through their central banks.

At this juncture, I would like to give a few quotes from prominent people, to back up what I am saying.

The powers of financial capitalism had (a) far-reaching aim, nothing less than to create a world system of financial control in private hands **able to dominate the political system of each country and the economy of the world as a whole. This system was to be controlled in a feudalist fashion by the central banks of the world acting in concert, by secret agreements arrived at in frequent meetings and conferences.** The apex of the system was to be the Bank of International Settlements in Basel, Switzerland, a private bank owned and controlled by the world's central banks which were themselves private corporations. **Each central bank... sought to dominate its government by its ability to control Treasury loans, to manipulate foreign exchanges, to influence the level of economic activity in the country, and to influence cooperative politicians by subsequent rewards in the business world.**

Tragedy and Hope (324—325)

If the American people ever allow private banks to control the issue of their money, first by inflation and then by deflation, the banks and corporations that will grow up around [the banks], will deprive the people of their property until their children will wake up homeless on the continent their fathers conquered.

Thomas Jefferson

Just taking an interest in my fellow man

At this point, a few things should be explained about money, interest on money and the philosophy behind interest. Did you ever think about what money is and what purpose it has? Economists do and it is important to understand this question. If we do, then we can more fully understand the fraud that the bankers have perpetuated on us. This is not a thorough explanation of the subject, but crucial to proceed beyond this point.

The text book definition of money is that it is a medium of exchange. That means that it came into being as a way of standardizing barter exchanges among people. Can you imagine the headache in only living by barter? For example, how many chickens is a computer worth? Or sacks of wheat for a steel belted radial? Or suppose that all you had to exchange was rice, and the person with whom you wanted to exchange it for had plenty of rice but wanted some socket wrenches. Or something else—suppose you had nothing but your services to barter with. How would a history professor barter his services for a car? Which car manufacturer would want history lessons in exchange for a car? The barter system is extremely inefficient by all accounts.

That made the introduction of a standardized intermediary exchange against which all exchanges could be measured, and which was accepted by all, an evolutionary shoo-in. That way, one could exchange his chickens for this "something" with full confidence that someone else would accept that "something" for whatever the chicken man wanted to buy. That "something", of course, was money and the world has been better off since its adoption.

But we have to understand a critical point here. The man who raised the chickens produced the chickens; the manufacturer produced the steel belted radial and the history professor produced a lecture. Money by itself, though, does not represent the production of anything (aside from its minting and/or stamping) but is only in existence to facilitate the exchange of produced goods or services.

Economically speaking, only produced goods and services are called wealth. That is, the country that has produced the most goods like cars, houses, manufacturing plants and Big Macs; or services like electricians, piano tuners, computer programmers or ditch diggers, has the most wealth. Notice that no mention was made about money. Money is not wealth. A society could have all the gold in the world minted into coins, but if there were no goods or services to exchange them for, they, being inedible, would have little worth. Money truly is just a standardized medium to facilitate the exchange of wealth (goods and services).

The point is expounded upon in the following quote:

> Money being naturally barren, to make it breed money is preposterous, and a perversion from the end of its institution, which was only to serve the purpose of exchange and not of increase...Usury is most reasonably detested as the increase arises from the money itself and not by employing it to the purpose for which it was intended.
>
> Aristotle on Usury in 350 BC

Since money does not represent wealth (produced goods or services), then to use it to create more money (through interest) is to increase one's amount of the medium of exchange without having produced anything. And since the medium of exchange can then be used to procure goods and services; if one increases the amount of money he possesses by interest, he can procure wealth (goods and services) without producing anything. That, in one sense, is robbery. To steal lots of money so as to procure goods and services without work or production is the robber's philosophy. That being so, then to charge interest is a way of robbing one's fellow man.

The international bankers know this. They also know one other subtle thing about interest. Interest represents the gradual transfer of money and wealth from society at large to the bankers. They become richer while society becomes poorer.

Here is where the fractional reserve banking system, or the world wide system now is use, comes in. For all money deposited with a bank, a certain fraction (it used to be 15%) had to be kept in reserve in the banks vaults, so that they could use it to keep the normal ebb and flow of deposits and withdrawals at an even keel. That helped to stem occasionally high withdrawal periods from becoming a run on the bank.

But the remainder (85%) was free for lending purposes. If you were to deposit $1,000 in your bank using these numbers, the bank could issue $850 of it out on loan. If the person who took out that loan were to redeposit it, then that person's bank could re-issue 85% of that $850, or $722.50 on another loan. By going through this process a number of times, the original $1,000 could be expanded to over $20,000 in loans. The money that is loaned out, however (the $850, the $722.50 and so forth), is not physically given out. It is retained by the bank. The loans are merely bookkeeping entries. That is, the person securing the loan has his or her checking account increased by the principal simply by making an entry on the computer. Another way of saying it is that they <u>create</u> the money out of nothing. If anyone else tried to do that, it would called counterfeiting. But every bank does it.

So the process goes like this—a person asks for a loan, the loan officer approves it and tells someone to type in the amount of the loan to the person's account. Then the lendee repays the principal (created out of nothing) plus interest (which comes out of the economy.) *That* money is real money which gradually, over a long period of time, is transferred from the economy at large to the bankers. And that means that as time goes by, the bankers will grow richer and the rest of society will become poorer. That is how money and wealth is transferred to the bankers.

For instance, back in the 1920's-1940's, when people were more in the habit of saving up to make a purchase, 85-90% of the population outright owned their own homes. If they bought a house through the bank, they paid it off in 10 or 15 years. That's what happened with my father when I was a kid. He paid it off in ten or twelve years.

How different it is today! 30 year loans are very common, and when it is finally paid off, the purchaser has paid for it 2 to 3 times over. So a $100,000 home will wind up costing about $200,000-300,000 in the end. And today, 85% to 90% of the population is either paying off their mortgage, rather than owning the house outright, or is renting. Housing costs are going through the roof. In the future, most Americans will be unable to purchase a house due to the cost.

Also, back in the "good old days", a man could comfortably support his family on one income, leaving the mother free to be the home-maker. But that is no longer possible in most cases. The family needs two incomes just to make ends meet these days.

In other words, we are gradually becoming poorer as a whole. That, of course, is not true in every case. But for every Bill Gates that could be cited as a local boy making good, there are literally millions of people having to work harder at making a living, and many people are literally not able to make a living anymore. It is <u>no</u> coincidence that the number of homeless persons throughout the world is on the rise.

The end result of this cunning and gradual transfer of money and wealth, if you haven't guessed it by now, is that the banks will eventually wind up with <u>all</u> the wealth and everyone else will be totally dependent on them. That is not just my opinion. Let me quote:

> When the Babylonian civilization collapsed, three percent of the people owned all the wealth. When old Persia went down to destruction, two percent of the people owned all the wealth. When ancient Greece went down to ruin, one-half of one percent of the people owned all the wealth. When the Roman Empire fell by the wayside, two thousand people owned the wealth of the civilized world...It is said at this time that less than two percent of the people control ninety percent of the wealth of America.

> Dr. R.E. Search, from <u>Lincoln money Martyred</u>

But the corker is that the bankers <u>know</u> what is happening. They know that they are secretly gaining the total wealth of the world. They've known it for years. They are incredibly wealthy. They are trillionaires and they acquired their money by creating it out of nothing and lending it at interest. Here is a quotation from an inside source to confirm the fact that the bankers are deliberately trying to take over all wealth:

> ...But toward securing this millennium Mr. Rhodes (Cecil Rhodes, a conspirator, who will be introduced later) believed the most powerful factor would be a "secret society, organized like Loyola's, **supported by the accumulated wealth of those whose aspiration is a desire to do something,"...**

> ...it may convey the discovery of an idea which will ultimately lead to the cessation of all wars, and one language throughout the world, the patent being **the gradual absorption of wealth and human minds of the higher order to the object.**

> ...What an awful thought it is that if, even now, we could arrange with the present members of the United States Assembly and our House of Commons the peace of the world would be secured for all eternity! We could hold a Federal Parliament, five years in Washington and five in London." Mr. Rhodes added: "The only thing feasible to carry out this idea is a secret society **gradually absorbing the wealth of the world, to be devoted to such an object."**

> *New York Times*, April 9, 1902, Front page article
> "Mr. Rhodes's ideal of Anglo—Saxon Greatness"

Now that you have an idea of what is really going on in this world as far as money is concerned, you may well ask what does that have to do with America? We don't have a central bank like those in Europe. Our government owns our bank, not some outside interest. After all, it is the **Federal** Reserve System. Well, the answer to that leads up to the next topic. The good old USA.

Charity begins at home

Here is a revelation, if you haven't guessed by now. The so called

29

Federal Reserve System is <u>not</u> part of the federal government. It is a private stock owned lending institution, and most of the stockholders are non-American. Here's another revelation. The Rothschild banking dynasty is one of the stockholders. Surprise, surprise! First they either created or took over the central banks of Europe and here they are establishing control over the American central bank, the Fed. Here is a list of the original owners of the Fed.

Rothschilds	London
Warburgs	Berlin
Lazar Brothers	Paris
Israel Moses	Italy
Loeb	New York
Lehman Brothers	New York
Rockefellers	New York

Remember these names. We will come across them again in other areas besides banking. They and their friends are wide spread in the areas of politics, media, education and economics.

In all, about 300 people were the original owners of the stock at $100/share. The stock is not publicly traded, and never will be. Today, that list has been expanded, but still the stockholders are all family or banks owned by the original owners.

If there are still skeptics out there who don't believe that the Federal Reserve is privately owned, then here is a challenge. Go to any university and ask any economy professor two questions: 1. "Is the Federal Reserve System part of the Federal Government, or is it privately owned"? 2. "Doesn't that at least suggest a situation that could be termed a conflict of interest? After all, if a private institution owns the money supply in the United States, isn't it at least possible for them to raise or lower interest rates and/or increase or decrease the money supply at the right time in order to personally profit from it?"

Well, I did that and was told by my economics professor that he didn't think there was a problem because the Congress had oversight of the Fed and would not let the Fed do anything that could be termed a conflict of interest. After all, in the Act of Congress authorizing the creation of the Fed, Congress was given oversight responsibility and could indeed abolish it if it chose to do so.

To rebut, it is true that Congress can vote to regulate, audit or even abolish the Fed. As a matter of fact, the Fed itself brags about that as if to assure the public that they really are controlled by the Government, but that assurance is more shadow than substance. The reality is quite the reverse. The Fed controls the Government, at least in the area of finance, fiscal policy and economic growth.

The Fed has never been audited in all the years of its existence and will never *allow itself to be audited*. The Fed and the international bankers who hold its stock understand that the Fed is a golden goose for them, allowing them to acquire literally billions of dollars each year through dividends on the stock in the Federal Reserve System. For that reason, plus the fact that they can control Government policies by being creditors to the Government means that they will *never* allow that gravy train to be destroyed. They have enormous influence in Congress and through that influence have fended off various attempts by individual congressmen who know the true threat the Fed poses to the Government and have tried to introduce bills in Congress to abolish the Fed.

The chairman of the Fed meets with various Senate and House committees on banking from time to time, to explain various Fed policies or to consult with them about the growth of the country, but that's not the same as a formal audit. Their books have never been opened, their shareholders dividends have never been seen, where their money goes and who it goes to, and even their policy meetings are closed to the public and government. There have been attempts at an audit before, but the Fed, with their power and influence, stopped all such proceedings.

The Federal Reserve Bank of New York is eager to enter into a close relationship with the Bank of International Settlements...The conclusion is impossible to escape that the State and Treasury

Departments are willing to pool the banking system of Europe and America, **setting up a world financial power independent of and above the Government of the United States.**

Rep. Louis McFadden, Chairman of the House Committee
on Banking and Currency quoted in the New York Times June 1930

Here is an aside about the above quotation. There were two failed attempts on Rep. McFadden's life, one by poisoning, the other by gunfire and he died after a third attempt of suspected poisoning after attending a banquet.

But how could something like this happen? The Constitution gives Congress express authority over the coining and issuance of money. So how could such a loss of sovereignty come about? Let us look at how the international bankers hoodwinked the country. We'll delve into the origins of the Fed.

Jekyll and Hyde in Plain Sight

The reason this secret combination is so successful is that it hides in plain sight. You will see that as we discuss the origins of the Federal Reserve System. To do this, here is a quote directly from the book, *Secret Combinations Today, a Voice of Warning* by Robert E. Hales, Horizon Publishers, 1996, starting on p. 113.

In...a Georgia State park located on Jekyll Island, Georgia, is a private hunting club house and winter resort formerly owned by J.P.Morgan. On one of the doors to the rooms in this elaborate castle—like building stands a plaque declaring, "In this room, the Federal Reserve System was Created."

The plaque refers to an infamous, and at the time, secret meeting held by seven people in the year 1910. These seven people represented the worlds richest organizations and individuals. Together, it is estimated that the participants in this 1910 meeting represented one—quarter of all the world's wealth. The result of that meeting was the establishment of the Federal Reserve System, a partnership between the United States Congress as the first party and the national and international money interests as the second party. Many of the participants in this then—secret meeting were competitors in the world of finance. The participants were:

Nelson Aldrich, the Chairman of National Monetary Commission, whose duty it was to recommend to Congress any principles advisable to reform banking;

Abraham Andrew, who was the Assistant Secretary of the United States Treasury;

Henry Davidson, the Senior Partner of the J.P.Morgan Company;

Charles D. Norton, President of J.P. Morgan's First National Bank of New York;

Benjamin Strong, the head of J.P. Morgan's Banker's Trust Company, and who would later be named as the first chairman of the Federal Reserve Board;

Frank A. Vanderlip, the President of National City Bank of New York, the most powerful bank then in existence, and who was also spokesman for William Rockefeller and for the international investment banking house of Kuhn, Loeb & Company; and

Paul M. Warburg, partner in Kuhn, Loeb & Company, a representative of the Rothschild banking dynasty in England and France and brother to Max Warburg who was head of the Warburg banking consortium in Germany and the Netherlands.

Three important aspects of the United States financial setting for the meeting are very important (to know). (1) Money was being shifted toward the West where many new banks were opening. In fact, a majority of deposits in the United States domiciled banks were in other than the New York banks. The trend was for more banks and a continued shift of control away from the current money powers. (2) The economy, still based on the gold standard, was growing from internal profits rather than from debt. Profits were being used to expand because it was less costly than paying interest rates. Gold, because of its rarity, provided a too-limited source of allowing debt to operate as the medium of growth. (3) Banks were failing, which would cause the public to lose confidence in the banking system. The bank failures were the result of the individuals bank's ability to lend more than it held in deposits, causing the potential for runs on the bank.

The simple answer to these problems was to create a Central Bank such as that housed in many European countries. However, the American people were against any type of a monopoly as anti-productive under our free enterprise system. Therefore, the participants agreed that their creation must not appear as an agreement among competitors. Accordingly, the men at Jekyll Island needed to come up with a plan which would stop the loss of control over the deposit money, eliminate the appeal of using profits rather than debt as the basis for issuing credit, and find a way to assure that the American people would accept the new concept.

The answer was the Federal Reserve System. This name is appropriately deceptive from the viewpoint that the activities of the organization mislead the American public.

The term "Federal" incorrectly implies government control and monitoring as well as responsibility by government entities. In fact, the Federal Reserve System is exempt from government control, its officers are beyond voter reach, and the organization is in fact private, not public.

The term "Reserve" implies that there are reserves to back up and support the value of the notes issued by the Federal Reserve System. In fact, there are no reserves, never were, and never will be. The public has been mislead to believe that the federal reserve note has the same credibility as the silver certificate or the $20 gold piece.

The term "System" indicates that the banks in the West South, North and East are all participants in the process and that the benefits are the same to all citizens. In fact, this may be the only truth associated with the name as the system is now in control of all financial transaction in the United States.

From *Secret Combinations Today*, (114, 115)

The Federal Reserve [Banks] are one of the most corrupt institutions the world has ever seen. There is not a man within the sound of my voice who does not know that this Nation is run by the International Bankers.

Rep. Louis McFadden

After the Federal Reserve Act of 1913 was passed, President Wilson later regretted the decision to sign it into law. He said, referring to the FED, "I have unwittingly ruined my country."

Now you know why this book is named, "Hiding in Plain Sight." Everybody has heard of the Fed, but at the same time, almost everybody has been mislead into thinking that it is just another government institution. Therefore, it can carry out its mission of controlling our government finances and financial policies through controlling its debt in open view. The news media downplays the fact that it is independent of the federal government. It is amazing how brazen they are. They truly do hide in plain sight.

In addition to the Federal Reserve System, there are other institutions that belong to the financial side of the conspiracy. One of those organizations is the Bank for International Settlements in Basel, Switzerland. It may be termed the central banker's bank. It is at the apex of the world financial pyramid. It is a privately owned bank, just like the Fed, the Bank of England, the Bundesbank and all other central banks throughout the world. But it is the bank other central banks go to for loans and other financial securities. And it is the bank that directs and coordinates the actions of the other central banks, in order to help them dominate their respective governments.

On June 28, 1998, *The Washington Post* published an article about the Bank for International Settlements (BIS) titled, "At Secret Meetings in Switzerland, 13 People Shape the World's

Economy," which describes these individuals as "this economic cabal...this secretive group...the financial barons who control the world's supply of money."

Secret Records Revealed

by Dennis Laurence Cuddy, Ph.D.

Hearthstone Publishing Ltd. 1999, (5)

Two more organizations will be mentioned here. They are the International Monetary Fund (IMF), and the World Bank (WB). They were created by the Council on Foreign Relations and the Royal Institute for International Affairs in the 1940's. The CFR and the RIIA will be discussed in chapter 4. The purpose of the IMF and the WB is to make loans to third world nations, get them into a debt so large that they will never be able to repay, then destroy their economies. By doing that the international bankers will make these nations completely dependent on them, and make it easier to integrate the third world into the New World Order.

The bankers destroy the economies of these countries via a two-pronged attack. 1) They loan large amounts of money at interest, (of course), that a small country will never be able to repay, and 2) As a condition of repayment, the international bankers then impose upon this country what are called "Austerity Measures." These measures ostensibly are imposed to help the indebted nation repay their loans, but in reality have the opposite effect. The measures vary from nation to nation and even decade to decade, but all have the consequence of destroying the economies of the nations involved and making them poorer.

Sometimes the austerity measures take the form of socialism. That is, regulations like wage and price controls, five year production plans, production quotas and so forth. The bankers know these measures will not work. Socialism, as an economic system, is a total failure and always has been. But their purpose is not to help them, as already stated, but to wreck the economies of the countries involved.

Modern austerity measures include the forced opening of borders to "free trade" and joining NAFTA, GATT or other trading treaties. The bad thing about the "free trade" facade is that the international bankers and their multinational corporations then go into these poor countries, pollute and destroy their natural resources, cut down their forests, pay the citizens slave wages and secure all the profits for themselves. The country is left poorer than when the corporations came in. The IMF and WB are indeed evil organizations but the people of the world are beginning to see that, as witnessed by the demonstrations against them when they met in Washington D.C. in the spring of 2000. We the people are beginning to see these organizations for what they really are.

Going along with the theme of this chapter which is financial combinations, a financial swindle which was perpetuated on the American Public was the Income Tax Amendment and the Internal Revenue Service (IRS). The Income Tax Amendment was not ratified by 3/4 of the states in 1913, as is commonly reported. Philander Knox was the Secretary of State in charge of certifying whether enough states ratified the Amendment (three-fourths of the states must ratify an amendment to the Constitution in order for it to be accepted into the Constitution). But it is a fact that Kentucky's legislature rejected the amendment, still Knox certified that they had ratified it. Oklahoma changed the amendment to mean just the opposite of what it said, then ratified the changed amendment, but Knox counted them as having ratified the original amendment. Minnesota did not submit any results or a copy of their vote to Knox, yet he counted them too. It would be instructive for anyone to investigate for themselves as to whether the Income Tax Amendment was ratified or not.

The Amendment has more than one purpose, but the primary purpose is NOT to fund government spending, as is commonly believed, but to make the general population poorer through taxation and further enslave them financially. Philander Knox was formerly a lawyer for many of the richest men in America, including Morgan, Carnegie, Rockefeller and Vanderbilt. The Amendment was sponsored by Senator Aldrich, who helped pass the Federal Reserve Act, and by Colonel Edward Mandell House, whom we shall meet later.

Having said that, I will now discuss the Income Tax Amendment in another light. On September 9, 1975, the First Presidency of the Church of Jesus Christ of Latter-day Saints issued a letter to all Stake and Mission Presidents which was read from the pulpit of all wards and branches during their respective sacrament meetings. Here it is:

TO ALL STAKE AND MISSION PRESIDENTS IN THE UNITED STATES:

Dear Brethren:

We have received several inquiries about our view towards the Federal Income Tax law and about the status of Church members who refuse to pay income tax or who may be convicted for failure to pay income tax.

The United States Supreme Court consistently has upheld the constitutionality of the income tax law. Until these decisions are reversed by the Supreme Court, or until Congress changes the income tax law by legislation, they represent the constitutional law of the land. Therefore, all Latter-day Saints are obligated by the Twelfth Article of Faith to observe this law, and members who deliberately refuse to pay income tax are in direct conflict with the teachings of the Church.

If one disapproves of the income tax law, his remedy is not to disobey or to ignore it, but rather to attempt to challenge it in the courts or to have it changed by legislation or constitutional amendment.

It is apparent that if all persons were to refuse to obey the laws of which they disapprove, a state of anarchy would exist.

Under these circumstances, a member who deliberately refuses to pay income tax or to comply with any final judgment rendered in an income tax case, is out of harmony with the teachings of the Church and should, for this reason, be denied a temple recommend. Furthermore, we feel that such a person should not be called to a position of principal responsibility in the Church.

We also feel that a member who is convicted of violating the income tax law should be disciplined by a Church court to the extent warranted by the circumstances.

That says everything. It is the author's assertion that the Income Tax Amendment is evil and was imposed in an illegal manner. Nevertheless, the First Presidency of the Church of Jesus Christ of Latter-day Saints have unequivocally stated that we should comply with the legal requirements of the income tax law. Because of that, I also lend my voice in unison with the Brethren and urge all members and citizens to live this law. Like Christ, we can learn obedience through the things which we suffer.

There are many who are striving to legally change the Constitution by repealing the Income Tax Amendment, and I wish them luck. Changing the law is the correct course of action (as opposed to not paying), as stated by the Brethren. However, they are missing the target. The root problem when discussing national finances is not the legality or illegality of the Income Tax Amendment, but the constitutionality of the Federal Reserve System. The Congressional Act which created the Fed in the first place almost demanded the necessity to impose the Income Tax Amendment, which would supplement the resultant increase in governmental spending that would arise from that very Act. In other words, the Fed is the necessity that demanded the invention of the income tax.

The Fed is at the root of the problem. Those who wish to destroy the onerous Income Tax Amendment should tackle the root, not the branches. They should get rid of the Federal Reserve by getting Congress to repeal the Act which created the Fed in 1913. There is much to recommend this course of action. You see, it is very, very difficult to change the Constitution. The founding fathers wanted the Constitution to be a stable agent of sovereign law and therefore made the Constitution relatively impervious to change. A new amendment to nullify the Income Tax Amendment must have 2/3 of the members of both houses of Congress to ratify it, plus 3/4 of the various state legis-

39

latures that make up our country. That is one hard row to hoe. However, an act of Congress may be repealed by a simple majority vote of the members of both houses of Congress. Logically speaking, that is much easier to do.

If the Federal Reserve Act of 1913 is repealed by Congress, it is my humble opinion that the Federal Government will stop deficit spending of necessity and be forced to live in a more fiscally prudent manner. Then the Income Tax Amendment will shrivel up an die almost of its own accord. Hopefully readers of this book involved in the attempt to overturn the Income Tax Amendment could take this advice to heart and tackle the root of the problem.

In the next chapter, we'll explore the question: Why don't more people know about these conspirators? How have they been able to hide in plain sight so successfully?

Chapter 3

It is difficult for them to see whose paycheck depends on them not seeing. —Upton Sinclair

"All the News That's Fit To Print"

The above quote is found on the front page of the New York Times. It seems to convey the impression that the New York Times will tell it all, not hold anything back, and let the people judge for themselves. Walter Cronkite (former CBS News anchor man) used to say, "That's the way it is, Friday, June 3rd, 1964." He was telling the public that his newscast was truthful and accurate. That this is the way the world really is. It is meant to give us a sense of trust in the media.

In his day, Walter Cronkite was called the "Father" of broadcast news because he portrayed a kindly, knowledgeable father figure. That image was deliberately created and carefully cultivated for just that effect. Today's anchors images are similarly refined and polished to give the impression of trust, friendliness and sincerity. But can it really be said that 'That's the way it is' when it comes to the polished news-cast we see every night? Can we trust those friendly figures who tell us the news? Can we trust the truthfulness of their reports? More and more people are beginning to wonder. Here is one dissident voice from a prominent newscaster:

My worldview was really shaped by Theodore Roosevelt, who got it right about power in America. Roosevelt thought the central fact of his era was that economic power had become so centralized and dominant **it could chew up democracy and spit it out**. The power of corporations, he said, had to be balanced in the interest

41

of the general public. Otherwise, America would undergo a class war, **the rich would win it, and we wouldn't recognize our country anymore. Shades of déjà vu. Big money and big business, corporations and commerce, are again the undisputed overlords of politics and government...**

The founders didn't count on the rise of mega—media. They didn't count on huge private corporations that would own not only the means of journalism but also vast swaths of the territory that journalism should be covering. According to a recent study done by the Pew Research Center for the People and the Press for the Columbia Journalism Review, more than a quarter of journalists polled said **they had avoided pursuing some newsworthy stories that might conflict with the financial interests of their news organizations or advertisers. And many thought that complexity or lack or audience appeal causes newsworthy stories not to be pursued in the first place...**

Bill Moyers
The Nation Magazine, May 7, 2001

Think about that. For one of journalism's best news reporters to say that journalism might be tainted or unobjective is like a doctor turning against the medical profession, or a lawyer denigrating the ABA. It doesn't happen very often. So if Moyers casts aspersions about his own profession, that is news indeed. But he isn't the only one. There are and have been others. And their stories are mysteriously absent from the national limelight. Does that surprise you?

Here is another insightful comment from one of America's best journalists of his day:

There is no such thing, at this date of the world's history, in America, as an independent press. You know it and I know it. There is not one of you who dares to write your honest opinions, and if you did, you know beforehand that it would never appear in print. I am paid weekly for keeping my honest opinion out of the paper I am connected with. Others of you are paid similar salaries for similar things, and any of you who would be so foolish as to write honest opinions would be out on the streets looking for another job. If I allowed my honest opinions to appear in one issue of my paper, before twenty-four hours my occupation would be gone. The business of the journalists is to destroy the truth; to lie outright; to pervert; to vilify; to fawn at the feet of mammon, and to sell the country for his daily bread. You know it and I know it and what folly is this toasting an independent press. **We are the tools and vassals of rich men behind the scenes. We are the jumping jacks, they pull the strings and we dance**. (*Punch and Judy*) Our talents, our possibilities and our lives are all the property of other men. We are intellectual prostitutes. (Comment added).

John Swinton, former Chief of Staff of the New York Times, when asked to give a toast to the "free press" at the New York Press Club in 1953.

John Swinton was one of New York's best known and respected newspapermen. He was called by his peers "The Dean of his Profession." This is to let you know that this statement is not by some "off the wall" screwball, but by one of America's finest journalists. There have been some discrepancies on the date of this speech as well as some of the words used, but this statement is essentially correct.

So how can the above quotations be reconciled with the idea of an "independent press?" After all, the press in this country has <u>howled</u> whenever the government tried to censure or in other ways limit them. They boldly proclaim their 'freedom' and 'independence' as 'servants of the people.'

The truth is that all major news media in this country is controlled, not by the government, but by trans-national corporations whose owners have their own agenda for the country. They purposely block out what they don't want us to hear. In support of that, here is an unusually candid quotation:

We are grateful to The Washington Post, The New York Times, Time Magazine and other great publications whose directors have attended our meetings and respected their **promises of discretion for almost forty years. It would have been impossible for us to develop our plan for the world if we had been subject to the bright lights of publicity during those years**. But, the world is now more sophisticated and prepared to march towards a world government. **The supranational sovereignty of an intellectual elite and world bankers is surely preferable to the national auto determination practiced in past centuries.**

David Rockefeller, founder of the Trilateral Commission, before that body in Baden-Baden Germany, June 1991.

Only if one had the control necessary to back it up could one assay such a comment. The control of the media came when super-rich businessmen and international bankers gradually and quietly purchased the media through the decades of the twentieth century. The new owners then fired, screened out or retired the publishers and editors who didn't share the 'right' views or who insisted on going after any story merely because it is newsworthy. At other times, stories embarrassing to the owners were quietly shelved without comment and the journalist responsible assigned to some other story. The owners thus silently managed to stifle the truth about the one world government they were trying to achieve. Even now, occasionally, reporters bring up stories which could be damaging to the conspiracy, but most are effectively squashed.

As an example of news suppression, one of the semi-secret organizations, the yearly Bilderberg Conference, took place in Portugal in May of 1999. About 120 of the most influential people in the world were present. They represented heads of state, CEOs of international corporations, owners of mass media, politicians and other powerful people. They most decidedly do *not* like news coverage.

A reporter from the Sunday Herald in Edinburgh, Nic Outterside, was called on by his editor to run a story about the Bilderberg conference held in Sintra, Portugal. Nic Outterside is not just another reporter. He was twice Scottish Journalist of the year and winner of seven other journalism awards. The editor wanted a bland whitewash of the Bilderberg Conference. But Nic put together a news article that told the truth, embarrassing the Bilderbergers. He submitted his story to his editor, which was then re-written without his permission and published under his by-line.

When Nic learned of this blatant plagiarism, he called George Rosey, the deputy editor at the Herald. After a heated argument about changing Nic's original story, George slammed the phone down on Nic. Nic resigned as a result. This was, in Nic's own words, a "sinister abuse of my journalistic integrity." It is evidence of the extent of the conspirator's power behind the scenes to suppress whatever they don't like. So much for the illusion of freedom of the press. To see the full text of Nic Outterside's article and his editor's version, see Appendix A.

The conscious and intelligent manipulation of the organized habits and opinions of the masses is an important element in democratic society. **Those who manipulate this unseen mechanism of society constitute an invisible government which is the true ruling power of our country.**

We are governed, our minds are molded, our tastes formed, our ideas suggested, largely by men we have never heard of...

Our invisible governors are, in many cases, unaware of the identity of their fellow members in the inner cabinet.

...it remains a fact that in almost every act of our daily lives, whether in the sphere of politics or business, in our social conduct or our ethical thinking, **we are dominated by the relatively small number of persons...it is they who pull the wires which control the public mind, who harness old social forces and contrive new ways to bind and guide the world.**

45

As civilization has become more complex, and as the need for invisible government has been increasingly demonstrated, the technical means have been invented and developed by which opinion may re regimented...

The minority has discovered a powerful help in influencing majorities. It has been found possible so to mold the mind of the masses that they will throw their newly gained strength in the desired direction.

Propaganda, by Edward Bernays
Liveright Publishing Corporation,
New York, 1928, excerpts from p.9–19

Edward Bernays was the chief advisor to William Paley, the CEO of the Columbia Broadcast System (CBS). Ed Bernays was so influential that when he died, a New York Times obituary called him the "Father of Public Relations."

As mentioned before, the conspirators bought the media quietly over the years, using front organizations and individuals. The huge amounts of money needed to do this came from their business enterprises and through central bank money lending. Some of it even came from drug money. The connection between the secret combinations and drug cartels will be discussed later.

They did not have to buy 51% of the stock to take over a news organization. Any stock broker will tell you that as far as large, publicly traded news corporations are concerned, (for instance, The Los Angeles Times), all that is necessary to obtain effective control of the corporation is to purchase about 5% of the outstanding stock. Since there are many hundreds of stockholders, the person with 5% usually is the single largest stockholder, so he can effectively control the company through the votes that represent the power of this single block of stock. There is not a single major source of news or entertainment that they don't own or control. Then in the stockholders meetings the majority stockholders would vote in their own managers and CEO's. The companies thus bought out include newspapers, news as well as other magazines, encyclopedias, book publishers, Hollywood movie companies, journals, wire services, etc.

For instance, in July, 1968, the House Banking Subcommittee reported that Rockefeller (remember that family as one of the owners of the Fed) through Chase Manhattan Bank, controlled 5.9% of the stock in CBS. Furthermore, the bank had gained interlocking directorates with ABC. In 1974, Congress issued a report stating that the Chase Manhattan Bank's stake in CBS rose to 14.1% and NBC to 4.5% (through RCA, the parent company of NBC.) The same report said that the Chase Manhattan Bank held stock in 28 broadcasting firms. The report, entitled "Disclosure of Corporate Ownership," was the result of more than two years of investigation and was published by the Senate subcommittee on intergovernmental relations. After that, Chase obtained 6.7% of ABC, and today the percentage could be much greater.

"En Route to Global Occupation" by Gary H. Kah, p.56-57.
(Comment added.)

That does not mean that control over the news media commenced about 1950 or so. It actually began much earlier but just solidified in the 50's and 60's.

In March, 1915, the J.P.Morgan interests, the steel, shipbuilding, and powder interest, and their subsidiary organizations, got together 12 men high up in the newspaper world and employed them to select the most influential newspapers in the United States and sufficient number of them **to control generally the policy of the daily press... They found it was only necessary to purchase the control of 25 of the greatest papers.** The 25 newspapers were agreed upon; emissaries were sent to purchase the policy, national and international, of these papers; an agreement was reached; the policy of the papers was **bought**, to be paid for by the month; an editor was furnished for each paper to properly supervise and edit information regarding the questions of preparedness, militarism, financial policies, and other things of national and international nature **considered vital to the interest of the purchasers... This policy also included the suppression of everything in opposition to the wishes of the interests served.**

U.S. Congressman Oscar Callaway,
The Congressional Record, Feb. 9, 1917
Vol. 54, (2947–48)

But the control over the media is even more subtle and profound than just owning the stock. The members of the Federal Reserve Board are owners of a number of large, supranational corporations in the US and throughout the world, which are the source of huge advertising revenues for broadcasting firms, newspapers and magazines. They also are on the boards of directors of others. They significantly influence what the media reports through advertising alone, as was stated in the quotation by Bill Moyers at the beginning of the chapter. Because of these facts, it actually becomes very clear why their conspiracy receives little or no press attention.

Now here are more examples of how this news media blanket works. You remember the book, *Tragedy and Hope* by Carroll Quigley mentioned in the last chapter. The history of the book is very interesting and will shed light on how they control what we see and hear.

Carroll Quigley was a professor of history at Georgetown University. He was a member of this international cabal and was proud of it. So much so that he wrote a major history book, *Tragedy and Hope*, in which he put forth the real history of western Europe from about the time of Columbus to the present. In this tome, about 1300 pages long, he patiently and in great detail explained how the international bankers beginning with the Rothschilds, gradually came to control first the central banks of Europe, and through them, the governments of Europe. He showed how they formed groups like the round tables groups (I will cover that in the next chapter), the Council on Foreign Relations and their counter organizations in other countries, and their acquisition of the major media and major corporations around the world. He was quite proud of this book. Here he makes his famous confession:

> **...There does exist, and has existed for a generation, an international Anglophile network which operates, to some extent, in the way the radical Right believes the Communists act.** In fact, this network, which we may identify as the Round Table Groups, has no aversion to cooperating with the Communists, or any other groups, and frequently does so. **I know of the operations of this network because I have studied it for twenty years and was permitted for two years, in the early 1960's, to examine its papers and secret records. I have no aversion to it** or to most of its aims and have, for much of my life, been close to it and to many of its instruments. I have objected, both in the past and recently, to a few of its policies...but in general my chief difference of opinion is that it **wishes to remain unknown, and I believe its role in history is significant enough to be known.**
>
> *Tragedy and Hope,* (950)

Do you understand the significance of that statement? It came not from an outsider but from an *insider who was willing to talk.*

Because of his influence with the conspirators, Quigley got his book published by Macmillan Co., one of the foremost book publishers in the U.S. That act was one of the conspiracy's occasional mistakes. The first printing was for 5,000 copies, and they sold out in short order. That was in 1966. So what do you think a book publisher normally does when the first printing of a book sells so well? They do a bigger printing, of course. But when they saw that the book revealed much of the history of their conspiracy, which revelation was discovered after the fact, they refused to reprint it! This book had all the earmarks of being a best seller. But they, along with every other major book publisher, refused to reprint it. And the press ignored it. Surprise, surprise.

Quigley himself came to the same conclusion that his book was suppressed:

> "...I am now quite sure that *Tragedy and Hope* was suppressed although I don't know why or by whom..."
>
> Carroll Quigley
> in a letter to a friend

If you want to get a copy of it today, you have to get it through small, out of the way publishing companies. Nevertheless, it is obtainable. You may purchase your own copy of *Tragedy and Hope* from booksellers on the internet. Learn about this secret combination from someone on the inside. To this day, this important book is ignored by the media. They try to pretend that it doesn't exist. So the news media blanket succeeded in keeping most Americans ignorant of the truth. This blanket of secrecy is very effective.

Quigley was mentioned in Ripley's Believe-it-or-Not as the youngest person ever to graduate with a Ph.D. from Harvard. He was a respected professor and an influential character in the conspiracy. He was one of their top recruiters who, as a university professor, quietly brought into the conspiracy fresh young minds. Some students, upon hearing about the conspiracy, are eager to become part of this great secret while others gradually warm up to the idea.

One of his most successful recruits was William Jefferson Clinton, who was inducted into the conspiracy while a Rhodes scholar at Oxford University in England. Quigley was instrumental in helping Clinton get this scholarship. The conspirators use the Rhodes Scholarships to introduce fresh minds to the conspiracy. That does not mean, necessarily, that all Rhodes scholars become part of the conspiracy. Some students do not work out as potential recruits. They may, for instance, balk at the last minute and reject the idea of rule by the few. In that case, they are allowed to just finish their education and go on with their lives without even knowing that they were being tested to become a part of this great latter-day secret combination.

Clinton regarded Quigley as his mentor in politics. Clinton was so influenced by Quigley that when he gave his first inaugural speech in

1992, he mentioned the fact that he (Clinton) studied under professor Quigley while a student at Georgetown University and considered Quigley to be one of the most influential characters in his life.

Here is yet another quote supporting the idea that the media is controlled:

It was this group of people, whose wealth and influence so exceeded their experience and understanding, who provided much of the framework of influence which the Communist sympathizers and fellow travelers took over in the united States in the 1930's.

It must be recognized that the power that these energetic Left-Wingers exercised was never their own power or Communist power but was ultimately the power of the international financial coterie, and, once the anger and suspicions of the American people were aroused, as they were by 1950, it was a fairly simple matter to get rid of the Red sympathizers.

Before this could be done, however, a congressional committee, following backward to their source the threads which led from admitted Communists like Whittaker Chambers, through Alger Hiss, and the Carnegie Endowment to Thomas Lamont and the Morgan Bank, **fell into the whole complicated network of the interlocking tax-exempt foundations.**

The Eighty-third congress in July 1953 set up a Special Committee to investigate Tax Exempt Foundations with Representative B. Carroll Reece, of Tennessee, as chairman. **It soon became clear that people of immense wealth would be unhappy if the investigation went too far and that the "most respected" newspapers in the country, closely allied with these men of wealth, would not get excited enough about any revelations to make the publicity worth while, in terms of votes or campaign contributions.** An interesting report showing the Left-wing associations of the interlocking nexus of tax-exempt foundations was issued in 1954 rather quietly. Four years later, the

Reece committee's general counsel, Rene A. Wormser, wrote a shocked, but not shocking, book on the subject called *Foundations: Their Power and Influence*.

Tragedy and Hope, (954—955)

Actually, there are many stories the media deletes. Here is yet another:

"If the Bilderberg Group is not a conspiracy of some sort, it is conducted in such a way as to give a remarkably good imitation of one."

These are the words of C. Gordon Tether, published on May 6, 1975, in "Lombard", a prestigious and influential column which he wrote daily for the (London) Financial Times. It was to be Tether's last reference to the Bilderberg Group in the FT. **All subsequent articles mentioning Bilderberg were barred from appearing in his financial and banking column by the editorial management.**

Tether was finally dismissed by the FT in August 1976 after a censorship battle which raged for well over two years. "Lombard", which Tether created and which has earned a place in the Guiness Book of Records for being the longest running daily column in the British Press, is now written by different specialists from the FT's staff. **There is no hint of Bilderberg these days.**

It is perhaps significant to note that **FT editor Fisher is a member of the Trilateral Commission,** (another secret group discussed later) **an organization closely related to Bilderberg...**

In fact, most editors of the "establishment" Press in Britain, Europe, and the United States have attended Bilderberg Conferences. Some are even members of the international steering committee which governs

Bilderberg.

Robert Eringer

The Global Manipulators, extract from Chapter four

Eringer goes on to say that the reason journalists are asked to attend Bilderberg and other secret meetings is that they are then bound by the same rules as members, that is, not to write about the proceedings.

Isn't it interesting to see for yourself just how much information is suppressed? It's like opening up a whole new world of truth. It helps one gain a true perspective of what the media is really like.

But there's more. On February 17, 1950, James Warburg, (his kin, Paul Warburg, helped set up the Federal Reserve System on Jekyll Island in 1910) Council on Foreign Relations member and international banker, stated before a Senate Foreign Relations Committee, **"We shall have one world government whether or not you like it, by conquest or consent."** What a provocative statement! But did you ever hear one word about it from the news media? Nobody did.

Or this: In the April 1974 issue of the Council on Foreign Relations quarterly magazine, *Foreign Affairs*, p. 558, Richard Gardener states that the new world order "will be built...but an end run around national sovereignty, eroding it piece by piece, will accomplish much more than the old fashioned frontal assault." When that was published by *Foreign Affairs*, Congressmen McDonald, Heinz and Tower stated that this is a conspiracy. But again, the news media was conspicuously silent.

The media will destroy good men's reputations without so much as a by-your-leave (as in the case of Ray Donovan, former Secretary of Labor under Reagan). They will viciously attack anyone who would try to tell the truth, (as in the case of Senator Joe McCarthy, who tried to point out Communists in the government and elsewhere). But they are conspicuously silent about their owners who are trying to destroy freedom throughout the world. Upton Sinclair had it right—"It is difficult for them to see whose paycheck depends on them not seeing."

The Bull Ring Syndrome

The Bull Ring Syndrome doesn't refer to matadors or the spectacle of a bull fight. Instead, it has reference to the ring that is often inserted through the nose of a bull so that he can be handled more easily. Unfortunately, the American public suffers from this syndrome and we don't even know it. We have been led around by the nose for a long time by the media. All too often, we have come to accept ideas that they want us to accept, fed to us gradually, subtly and persistently.

You see, there is more to the function of the media than just keeping silent about the treasonous activities of the global conspiracy. The media, in fact, has four main functions laid down by their bosses, the conspirators.

-The media are charged with keeping the conspiracy off the air.

-The media try to gradually indoctrinate us into accepting the idea of one-world government. They do this by promoting one-world government concepts and minimizing ideas of nationalism or patriotism. The aforementioned concepts originate in their think tanks like Tavistock Institute and are given to the media for dissemination to the masses. We are gradually being conditioned to think favorably about the idea of nations without borders and the scrapping of outmoded national constitutions.

As evidence of the above, here are quotations worth examining from none other than the dean of American journalism himself, Walter Cronkite. He recently wrote a book called *A Reporter's Life*, 1996, published by Alfred A. Knopf and Random House in which the following appears:

If we are to avoid that catastrophe (nuclear devastation), a system of world order—preferably a system of world government—is mandatory. The proud nations someday will see the light and, for the common good and their own survival, **yield up their**

precious sovereignty, just as America's thirteen colonies did two centuries ago.

When we finally come to our senses and establish a world executive and parliament of nations, thanks to the Nuremberg precedent we will already have in place the fundamentals for the third branch of government, the judiciary.

And how about this statement, same author, same book:

There is going to be a social and political and economic evolution, which will explode with such suddenness as to have the character of revolution. The revolutionary forces are already at work today, and they have humankind's dreams on their side. **We don't want to be on the other side**.

The last sentence sounds ominous, as well it should. Here we have an example of a planned leak by the controlled media telling us what is coming in the future. If you want, begin looking through newspapers, books and other media observing hints dropped here and there as to what are the insider's future plans.

-The entertainment media is used to promote drugs, promiscuity, homosexuality, Satanism, Witchcraft, divorce, violence and every other evil influence calculated to destroy the family unit and degrade society as a whole. Sometimes this promotion is quite subtle. This vile promotion scheme is a subplot of the conspiracy's overall connivance of world domination. This subplot is called the "Aquarian Conspiracy." The origins of the Aquarian Conspiracy will be dealt with in another chapter.

-And, lastly, the media manipulates us into fighting created wars. These concocted conflicts are considered by the conspirators to be necessary to eliminate their enemies and to depopulate the world, if you can believe it.

Sound Orwellian? It's not really that outrageous when one reads this quotation from Jerry Spence:

> ...we have delivered our freedoms to a new master, the corporate and governmental conglomerate, ...'the New King.'

> ...we have achieved the **Orwellian prediction**—enslaved, the people have been programed to love their bondage and are left to clutch only mirage like images of freedom, its fables and fictions.

> The new slaves are linked together by vast electronic chains of television that imprison not their bodies but their minds. **Their desires are programed, their tastes manipulated, their values set for them.** Whereas the Black slave was chained to a living master, the new slave has become a digit, a mere item of production that is expended by an invisible master without heart or soul.

From the foreword to his book
From Freedom to Slavery

What a horrendous thought! That we, who consider ourselves knowledgeable about the world because we think we have a "free press", could ever be manipulated into accepting things we haven't considered or even wanted! But this manipulation happens all the time.

One of the many ways the conspirators control us is to manipulate us into hating some enemy they want us to hate. This sounds like something straight from 1984, and in some ways, it is. Usually the object of hatred is some dictator or even a prominent person like Senator McCarthy in the 1950's who was not controlled by them. Then when we have been beguiled into disliking the 'bad guy', we help subdue the enemies of one—world government by giving our blessing, through public opinion polls, for our government to make war with the enemy.

That is, our opinion is manipulated, by carefully controlled newscasts and pollsters, into agreeing with the conspirators that some head of state they don't like is "bad" and must be punished. After being brainwashed with subtle, negative stories about this "tyrant" for a sufficient length of time, the public is then asked for their opinion, through public opinion polls that are precisely worded to evoke the "correct" response. That then gives the conspirators the appearance of public support they want so as to be able to make war on the poor schmuck who happens to be on the blacklist.

Amazingly, the people who control us have need of public support. Don't think that the conspirators suppose that they can do whatever they want and public opinion be damned!

The conspirators will not send the sons of the masses out to be slaughtered unless the public is first blinded into believing that the war they are to engage in is a "patriotic war." The cabalists know that, at least for the time being, they need to have public support for the wars they pursue. That is because the conspirators know that they do not yet have one—world government. They know that if the masses ever found out what was really going on, the conspiracy would be overthrown.

But the important thing to remember is that the "enemy" is always *carefully selected for us.* This is right out of the book, 1984. There are many dictators and heads of state who know the New World Order for what it is, and resist it. If these dictators don't go along with what the NWO wants, they are set up by the media as the "new" Hitler and slandered, thus setting them up for elimination.

As an example, in Desert Storm, the bad guy was Saddam Hussein. We were conditioned, with every newscast, to think negatively about this "monster." The media subtly cast him as the enemy. Does that mean that Saddam is a nice guy? No! But think. There are many dictators that would make Saddam look like a boy scout if we were allowed to see the truth about them. (The heads of Communist China come immediately to mind). These others are ignored because they are controlled by, or are active supporters of the conspiracy. So we are conditioned to go to war with the people the New World Order wants to control or destroy. We are being herded down a certain path. We are allowed to see a only a planned, orchestrated production.

Let me show you how that was done in the case of the Gulf War.

Transcript of Meeting Between Iraqi President, Saddam Hussein and U.S. Ambassador to Iraq, April Glaspie. —July 25, 1990 (Eight days before the August 2, 1990 Iraqi Invasion of Kuwait)

[Comment—there is some dispute as to the date of this meeting. At the end of this piece, the date suggested is July 29, 1990.]

July 25, 1990 — Presidential Palace — Baghdad

U.S. Ambassador Glaspie —

I have direct instructions from President Bush to improve our relations with Iraq. We have considerable sympathy for your quest for higher oil prices, the immediate cause of your confrontation with Kuwait. (pause) As you know, I lived here for years and admire your extraordinary efforts to rebuild your country. We know you need funds. We understand that, and our opinion is that you should have the opportunity to rebuild your country. (pause) We can see that you have deployed massive numbers of troops in the south. Normally that would be none of our business, but when this happens in the context of your threats against Kuwait, then it would be reasonable for us to be concerned. For this reason, I have received an instruction to ask you, in the spirit of friendship—not confrontation—regarding your intentions: Why are your troops massed so very close to Kuwait's borders?

Saddam Hussein —

As you know, for years now I have made every effort to reach a settlement on our dispute with Kuwait. There is to be a meeting in two days; I am prepared to give negotiations only this one more brief chance. (pause) When we (the Iraqis) meet (with the Kuwaitis) and we see there is hope, then nothing will happen. But if we are unable to find a solution, then it will be natural that Iraq will not accept death.

U.S. Ambassador Glaspie —

What solutions would be acceptable?

Saddam Hussein —

If we could keep the whole of the Shatt al Arab—our strategic goal in our war with Iran—we will make concessions (to the Kuwaitis). But, if we are forced to choose between keeping half of the Shatt and the whole of Iraq (i.e., in Saddam's view, including Kuwait) then we will give up all of the Shatt to defend our claims on Kuwait to keep the whole of Iraq in the shape we wish it to be. (pause) What is the United States' opinion on this?

U.S. Ambassador Glaspie —

We have no opinion on your Arab-Arab conflicts, such as your dispute with Kuwait. Secretary (of State James) Baker has directed me to emphasize the instruction, first given to Iraq in the 1960's, that the Kuwait issue is not associated with America. (Saddam smiles)

On August 2, 1990 four days later, Saddam's massed troops invade and occupy Kuwait.

Not only that, but according to Ramsey Clark's "The Fire Next Time," pp. 23-24, April Glaspie lied to the Congress in March 1991, claiming that she had repeatedly warned Saddam Hussein that the U.S. would not tolerate any use of violence by Iraq to settle its dispute with Kuwait, but she was proved wrong when her cables to the State Department were released in July 1991.

Saddam was set up, that is, he was lied to by Ms. Glaspie into thinking that America had no interest in a Iraqi-Kuwaiti conflict. But we know from history that as soon as Iraq invaded Kuwait, America began frothing at the mouth with hypocrisy about the "war-mongering" Hussein. So why did America prod Hussein into starting a war, then expend American and Arab lives to fight it, when the Yanks could have easily prevented said war just by telling Saddam to back off in the first place? There is actually more than one answer to that question, but one notion is the same with all wars. That is, war is immensely profitable.

All wars promoted by the cabal are aimed at profit. The fact is, the conspirators sell armaments to both sides of all wars and make double profits thereby. Wars are at least as profitable as drugs and the international businessmen know this. But there are other reasons to promote armed conflicts.

To help explain other reasons for war, here is a quotation from Dr. Coleman's book, *The Conspirator's Hierarchy: The Story of the Committee of 300* that is an eye opener:

> We are close to the point where **the United States will send its military Forces to settle any and all disputes brought before the United Nations...This is an important step along the road to a One World Government.**

So the United States is being increasingly used as the world's policeman, with each conflict becoming larger and more involved with NATO or the U.N. By doing that, the lines of national self—interest become blurred and slowly merged with international goals. In the future America will no longer object to the formal merging of her armed forces with a world army. At least, that seems to be the goal of the conspirators. However, American public opinion seems to go against that idea, in spite of the media propaganda to the contrary.

Here's another quotation to reinforce the above sentiment:

> On a CNN program in late July, 1991, CFR member and former CIA director Stansfield Turner (Rhodes Scholar), when asked about Iraq, responds:

> We have a much bigger objective. We've got to look at the long run here. This is an example—the situation between the United Nations and Iraq—where the United Nations is **deliberately intruding into the sovereignly of a sovereign nation...Now this is a marvelous precedent (to be used in) all countries of the world...**
>
> *Secret Records Revealed*
> op cit, (142)

The very idea of using American forces to be the world's policeman will be further discussed in the next chapter. As America evolves into the world's policeman, the world, in return, will come to resent America more and more. The natural result of such increasing interference in the internal affairs of other nations will be that the world just might avenge themselves on us. World opinion is extremely hateful of America at the present time. The conspirators *know* this and are using American military might to exacerbate just such resentment. The conspirators are doing this to provoke someone, such as Russia, into attacking America, thus causing WWIII. This is a distinct possibility. By moving our nation in this direction of the world's policeman, thus causing resentment in other nations, an international war against the U.S. is the natural consequence. Such a move will be used as a pretext to help the conspirators grab power over the world.

From the book, *Conspirators' Hierarchy, the Story of the Committee of 300*, Dr. John Coleman says the following:

It is the job of the polling companies to mold and shape public opinion in the way that suits the conspirators. Polls are constantly being taken by CBS-NBC-ABC, the New York Times, the Washington Post. Most of these efforts are coordinated at the National Opinion Research Center where, as much as it will amaze most of us, a psychological profile was developed for the entire nation.

Findings are fed into the computers of Gallup Poll and Yankelovich, Shelley and White for comparative evaluation. Much of what we read in our newspapers or see on television has first been cleared by the polling companies. WHAT WE SEE IS WHAT THE POLLSTERS THINK WE SHOULD SEE. This is called "public opinion making." The whole idea behind this bit of social conditioning **is to find out how responsive the public is to POLICY DIRECTIVES handed down by the Committee of 300.** (More on them in a later chapter). We are called "targeted population groups" and what is measured by the pollsters is how much public resistance is generated to what appears in the "Nightly News.''...

...Today our people believe they are well—informed but what they do not realize is that the opinions they believe are their own **were in fact created in the research institutions and think tanks of America** and that none of us are free to form our own opinions because of the information we are provided with by the media and the pollsters.

Polling was brought to a fine art just before the United States entered the Second World War. Americans, unbeknown to themselves, were conditioned to look upon Germany and Japan as dangerous enemies who had to be stopped. In a sense, this was true, and that makes conditioned thinking all the more dangerous, because based on the INFORMATION fed to them, the enemy did indeed appear to be Germany and Japan. Just recently we saw how well (the) conditioning process works when Americans were conditioned to perceive Iraq as a threat and Saddam Hussein as a personal enemy of the United States...

One of the most respected of all pollsters is Committee of 300 member Daniel Yankelovich, of the company, Yankelovich, Skelly and White. Yankelovich is proud to tell his students that **polling is a tool to change public opinion...**

I've saved the best for last. Here is an example of outright lying from NBC news using a popular radio show. The conspirators really hate that part of the Constitution, the Second Amendment to the Bill of Rights. Their aim is to disarm American citizens. Among other things, they try to shade the news against gun ownership. This was sent to the Drudge Report which can be accessed on the internet.

Dear Mr. Drudge,

Howie Carr and The Howie Carr Show had an interesting experience with NBC's Nightly News with Tom Brokaw on Tuesday. NBC called us and asked if we would discuss the topic of the effect of the Littleton shootings on our listeners attitudes towards gun ownership. Lisa Myers had a piece scheduled for that nights news broadcast and she wanted popular reaction footage to complete her piece.

We agreed. In the first hour of the show Howie asked the listeners how they were effected if at all while the NBC cameras rolled. **We took 33 calls. 30 of those calls said the effect of the shootings was to make them want to own a gun for protection and not tighten up the laws.**

When the story aired on NBC that night Lisa Myers said that **according to polls (which ones she never identified) and popular reactions on talk shows most people were in favor of stricter gun laws and were against gun ownership. She went on to play one of the 3 anti-gun phone calls from our show completely ignoring the 30 calls which did not agree with her premise.**

This skewing of the actual poll results from our show has caused quite a stir among our listeners who...heard the gun hour and then witnessed the blatant misrepresentation of what the majority response was on NBC news. It has left much of our audience feeling mistrustful and angry with network news in general and NBC specifically...

Thanks for letting us vent.

> Nancy Shack, Executive Producer The Howie Carr Show.
> News Manipulation Noted at NBC on Gun Issues
> Letters to Drudge 6/10/99 From Nancy Shack

More Quotations About the Media

Herman Dinsmore becomes foreign editor of *The New York Times*, and will remain in that position until 1960. In his book, *All the*

News that Fits (1969), he will write:

The New York Times today is deliberately **pitched to the so-called liberal point of view**...Positively and negatively, the weight of *The (New York) Times* has **generally on the side of the communists since the end of World War II.**
Secret Records Revealed, op cit, (85—86)

Pope Paul VI writes in *Populorum Progressio* calling for a "new juridical order" and stating:

Who can fail to see the need and importance of thus gradually coming to the establishment of a world authority capable of taking effective action on the juridical and political planes?...Delegates to international organizations, public officials, **gentlemen of the press**, teachers and educators–all of you must realize that you have your part to play in the construction of a new world order.
Ibid, (108)

The Real War by former President Nixon is published (1980), in which he explains:

The nation's immediate problem is that while the common man fights America's wars, the intellectual elite sets its agenda. Today, whether the West lives or dies is in the hands of its new power elite: those who **set the terms of public debate, who manipulate the symbols, who decide whether nations or leaders will be depicted on 100 million television sets as "good" or "bad."** This power elite sets the limits of the possible for Presidents and Congress. It molds the impressions that move the nation, or that mire it.
Ibid, (125)

In the next chapter, we discover what the conspiracy has done in the realm of direct political intervention.

Chapter 4

In politics nothing happens by accident. If it happens, you can bet it was planned that way.
—Franklin Delano Roosevelt

'The Buck Stops Here'—Harry Truman

We dealt with international banking and finance in the second chapter. The third was an expose of the national and international news media. This chapter deals with direct political control of the Presidency from behind the scenes, plus considerable influence in Congress as also the Supreme Court.

The case for direct political control of governments from behind the scenes is not new. It started in antiquity, and had many faces. Perhaps the best known example was the triumvirate of Crassus, Pompeii and Julius Caesar. They conspired to overturn Rome's Republic and establish an Empire with Crassus as Praetor first then Julius Caesar became the first Emperor. How will be covered later.

The Book of Mormon gives an example of how the Gadianton Robbers (a secret combination founded by Gadianton) managed to overturn the freely elected Nephite rule of Judges and place a member of their secret order on the throne as Chief Judge. This is found in Helaman 7:4,5. Chapter 2:13 says:

> And behold, in the end of this book ye shall see that this Gadianton did prove the overthrow, yea, almost the entire destruction of the people of Nephi.

So the idea that nations are controlled from behind the scenes is nothing new.

New York—"Do you smell something in the halls here?" Joseph V.

65

Reed asks a visitor to the plushly furnished 17th floor of One Chase Manhattan Plaza, where the office of Mr. Reed's boss and Chase's chairman, David Rockefeller, is located. "Do you know what it is?" presses the aide-de-camp, lowering his voice. "It is the smell of power."

"That man in there," pronounces Mr. Reed grandly, nodding toward Mr. Rockefeller's office, "is the equivalent of a head of state. He is the chairman of the board of the Eastern Establishment." (i.e., head of the Council on Foreign Relations).

Julie Salamon
The Wall Street Journal, front page
April 3, 1981 (Comment Added).

The power behind the political scene in America is exercised through an organization called the Council on Foreign Relations, or the CFR. The CFR, often called the "Establishment" by most Americans, is not the supreme organization for world government but is controlled by, and part of, a higher organization called the "Round Table." These groups and others that sprang up through of them are the subjects of this chapter.

To show evidence supporting the view that the Presidency is run via the CFR, please consider this quotation:

For a long time I felt that FDR had developed many thoughts and ideas that were his own to benefit this country, the United States. But, he didn't. **Most of his thoughts, his political ammunition, as it were, were carefully manufactured for him in advance by the Council on Foreign Relations One World Money group...**Brilliantly, with great gusto, like a fine piece of artillery, he exploded that prepared "ammunition" in the middle of an unsuspecting target, the American people, and thus paid off and returned his internationalist political support.

...My feeling is that he accepted that support merely as a practical means to gain and retain for himself more personal and political power.

Curtis Dall, FDR's son in law as quoted in his book,
FDR My Exploited Father in Law
Christian Crusade Publications 1968 (185)

Curtis Dall expressed the view that his father-in-law (Franklin Delano Roosevelt) was manipulated from behind the scenes. Does that surprise you? But Dall wasn't the only one to think of behind the scenes control. Here's a quote from Woodrow Wilson:

> Since I entered politics, I have chiefly had men's views confided to me privately. Some of the biggest men in the U.S., in the field of commerce and manufacturing, are afraid of something. They know that there is a power somewhere so organized, so subtle, so watchful, so interlocked, so complete, so pervasive, that they had better not speak above their breath when they speak in condemnation of it.
>
> Woodrow Wilson
> *The New Freedom,* Doubleday, 1913 (13, 14)

The House that House Built

The Council on Foreign Relations was officially formed on the 29th of July, 1921 in Paris France. The men who made up this original meeting of the CFR met the approval of Baron Edmond de Rothschild of France. It was Baron de Rothschild who dominated this conference. (*The Unseen Hand*, R. Epperson). So Rothschild was involved with the formation of the Federal Reserve System, and now with the CFR. It seems that the people who rule us run in a small circle. Notice the other names in this paragraph. Most were also involved in the formation of the Fed. Money for the founding of the CFR came primarily from J.P.Morgan, Bernard Baruch, Jacob Schiff, Paul D. Warburg and John D. Rockefeller, among others. (What is Mystery Babylon? By Rev. R.L. Meares).

One of the principal players in the formation of the CFR was Colonel Edward Mandell House. House was a friend and personal adviser of President Woodrow Wilson during his term of office. Writing in the July 17, 1926 issue of the *Saturday Evening Post*, Arthur D. Howden Smith presented a profile of House.

...Although few Americans beyond the rarefied realms of the political elite knew much of House, the austere Texan had played a decisive role in many of the most important policy decisions made by President Woodrow Wilson. On more than one occasion, Wilson described House as his "silent partner," his "second personality," his "independent self." Although his friendship would later disintegrate under the stress of political disappointment, during the eight years of the Wilson Administration, the President maintained of House that "his thoughts and mine are one."

House was enamored by the notion of forming a one world government with himself, of course, at the head. He believed that the Constitution, "...(a) product of eighteenth century minds and a quasi-classical, medieval conception of republics, was thoroughly outdated; that the country would be better off if the Constitution could be scrapped and rewritten."

Reflective of that viewpoint, House wrote a novel called *Philip Dru: Administrator* in 1912. In it, a man who calls himself an "idealistic" Marxist seizes control of the U. S. Government through a coup and installs socialist reforms by fiat. He envisioned "Socialism as dreamed of by Karl Marx, along with a "spiritual leavening." In that novel, Dru seeks to establish a "League of Nations" (his own term from the book) and the merging of the United States into a world government. It was published anonymously but House confided to friends in private letters that he, indeed, was the author.

As you might have already guessed, House was behind the League of Nations movement in America. As a matter of fact, he was one of the principle players to create the Treaty of Versailles, within which was placed the League of Nations charter. When the Senate saw that joining the League of Nations meant a loss of sovereignty, they rightly balked at the idea. Following the Senate rejection of enrollment in the League, House was heartbroken. He could see that the Senate was not "forward thinking" like himself. So he had to go back to the drawing board and start all over.

Such was the personality of the man who was close to not only Wilson, but FDR as well. He was responsible for a lot of evil in the early part of this century. He also had a hand in the creation of the Income Tax amendment to the Constitution which is another story in itself.

Again, from The New American "Conspiracy" Issue, 1997 edition, p. 11:

> When, in real life, the League of Nations was thwarted by the U.S. Senate, House and his colleagues found it necessary to continue their struggle by other means. Hose was part of a cabal called "The Inquiry," a group of 100 "forward-looking" social engineers who created the Versailles Peace Treaty...This group formed the nucleus of the Institute of International Affairs, which was to have branches in New York and London—the Council on Foreign Relations (CFR) and the Royal Institute of International Affairs, respectively. This is the basis of the "Anglophile network" described by historian Carroll Quigley in...*Tragedy and Hope*...

In the beginning, the CFR was not especially powerful. It had limited input in the decisions of government. But the CFR gradually assumed more power, until an event happened to propel it to the forefront of foreign policy decision making. That event was WWII.

> Several of the most important features of the international order after WWII—including the International Monetary Fund, the World Bank and the United Nations—were conceived by a small group of planners at the Council on Foreign Relations between the years 1939 and 1942. **Working under the auspices of the War and Peace Studies Project, the council developed close ties with the State Department and infused the government with its view of the "national interest" for the postwar era...**

> Immediately after WWII broke out in Europe in September, 1939, leaders within the Council on Foreign Relations began to think about what United States war aims should be. They also were

concerned to develop plans for the shape of the postwar world. **The executive director of the council and the editor of its magazine, Foreign Affairs, traveled to Washington two weeks after the war began** to express their concerns to State Department officials and to **gain official support for the council's proposal to study these problems**. The contact was made easily because of numerous direct links between the council and State, including the close relationship between Council president Norman H. Davis and Secretary of State Cordell Hull.

The Powers That Be

G. William Domhoff

Vintage Books Jan. 1979, p. 101—102

To paraphrase, the book goes on to say that funding for the study groups between the CFR and the State Department came from the Rockefeller foundation. At first the CFR influence within the State Department was limited to advisory capacity, but with Secretary of State Hull's help, the council began to gradually increase its involvement, scope and authority so that "By 1942, then, the study groups set up by the council in 1939 had been in effect merged into the State Department as its postwar planning apparatus...**The line between the allegedly independent state bureaucracy and the private policy-planning groups had become very hazy indeed.**" (*The Powers That Be*, p. 106-107). And from that day to this, the CFR controlled the State Department then spread its influence to other Cabinet Departments and to the Presidency itself.

Now, just how does the CFR influence our government today? The answer partially lies with a excerpt directly from the CFR's own publication, *Foreign Affairs*.

The purposes of the Council on Foreign Relations are several and overlapping: **to break new ground** in the consideration of international issues, **to help shape American foreign policy in a constructive, non-partisan manner; to provide continuing leadership for the conduct of our foreign relations;**

and to inform and stimulate the Council's membership, as well as **reach a wider audience, through publications and other means...**

To encourage a forthright exchange of ideas and full freedom of expression in Council meetings, it is the Council's tradition that participants will not later **attribute the statements of speakers and other participants to them in public media or forums or knowingly transmit them to persons who will.** Some meetings are open to selected guests or are announced as on-the-record.

> Council on Foreign Relations, Inc.-Summary Description,
> June 30, 1979 (5)

The Council on Foreign Relations is a semi-secret organization. It holds meetings, (sometimes open to selected guests), seminars, discussion groups, working luncheons and lectures about foreign policy. Sometimes they will allow some of their meetings such as formal dinners to be broadcast either over the radio and/or T.V., usually PBS. As topics are discussed, the CFR elicits as broad a range of opinions as possible from their membership or even from guests, and try to understand a topic from as many viewpoints as possible.

The CFR has considerable power in each Presidency, regardless of which party controls the White House, because both Democrats and Republicans staff almost all of the positions in each cabinet with CFR members. That is, almost all of the Secretaries of State from FDR to now have been CFR members. And that goes for the Secretary of Defense, the Secretary of Commerce, the Secretary of the Treasury, the Secretary of HUD, the Secretary of the Interior, the Secretary of Education, the head of the NSA, the head of the CIA, etc.

That is what Alexandr Solzhenitsyn was referring to in *Foreign Affairs*:

It is clear that Robert C. Tucker's essay reflects not only his personal opinions but the established views of a milieu which exerts a formative influence upon U.S. policy: **whether Democrats or Republicans are in power, and regardless of who is in the White House, the leading experts and advisers are drawn from these same circles.**

Foreign Affairs Fall 1980
"Mr. Solzhenitsyn and His Critics" (200)

Foreign Affairs, published quarterly, is the official periodical of the CFR, which may be purchased in almost any bookstore or found in any library. Because of this the CFR claims that they are not a secret organization since anyone can read about them. They say they are trying to "reach a wider audience, through publications and other means." (See the above quotation). But if that is really true, why don't they go on prime time T.V. or put themselves on the front pages of magazines and newspapers on a continual basis? Why doesn't the CFR openly allow media coverage of all their meetings? After all, that is what happens with Congress.

That is, the floors of both chambers of Congress have national T.V. coverage, plus coverage of selected committee hearings. In addition, all speeches given on the floor of either the House or Senate, plus all speeches that occur in all committee or subcommittee meetings, along with all investigations and everything that is said, excluding national defense secrets, are openly published in the *Congressional Record* for the public to see. The *Congressional Record* consists of about twenty thousand pages of national business conducted in Congress and published **each and every day** by the Library of Congress and is open to public inspection.

Contrast that with the 250 or so pages published each **quarter** through the CFR's publication, *Foreign Affairs*, when the membership of the CFR is about 3,000! The CFR claims they want to "reach a wider audience" and their membership roster is well represented by owners of major news media, including newspapers, magazines, journals, T.V., radio and the CEO's of major movie companies. These news makers could easily do a media blitz and deluge the general populace with infomercials or T.V. specials if they really wanted to "reach a wider audience." The CFR could become a household name with no problem.

So if that's true, and the CFR wants to "reach a wider audience," why is it that not one person in a thousand has ever heard of the CFR? The members occupy some of the most powerful positions in the country in finance, business, media, politics, education, religion and entertainment and yet the vast majority of Americans have no knowledge of who the CFR is or how much influence they wield.

The answer to that, of course, is that the CFR *doesn't* want the general populace to know about them and what they are really trying to do. Publicity provokes questions, and they know that there are questions that they can't answer. Like, for instance: Where is the CFR (or anything like it) mentioned in the Constitution? Or: What Supreme Court decision or constitutional amendment gave the CFR the right to occupy positions of power in our national government? Wouldn't such influence at the very least be considered a conflict of interest, or at worst, treason? What is the agenda of the CFR? And: Why do you overlook the views of the vast majority of Americans when you make your decisions?

However, the CFR also knows that if they were strictly secret, with absolutely no coverage of any kind and no at large publications, then the claim of secrecy that is leveled against them all the time could grow until it united people against them. So to deflect criticism, the CFR allows the public a small view, with no in depth reporting nor auditing done by the news media nor Congress. But the amount of exposure they allow is extremely limited considering their huge scope of influence.

They allow minimal media coverage such as occasional PBS specials, newspaper stories, and oblique references in magazines or newspapers. Less than twenty full—blown, in—depth newspaper and magazine articles have been published about them in the last fifty years. And even those were carefully scanned so as to give general information without really exposing anything important about the CFR.

The membership of the CFR consists almost exclusively of CEO's of multinational corporations and members of their respective boards of directors, billionaires and international bankers; owners of newspapers, magazines, book publishing companies and T.V. and radio corporations; movie personalities and famous entertainers; union presidents, presidents of national racial organizations, heads of national religious organizations; university presidents, foundation presidents and members of the Federal Reserve Board; nationally known reporters, journalists, editors, news anchors and publishers; presidential advisors, present and former cabinet members, members of the Joint Chiefs of Staff, Supreme Court Justices, present and former Presidents of the United States, Senators and Congressmen.

In other words, people with money, power and/or fame. The median income of the members of the CFR is sky high compared to the median income of the average American. That suggests rule by the rich and powerful (secretly, of course) with little or no representation from the middle class who characterize the vast majority of Americans.

As for the ideology of the members of the CFR, they come from all possible philosophies and political affiliations. There are republicans, democrats, liberals, conservatives and independents. There are Marxists, socialists, free—enterprise capitalists; religious persons as well as non—religious; agnostics, atheists, anarchists, nihilists, and every —ist you can think of. There are blacks, orientals, whites and all races represented. The leadership of the CFR goes out of its way to listen to and encourage all points of view. As a matter of fact, they actually encourage extreme points of view. The CFR then points out to critics that because the CFR is open to all ideas, that necessarily means they are democratic and open. But there are inconsistencies that destroy the concept of democracy or even the idea of pluralism in the CFR.

For instance, there are no poor people on the membership roster.

Or even the average middle class working stiff. Where are the truck drivers, the coal miners or secretaries? How about elementary school teachers, engineers or used car salespersons? Or even (Heaven forbid) an actual homeless person?

The scriptures give evidence of the relationship the poor have to secret combinations. This is found in Hel. 6:38-39:

> And it came to pass on the other hand, that the Nephites did build them up and support them, beginning at the more wicked part of them, until they had overspread all the land of the Nephites, and had seduced the more part of the righteous until they had come down to believe in their works and partake of the spoils, and to join with them in their secret murders and combinations.
>
> And thus they did obtain the sole management of the government, **insomuch that they did trample under their feet and smite and rend and turn their backs upon the poor and the meek and the humble followers of God.**

So that scripture says that the poor were downtrodden by the secret combination of the past. That suggests that today's secret combination would also be the enemy of the poor. And yet, they want us to think they are champions of the poor with grandiose social welfare give-away schemes. The problem is that the social welfare give-away schemes actually create more poor people through taxation to pay for the programs. They also create more poor people by taking money from them via the act of lending at interest. The effect of their various schemes suggests that they are trying to eliminate the middle class which would result in a small number of rich and a large majority of poor.

Another cogent point needs to be discussed. The CFR stresses that it considers all points of view from anyone it invites to its meetings. As far as it goes, that is true. A friend of mine was invited to a working luncheon of the CFR wherein they discussed various foreign policy initiatives they were considering at the time. He gave his input which was seriously considered. He was of the opinion that the meetings of the CFR are open to any suggestion. But how the CFR really operates goes deeper than that.

You see, even though they promote discussion on all points of view, the final decisions on any initiatives submitted to the President of the United States are always made by the *leadership* of the CFR, which is the Executive Committee. The membership of the CFR itself is never allowed to vote on final drafts of foreign policy initiatives. And forget about the participation of the American people at large. So no matter what points of view are considered, no matter what pains are taken to listen to all sides, the Executive Committee and the Executive Committee *only* decides the final agenda with little or no consideration for the viewpoints heretofore painstakingly elicited. That kind of makes the contention that the CFR is open to all viewpoints rather bogus. The leadership listens to all, then makes up its own mind. More will be said about the executive committee of the CFR in a later chapter.

Here is just a very small partial list of who's a member of the CFR. It reads like a who's who in America.

-Bill Clinton, President of the U.S.
-Anthony Lake, National Security Advisor
-Madeleine Albright, Secretary of State
-Warren Christopher, former Secretary of State
-Ruth B. Ginsburg, Associate Supreme Court Justice
-Sandra Day O'Connor, Associate Supreme Court Justice
-Donna Shalala, Secretary of Health and Human Services
-Laurence H. Silberman, Judge, U.S. Court of Appeals, D.C. Cir.
-John Norton Moore, Chairman, U. S. Institute for Peace
-Roger Altman, Deputy Secretary of the Treasury
-David Gergen, White House Chief of Staff
-Frank T. Rhodes, Board of Directors, National Science Foundation
-Thomas Graham Jr., General Council, U.S. Arms Control and

Disarmament Agency
-Thomas R. Pickering, U. S. Ambassador to Russia
-William S. Cohen, Senator (R-ME)
-Christopher J. Dodd, Senator (D-CT)
-Richard A. Gephardt, Congressman (D-MO)
-Newton L. Gingrich (R) GA, former speaker of the House
-Charles B. Rangel, (D-NY)
-Alan Greenspan, Chairman, Federal Reserve Board
-Katharine Graham, owner of the Washington Post

And so on and so on. There are approximately 3,000 total members. A membership roster as recent as 1995 can be found on the internet.

Another thing to consider is that many of the membership may be ignorant of the true nature of the one-world government promoted by the CFR. And they may also be ignorant of the true nature of the leaders of the CFR. We have not yet addressed the full extent of the evil in this organization. As they say, "You ain't heard nuthin' yet." The Council on Foreign Relations practices the old secret conspiracy tactic of having circles within circles (or secret groups within secret groups). But to go back to the subject at hand, let us see how they influence the government so easily.

After they have studied a certain aspect of foreign policy with discussion groups, seminars and workshops, they draft preliminary papers suggesting foreign policy initiatives. Then they have more discussions, seminars, etc. until they come up with a final draft. Then the Executive Committee makes the final decision, sometimes after consultation with the Royal Institute on International Affairs in London (a sister organization) or the Tri-Lateral Commission. After the final draft, the paper makes its way to the appropriate Cabinet Department Head it needs to go to so as to surface in a Cabinet meeting with the President. Sometimes it is accepted and acted upon as it is and sometimes it is further revised and changed by the President to meet changing conditions. But the initiatives themselves come from an organization that is outside the auspices of the Constitution of the United States. That is how the CFR side-steps the Constitution. They are in a position to use the President from behind the scenes to pass their agenda on to the public and make it look like it came from him.

And as long as the President is also a member of the CFR, that becomes easy to do. He will just go along with what they say. But what if he isn't a member? Were there any recent Presidents who were not members of the Council? If so, who were they and how could the CFR control them?

There was one. That was Ronald Reagan. He was not a member of the CFR, and yet was heavily influenced by them. That is an interesting story by itself.

When he ran for President in 1980, he was the front-runner for the Republican nomination for president. To get to that position, he made certain promises to certain people. According the late Gary Allen, just prior to the vote for the Republican Candidate for President in the Republican National Convention that year, Walter Cronkite and Henry Kissinger (two of the cabalists) came to Reagan and said that they would support his candidacy if he would do two things in return. 1. Nominate George Bush (conspirator) as his Vice Presidential Running Mate and, 2. Select people from the Council on Foreign Relations to be in his cabinet.

Other than that, they had no other demands. Kissinger and Cronkite stressed that they would not coerce Reagan in any way to make any decisions in his Presidency. He was free to make his own determinations as President. The two men then told Reagan that if he didn't go along with them, they would use their influence to see that he lost the nomination to George Bush, who at the time was his chief rival for the nomination for President. Kissinger said that if Reagan didn't believe he, (Kissinger), could sway the Convention in Bush's favor, he (Reagan) could go ahead and refuse these demands. Reagan would then find out for himself that Henry K. had the clout to do it. The pressure was intense. But because Reagan wanted the presidency so badly, and thought that he could make a difference only if he were President, he agreed. (How the conspiracy controls national nominating conventions for both the Republicans and Democrats will be shown later.)

So the question arises—how could the conspiracy control him when they don't directly tell him what to do? After all, he isn't a member of any of their organizations and the agreement was that he made his own decisions. That was emphasized repeatedly. During his presidency, no one called on Reagan to direct him in any way that I know of. So how could the conspiracy sway him?

Actually, the answer is surprisingly simple.

If you believe that the President of the United States is the only one that makes the decisions that run the country, you are in error. Actually, most of the decisions he makes, if he is not part of the cabal in the first place, are made for him. It may surprise you to know that our country is not run by the President alone but by his Cabinet also, to a large extent. That's because the President cannot possibly know all there is to know about every situation. He must rely heavily on his Cabinet to do research and perform services such as information gathering and viable suggestions that he can't do himself. And there's normally nothing wrong with that. Any CEO worth his salt will rely heavily on his Board of Directors to do the grunt work that is necessarily involved in any major decision. That is how any leadership position works. And major Cabinet involvement works well for the President, if there's not some hidden agenda on the part of the Cabinet. Here's an imaginary scenario of how Reagan was manipulated.

Let's say that Reagan was conducting one of his weekly Cabinet meetings. Let's suppose that some foreign policy emergency came up. Suppose it was some Middle East country that was harboring terrorists and we wanted them to stop. Reagan says to the Secretary of Defense, "What can we do militarily to make them kick the terrorists out of their country? Fix up a working paper on the situation, complete with the latest intelligence reports and suggestions of what we could do in the military area to persuade them to go along with us." The Secretary of Defense says, "Will do." Then he turns to the Treasury Secretary and says, "What kind of monetary assets does this country have in our banks? How about land titles, investments, securities, other holdings? What can we do with their holdings in our country to make them more compliant to our request? What can they do in retaliation? Give me a working paper on our options next week." The Secretary of the Treasury says, "OK, Mr. President." And so on to the Secretary of Commerce, the Secretary of State and others.

Each of these persons then goes back to their respective offices and, after sufficient research, come up with options for the President to consider for each of these contingencies. But the beauty of the conspirators method is that all the options they give President Reagan are *beneficial for the conspiracy*. So when they re-assemble again next week (or whenever) to give him their recommendations, *it doesn't matter what choices he makes, it will ultimately help the conspiracy*. He makes the final decisions, all right, and then honestly stands up before the American people and says, "The buck stops here. I am the ultimate authority in the land and nobody tells me what to do." And, in a sense, he's right! They don't call him on the phone and tell him how to run the country. They leave him alone in that respect and just run him quietly from behind the scenes via the Cabinet. It's very subtle, very secretive and very effective.

To quote again from the Summary Description of *Foreign Affairs*:

To encourage a forthright exchange of ideas and full freedom of expression in Council meetings, it is the Council's tradition that participants will not later **attribute the statements of speakers and other participants to them in public media or forums or knowingly transmit them to persons who will**. Some meetings are open to selected guests or are announced as on-the-record.

The above quotation embodies the famous "non-attribution rule" of the CFR. It means that no one who attends their meetings is allowed to attribute what is said to any particular person, so that discussion can be free and open. The thought being that if you say something at one of the meetings of the Council on Foreign Relations that later is attributed to you in tomorrow's news, that could stifle your desire to say anything at all in future meetings. The CFR implemented this rule to let members freely express themselves, knowing that what they say won't be reported abroad. But the real reason for the non-attribution rule is that it allows the CFR and other organizations to openly plot against their respective governments in their meetings.

Again, here is a quotation by David Rockefeller from the last chapter to reinforce this idea:

We are grateful to The Washington Post, The New York Times, Time Magazine and other great publications whose directors have attended our meetings and respected their **promises of discretion for almost forty years. It would have been impossible for us to develop our plan for the world if we had been subject to the bright lights of publicity during those years.** But, the world is now more sophisticated and prepared to march towards a world government. The supranational sovereignty of an **intellectual elite and world bankers is surely preferable to the national auto determination practiced in past centuries.**

David Rockefeller, founder of the Trilateral Commission,
before that body in Baden-Baden Germany, June 1991.

Here is one strong reason why the CFR and the Tri-Lateral Commission likes the anonymity the non-attribution rule gives. The following is a quotation by Henry Kissinger at a meeting of the Bilderbergs, which is another of the secret organizations to be discussed later:

Today Americans would be outraged if U.N. troops entered Los Angeles to restore order; **tomorrow they will be grateful!** This is especially true if they were told there was an outside threat from beyond **whether real or promulgated**, that threatened our very existence. **It is then that all peoples of the world will pledge with world leaders to deliver them from this evil.**

The one thing every man fears is the unknown. When presented with this scenario, **individual rights will be willingly relinquished for the guarantee of their well being granted to them by their world government.**

Henry Kissinger in an address to the Bilderberger meeting
at Evian, France, May 21, 1992.
Transcribed from a tape recording made by a Swiss delegate.

Think about that. What would the public do if this statement were paraded on the front cover of Time magazine? Henry Kissinger could be arrested and charged with treason. But the non-attribution rule, coupled with the ownership of the media, makes it possible for plotters to make bold statements like the above behind closed doors and not worry about being exposed. The above quotation is rather typical of what is really said in their closed meetings.

Even when the public gets access to these statements, it still is hard to get the word out because of the blanket the news media throws over any statements that are leaked. Even so, the word is growing throughout the country that there is something amiss with our leaders. This perception is due in large part to the internet which is mostly unregulated, and people are beginning to understand that the news media is controlled by the insiders.

However, every once and awhile, the truth comes out from some of their meetings. Here is one unbelievable example:

On July 12-13, the New York Council on Foreign Relations held, at is mansion-headquarters in Manhattan, a conference...What emerged as a dominant second theme reflecting the thinking of the CFR, was the enunciated policy that **many tens of millions of Africans should be allowed to die by being denied treat-**

ment for AIDS. As one participant put it, "Those with AIDS in Africa should die quickly."

Next came an interview with Richard Freeman, senior economic staffer of EIR and Peter Schwartz, formerly a director the Scenario Planning Department of Royal Dutch Shell, the founder of Wired Magazine and current head of the Global Business Network as well as a member of the CFR:

> Richard: Yesterday, at a session of the conference that you directed, you stated that we should not keep alive those who have AIDS in Africa. You are writing off part of that continent's population.

> Schwartz: In 1986, I did a study on this for AT&T, Royal Dutch Shell, and Volvo. We concluded that **people who have AIDS in Africa should not be kept alive; they spread the disease. It is better they should die quickly.**

> Schwartz then brought Robert Hormats into the conversation. Hormats, the former U.S. Assistant Secretary of State for Economic Affairs, vice-chairman of the international division of Goldman Sachs investment bank, and a major figure in the Gore campaign. After Schwartz made some more remarks about getting rid of persons with AIDS in Africa, Hormats concurred, "This is just natural selection." Schwartz beamed at the horrifying conclusion.

> Schwartz and Hormats represent the genocidal view of Lord Bertrand Russell, who in 1951 thought **"bacteriological war may prove effective"** in **"ridding" the world of non-white people. To achieve that objective, "a Black Death [should] spread throughout the world once in every generation."**
> CFR Bankers Plot...Genocide
> by Richard Freeman
> reported on Rense.com, 7-25-00

This is another example of what the CFR really talks about in their meetings. No wonder they have the non-attribution rule. For more detail about them, you can read *The Shadows of Power: The Council on foreign Relations and the American Decline* by James Perloff, American Opinion, 1988. A further treatment is: *The CFR, Conspiracy to Rule the World* by Gary Allen, American Opinion, 1969. Also, greater detail on how the CFR took over the State Department is contained in State Department Publication 2349, *Report to the President On The Results Of The San Francisco Conference* by Secretary of State Edward R. Stettinus (CFR) to President Harry Truman.

More Quotations about the CFR

...James K. Fitzpatrick would write on the editorial page of the national newspaper The Wanderer, November 18, 1993,:

Clinton told reporters in an interview that Quigley's work centered on the existence of a **permanent shadow government of powerful bankers and businessmen and government officials that controls the agenda of our political life from behind the scenes**. Clinton spoke in that interview of coming to the conclusion, while still a young man, that it was necessary for him to gain access **to the inner circle of this group** in order to become part of the decision-making process that shapes our world.

Secret Records Revealed
by Dennis Laurence Cuddy
Hearthstone Publishing Ltd., 1999, (5)

Another quotation:

The Power Elite by C. Wright Mills is published (1956). He is a leftist Columbia University sociologist, and in his book, he acknowledges:

There is...little doubt that the American power elite—which contains, we are told, some of "the greatest organizers in the world"—has...planned and plotted.

...Certain types of men from each of the dominant institutional

84

areas, more far-sighted than others, have actually promoted the liaison [of the power elite] before it took its truly modern shape...**Many higher events that would reveal the working of the power elite can be withheld from public knowledge under the guise of secrecy.**

Secret Records Revealed, op cit, (91-92)

Now we'll look at three other groups, all important to the overall effort of carefully leading the world to a one world government.

Chapter 5

...I'll bet that within the next hundred years...nationhood as we know it will be obsolete; all states will recognize a single, global authority...
-Strobe Talbott, Deputy Secretary of State,
Editorial, Time Magazine, July 20, 1992 p.70

The Round Table, the TLC and the Bilderbergers

The Round Table

There is another group that works with and is superior to the Council on Foreign Relations. To introduce this new group is Quigley's confession again, from *Tragedy and Hope*:

> **...There does exist, and has existed for a generation, an international Anglophile network which operates, to some extent, in the way the radical Right believes the Communists act.** In fact, this network, which we may identify as the **Round Table Groups,** has no aversion to cooperating with the Communists, or any other groups, and frequently does so. **I know of the operations of this network because I have studied it for twenty years and was permitted for two years, in the early 1960's, to examine its papers and secret records. I have no aversion to it** or to most of its aims and have, for much of my life, been close to it and to many of its instruments. I have objected, both in the past and recently, to a few of its policies...but in general my chief difference of opinion is that it **wishes to remain unknown, and I believe its role in history is significant enough to be known.**
>
> *Tragedy and Hope,* (950)

The following is a history of the Round Table Groups mentioned to in the above quotation. This is important because they are the originators, along with Colonel House and others, of the Council on Foreign Relations.

Until 1870 there was no professorship of fine arts at Oxford, but in that year, thanks to the Slade bequest, John Ruskin was named to such a chair. He hit Oxford like an earthquake, not so much because he talked about fine arts, but because he talked also about the empire and England's downtrodden masses, and above all because he talked about all three of these things as moral issues. Until the end of the nineteenth century the poverty-stricken masses in the cities of England lived in want, ignorance, and crime very much as they have been described by Charles Dickens. Ruskin spoke to the Oxford undergraduates as members of the privileged, ruling class. He told them that they were the possessors of a magnificent tradition of education, beauty, rule of law, freedom, decency, and self-discipline but that this tradition could not be saved, and did not deserve to be saved, unless it could be extended to the lower classes in England itself and to the non-English masses throughout the world. If this precious tradition were not extended to these two great majorities, the minority of upper-class Englishmen would ultimately be submerged by the majorities and the tradition lost. To prevent this, the tradition just be extended to the masses and to the empire.

Ruskin's message had a sensational impact. His inaugural lecture was copied out in longhand by one undergraduate, Cecil Rhodes, who kept it with him for thirty years. Rhodes (1853-1902) feverishly exploited the diamond and goldfields of South Africa, rose to be prime minister of the Cape Colony (1890-1896), contributed money to political parties, controlled parliamentary seats both in England and in South Africa, and sought to win a strip of British territory across Africa from the Cape of Good Hope to Egypt...Rhodes inspired devoted support for his goals from others in South Africa and in England. **With financial support from Lord Rothschild and Alfred Beit**, he was able to monopolize the diamond mines of South Africa as De Beers Consolidated Mines and to build up a great gold mining enterprise as Consolidated Gold Fields. In the middle 1890's Rhodes had a personal income of at least a million pounds sterling a year (then about five million dollars) which was spent so freely for his mysterious purposes that he was usually overdrawn on his account. These purposes centered on his desire to **federate the English-speaking peoples and to bring all the habitable portions of the world under their control...**

Among Ruskin's most devoted disciples at Oxford were a group of intimate friends including Arnold Toynbee, Alfred (later Lord) Milner, Arthur Glazebrook, George (later Sir George) Birchenough. These were so moved by Ruskin that they devoted the rest of their lives to carrying out his ideas. A similar group of Cambridge men including Reginald Baliol Brett (Lord Esher), Sir John B. Steeley, Albert (Lord) Grey, and Edmund Garrett were also aroused by Ruskin's message and devoted their lives to extension of the British Empire and uplift of England's urban masses as two parts of one project which they called "extension" of the English-speaking idea." They were remarkably successful in these aims because England's most sensational journalist William T. Stead (1849-1912), an ardent social reformer and imperialist, brought them into association with Rhodes. This association was formally established on February 5, 1891, when Rhodes and Stead organized a **secret society** (Quigley's words) of which Rhodes had been dreaming for sixteen years. In this secret society Rhodes was to be leader; Stead, Brett (Lord Esher), and Milner were to form an executive committee; Arthur (Lord) Balfour, (Sir) Harry Johnston, **Lord Rothschild**, (remember him in the Fed and the CFR?) Albert (Lord) Grey, and others were listed as potential members of a "Circle of Initiates"; while there was to be an outer circle known as the "Association of Helpers" (later organized by Milner as the **Round Table organization**)...

In 1909-1913 they organized semi-secret groups, know as Round Table Groups, (named after King Arthur's Round Table) in the chief British dependencies and the United States. These still function in eight countries...In 1919 they founded the Royal Institute of International Affairs (Chatham House) for which the chief financial supporters were Sir Abe Bailey and the Astor family (owners of The Times). Similar Institutes on International Affairs were established in the chief British dominions and the United States (where it is known as the Council on Foreign Relations) in the period 1919—1927...

The power and influence of this Rhodes-Milner group in British imperial affairs and in foreign policy since 1889, although not widely recognized, can hardly be exaggerated. We might mention as an example that **this group dominated The Times from 1890 to 1912 and has controlled it completely since 1912...Numerous other papers and journals have been under the control or influence of the group since 1889.** They have also established and influenced numerous university and other chairs of imperial affairs and international relations...

Tragedy and Hope
(130-133)

This is a bare bones history of the Round Table Groups. They, working in conjunction with some Americans (chiefly George Beer, Walter Lippman, Frank Aydelotte, Whitney Shepardson, Thomas Lamont, Jerome Greene, and Erwin Canham along with Colonel House), met together often until they came up with a working model for a front for the Round Table Group called the Council on Foreign Relations in America and the Royal Institute for International Affairs in England. This was in 1921.

For further information on the Round Table, the New York Times on Wednesday, April 9, 1902 (before they were taken over by the conspiracy) ran front page articles on Cecil Rhodes shortly after his death. Look it up in the library. The article openly discussed Rhodes idea of a "Wealthy Secret Society" to rule the world. Here are excerpts from the Times article:

> In its three columns of complex sentences the whole of Mr.Rhodes's international and individual philosophy is embraced. Perhaps it can best be summarized as an argument in favor of **the organization of a secret society, on the lines of the Jesuit order**, for the promotion of the peace and welfare of the world, and the establishment of an American-British federation, with absolute home rule for the component parts.

> ...The only thing feasible to carry out this idea is a secret society **gradually absorbing the wealth of the world, to be devoted to such an object.**

So where is the Round Table located with respect to the CFR in power? It is above the CFR which does the Round Table's biding. It is also controls the Royal Institute for International Affairs (RIIA). In fact, members of the Round Table are found in the Executive Committee of the CFR and the RIIA, along with all other foreign policy organizations throughout the industrialized world. But the important thing to remember is that the CFR is subservient to the RIIA. That means that our government, which is run by the CFR, actually takes its marching orders from the Royal Institute for International Affairs in Britain, which runs both our government and the British government. When the Americans defeated the British in the Revolutionary War, the International Bankers that controlled Britain at the time vowed to bring America back under British control, no matter how long it took. They succeeded.

All I need is a little TLC

Now we come to the Trilateral Commission (TLC). It was founded in 1973 by David Rockefeller (Fed and CFR). By now that name mentioned as the power behind an organization should not surprise you any more. The continual recurrence of the name Rockefeller, Morgan and Rothschild should begin to help you see how interlocked and closely connected the power elite is.

The TLC is a group dedicated to integrating the world's economies into one (or possibly three) economies. The reason for this is that the TLC feels that a world economic union would be the perfect precursor to a world political union. For that reason, the TLC has been behind each of the international trade agreements that have come to fruition. That includes NAFTA, GATT and all the others that are either completed or on the drawing board. GATT has been around before 1973, but the TLC is the main impetus behind it now. They are also helped with the Maastricht treaty for the European Union.

Their name is rather odd, but it comes from the fact that the world today is divided into three main economic areas. Those areas are: North America, Europe and the Pacific Rim of countries including Japan. The membership (a little over 300) comes from these areas and is even more exclusive than the CFR. It consists almost exclusively of politicians and CEOs of international corporations. The goal, as I said, is to integrate the world into one (or possibly three) economic blocs which will help with the overall effort to integrate it politically.

A complete list of the members of the Tri-Lateral Commission, current up to 1992, can be found on the internet.

Senator Barry Goldwater made some statements about the Tri-Lateral Commission.

He termed the Commission "David Rockefeller's newest international cabal" and said, "It is intended to be the vehicle for multinational consolidation of the commercial and banking interests by seizing control of the political government of the United States."

Also, concerning the presidential candidacy of Jimmy Carter, (a member of the TLC), Goldwater wrote, "David Rockefeller and Zbigniew Brzezinski found Jimmy Carter to be their ideal candidate. They helped him win the nomination and the presidency. To accomplish this purpose, they mobilized the money power of the Wall Street bankers, the intellectual influence of the academic community—which is subservient to the wealth of the great tax-free foundations—and the media controllers represented in the membership of the CFR and the Trilateral."

Senator Barry Goldwater,
from his book, *With No Apologies*.

President Bush was a member, Clinton is another and many more are part of it. The TLC tries to integrate the world's economies, pushes for legislation in all countries for the abolition of all import/export laws and regulations and subtly conditions the thinking of the world's people toward a one world economy. Their line goes like this: Since the world already has national economies that are interdependent on each other, why should there be tariffs, excise taxes, import duties or other activities by governments that dampen business activity? Immigration laws also should be eliminated so that workers can have free access to any employer they want. But, if all that were to happen, what then would be the use of national boundaries or even a national identity? Why not just merge the world into one super government and automatically eliminate all business stifling laws?

That is one of their approaches and the rebuttal to that idea is that if there were no national boundaries, then total political control (and dictatorship) over the world would be the result.

The TLC is a powerful part of the total global conspiracy. For more information on the Trilateral Commission, there is a three volume book, *Trilaterals over Washington* by Antony C. Sutton and Patrick M. Wood.

The Bilderbergers

Another major conspiracy group is called the Bilderbergers. They got this name from the Bilderberg Hotel in Oosterbeek, Holland, the site of their first meeting in 1954. The Bilderbergers have gotten together every year since, each time at a different location but always at a luxury hotel somewhere in the world. They recently completed a meeting in Sintra, Portugal in June of 2000. At these meetings, the hotel and grounds are completely secured, which means checking for bugs, surrounding the hotel with a perimeter fence, erecting a guardhouse with a security checkpoint, thus allowing only those with a pre-issued ID card through and even sending the management and staff home for the duration of the conference. The Bilderbergers then staff the hotel with their own people. These conferences usually last about three to four days.

The Bilderbergers are an imperialistic think tank for a group higher up on the pecking order. The Bilderbergers mainly control European Union politics, including the government of Russia. They also exercise some control over the U.S. Some of the members of the Bilderberg are also members of the TLC, the CFR, and other groups. All these organizations coordinate and reinforce each other in their global conspiracy efforts.

Here is something that came out of the first meeting in 1954.

The first meeting witnessed the gathering of ideologies, poles apart. The issue of McCarthyism was reaching its peak in the United States. European participants, exasperated with the McCarthy propaganda, saw in their American counterparts a clear political shift towards an ultra-right-wing fascist state. Memories of World War II still fresh in their minds, the Europeans found the concept rather repulsive.

C.D. Jackson (a member of the CFR), in an attempt to regain the international delegates' confidence, stated: "Whether McCarthy dies by an assassin's bullet or is eliminated in the normal American way of getting rid of boils on body politics, I prophesy that by the time we hold our next meeting he will be gone from the American scene."

Hatch, Alden, *H.R.H. Bernhard, the Prince of the Netherlands*, 1962

The McCarthy movement to identify communist agents in America was derailed the next year. They can and do pull strings and destroy lives in the process.

Here is a re-iteration of a quotation opener:

We are close to the point where **the United States will send its military Forces to settle any and all disputes brought before the United Nations...This is an important step along the road to a One World Government**.

To expand, about the same time this was written, the U.S. was engaged, or was about to be engaged, in the Gulf War with Saddam Hussein. President Bush had General Shwartzkopf lead an international army (the majority of which were Americans) against Iraq. Remember what Bush said at that time?

What is at stake is more than one small country, it is a big idea—a **new world order**...to achieve the universal aspirations of mankind...based upon shared principles and the rule of law... The illumination of a thousand points of light...The winds of change are with us now.

President Bush
In his State of the Union message
during the Gulf War.

The NWO gang was trying to accomplish an important step in their goal to bring the world under their complete control. The U.S. has become **the** armed forces of choice to quell hot spots in the world. We have become the world's policeman. I know that there is resistance in America to that thought, but we are constantly being bombarded by the elitists of the world to do it. The higher-ups in both the Republican and Democratic parties are telling us that although they don't like the idea of America being the world's policeman, that we still should go into such and such a country so as to "bring peace" to it. Never mind the fact that the conflict is usually nurtured by the conspirators in the first place, so as to allow the United States to intervene later.

In other words, they try to either create a conflict or augment an already existing one, foment trouble, bring it to the world's attention, then marshal public opinion to exterminate a problem they, the conspirators, created. Then they send in Uncle Sam, who beats up on some poor third world nation. That only creates more hatred for America, increasing the chance that terrorists or even other nations will exact revenge at some future date. Such a stratagem of playing people and nations against each other until they destroy each other strengthens and consolidates the conspirators drive for power.

We have gone into country after country both before and since the Gulf War, in an increasingly brazen manner, under Presidents who should have been looking out for our benefit, so as to fulfill the mandates of the Bilderbergers. The culmination of these efforts was the recently concluded Kosovo War which was waged mostly by American military aircraft. It was the most blatant subversion of American and international law yet known.

We deliberately intervened in the internal conflict of a sovereign nation without U.N. nor U. S. Congressional approval, and against NATO's own charter.

According the NATO charter, NATO forces may only by used in a **defensive** capacity. That is, if and only if a member state is attacked by some foreign power, NATO may use its armed forces to defend that member nation. But that was not the case in the Kosovo war. All parties on both sides of the conflict acknowledged that the Kosovo conflagration was entirely an internal Yugoslavian affair. That country threatened no other nation, period. But what does international law mean to the Bilderbergers who are basically amoral?

Here is another quotation which talks about the real role of NATO in the Kosovo war. The source is a high State Department official.

"It is important to the Bilderberg scheme for world government to get NATO out from the limitations of its own charter," said the source, a reliable observer for more than a decade.

The treaty limits the alliance to a defensive position, providing that if any member nation is attacked, all NATO countries would respond, he pointed out. The treaty has no authority for an unprovoked attack on a sovereign nation.

"By bombing Kosovo, the precedent is set," he said. "Despite the terms of the treaty, NATO now can go anywhere and attack anybody. This solidifies NATO's role as the UN's world army."

Giving NATO a global role instead of only a mission to defend Western Europe is part of both evolving a world army and conditioning the public mind to accept surrendering national sovereignty, he said.

War Seen Part of Plutocrats Agenda,
by James P. Tucker Jr.
Spotlight, 5/11/2000

The President used his ability to commit U.S. forces for sixty days without Congressional consent, at the end of which, under a Congressional/Presidential compromise, the President would have to withdraw troops unless or until Congressional approval and funding was passed. **But Clinton ignored Congress and continued the bombing up until seventy-eight days had passed.** That's when Milosevic capitulated. The funny thing is that Congress barely said a word about this blatant disregard for law. What will happen next time? Will the President commit U.S. troops one hundred days without Congressional approval? Will it be one year? Will it be indefinite?

The Constitution explicitly states that only **Congress** has the power to declare war. We, as a nation, have capitulated that right to our new Imperial Presidency. No approval of Congress was asked, none given. From now on the President, as he pleases, will commit American troops to fight wars he considers necessary. It is up to us to demand that Congress reclaim that right. The founders made the Congress responsible, not the President, for committing Americans to war, because they feared that America would become like the Roman Empire again, with Caesar able to conduct wars as he saw fit. The ability to unilaterally wage war is a huge usurpation of power. Not many republics have survived long after the fact.

We have all heard about that war in Yugoslavia. The Bilderbergers, along with the Council on Foreign Relations, was behind the NATO bombing. But what they never said about the Kosovo conflict was that it was a war of naked aggression by NATO, under the direction of the Bilderbergers, to acquire some property.

That is, the province of Kosovo is home to the richest mines (gold, silver, coal, lead, zinc and cadmium) in all of Europe. The Trepca mines were owned and run, prior to the Kosovo war, by the Federal Republic of Yugoslavia, (FRY). In other words, it was a nationalized mining company. The mines were coveted by the Bilderbergers and they decided to steal it for themselves, (e.g., the CEO's of international corporations that make up the majority of the Bilderberg group), using NATO as a front.

The official party line on the Kosovo war was that bombing was necessary because Milosevic refused to "negotiate" over Kosovo autonomy, which is a mostly ethnic Albanian province of Serbia. The fact that Kosovo was a legal province of Serbia was well known to and accepted by everyone, even the Kosovo Albanians themselves. The powers of NATO wanted to "negotiate" an autonomy for Kosovo, so that they would be independent of Serbia, which is mostly Slavic in population. The Serbs were killing the Albanian Kosovars. That is what we were told by the national news media.

Originally, Serbia came to the negotiation table with the idea that Kosovo could achieve some degree of autonomy, which the Serbs did not oppose in principle. But after the meeting started, at Wright-Patterson Air Force Base in Dayton Ohio, the real purpose became apparent.

The truth is, there were no "negotiations." There was only the Rambouillet Agreement, prepared by the Bilderberg Group before-hand and handed over to Milosevic by Madeline Albright and other U.S. officials with the ultimatum—agree to it or get bombed.

The Serbs weren't allowed to "negotiate" the Rambouillet

Agreement at all. Albright rammed home the point over and over again that there was no room for discussion on its terms.

And very few people knew what were the real terms of the Agreement. Certainly no one in the news media. They weren't trusted with the terms until later, two weeks after the bombs began falling on Serbia. But a careful examination of the actual document reveals why no independent state, including the United States, would ever accept its dictatorial and barbarous terms. The official Rambouillet Agreement can be seen on the internet. Here are some of the actual stipulations of this agreement. They are quite revealing.

> Article 8 of this Appendix reads: "NATO personnel shall enjoy, together with their vehicles, vessels, aircraft, and equipment, free and unrestricted passage and unimpeded access throughout the FRY (Federal Republic of Yugoslavia) including associated airspace and territorial waters. This shall include, but not be limited to, the right of bivouac, maneuver, billet, and utilization of any areas or facilities as required for support, training, and operations."

> Article 6 gives NATO absolute immunity: "NATO personnel, under all circumstances and at all times, shall be immune from the Parties' jurisdiction in respect of any civil, administrative, or disciplinary offenses which **may be committed by them in the FRY.**"

So that means that NATO forces can go anywhere they want throughout Yugoslavia then commit any offenses they want and be immune from prosecution. Would you agree to that?

The following is from a column by Richard Becker:

> The agreement also provided for a type of "autonomy" (for Kosovo) never before seen. Kosovo would have its own constitution, president, prime minister, legislature and supreme court and be able to make virtually all of its laws. The new "provincial" Kosovo government, as envisioned, would be able to overrule any federal laws it

wished, unlike U.S. states whose laws are subordinate to federal legislation. The Supreme Court of the FRY would be required to enforce legislation passed by the Kosovo parliament.

Kosovo would also be allowed to conduct its own foreign policy under the accord—something not granted to any other autonomous region anywhere in the world.

All Yugoslav federal army and police forces would have to be withdrawn, except for a three-mile-wide area along the borders of the province. A new Kosovar police force would be trained to take over internal security responsibilities. Members of the KLA, which are supposed to disarm under the agreement, could join the police units.

But the real kicker is that even though Kosovo would be autonomous from Yugoslavia, they would still be under NATO control. So the sovereignty in Kosovo would not reside in Kosovo itself but NATO. To quote again from Richard Becker:

A 28,000-strong NATO occupation army,...would be authorized to "use necessary force to ensure compliance with the Accords," according to a U.S. State Department fact sheet issued on March 1.

"The international community will play a role in ensuring that these provisions are carried out, through a civilian Implementation Mission, an ombudsman and constitutional court judges selected under international auspices, OSCE/EU [Organization for Security and Cooperation of the European Union] supervision of elections, and an international military presence," said the State Department.

The OSCE/EU also could remove officials from office and shut down or censor the media.

The most telling part of this power play is the following: Kosovo would be required to have a "free market" economy. We in the U.S. think that is a great idea, but that idea was used to justify theft on a grand scale. Remember, the Yugoslavian Government nationalized the mines in Kosovo. The requirement that Kosovo have a "free" economy meant that the Government had to sell the mines on the open market which allowed the Bilderbergers, through fronts, to buy up the shares offered and add them to their other multinational interests. So much for the war in Kosovo being about helping the Kosovo Albanians. It was just plain greed passing for humanitarianism.

The Bilderberg Group is superior to the CFR and The TLC as well as the Royal Institute for International Relations, (Britain's CFR). They are superior to the Round Table Group. These take their marching orders from the Bilderbergers. But the Bilderbergers are not the superior or dominant group in the world. There is another cabal that we will address later that ties or binds all the secret groups together. They either act like an information clearinghouse to coordinate the efforts of the various groups working together, or they have power over the other groups and order them around. In either case, they are what one may term the apex of the pyramid of power as far as the secret combinations are concerned.

There are literally dozens if not hundreds of other groups that work together. Some of them are think tanks (like the Heritage Foundation), some are professional associations (like the Institute for Pacific Relations), some are fraternal organizations (like the Freemasons), some are Universities that have conspirators on their Boards of Regents (like Harvard and Yale), some are tax exempt foundations (like the Ford Foundation), some are religious organizations (like the World Council of Churches), some are political organizations (like the United Nations), some are military organizations (like NATO) and some are aristocratic associations (like the Black Nobility of Europe). The ones mentioned above are some of the most important in history.

More Quotations on the TLC

In my view the Trilateral Commission represents a skillful, coordinated effort to seize control and consolidate the four centers of power—political, monetary, intellectual, and ecclesiastical. All this is to be done in the interest of creating a more peaceful, more productive world community. What the Trilateralists truly intend is the creation of a worldwide economic power superior to the political governments of the nation—states involved.

Secret Records Revealed, op cit, (125)

In the next chapter we'll will see the formation of yet another secret combination, but this one is particularly bad. It is violent and deadly. It is the Illuminati.

Chapter 6

Sin is only that which is hurtful, and if the profit is greater than the
damage, it becomes a virtue.
—Adam Weishaupt, founder of the Illuminati

The "Enlightened Ones"

The subject of the Illuminati is very important to this book. The
name means the "Enlightened Ones." It also has another name,
"Moriah Conquering Wind," given by it's superiors. The Illuminati was
formed by a man who was deep into the occult. Adam Weishaupt was
a professor of canon law at Ingolstadt University in Bavaria, Germany.
He was called "a human devil" by Abbe Barruel and "the profoundest
conspirator that ever existed" by Professor John Robison.

The following biographical sketch is by Joseph Trainor:

Adam Weishaupt was born on February 6, 1748 in Ingolstadt,
Bavaria, Germany which was an independent kingdom at the time.
When he was a baby, his parents who had been Orthodox Jews,
converted to the Roman Catholic Church. Instead of attending the
yeshiva, Adam attended monastery schools and later a hochshule
(high school) run by the Society of Jesus.

As a Bavarian, Adam learned Czech and Italian as a child, and in
school, he soon mastered Latin, Greek and, with his father's help,
Hebrew...(he) became the professor of canon law at the University
of Ingolstadt...He read every ancient manuscript and text he and
his associates could lay hands on. Adam grew interested in the
occult, becoming obsessed with the Great Pyramid of Giza.

He was convinced that the edifice was a prehistoric temple of initiation. In 1770, he made the acquaintance of Franz Kolmer, a Danish merchant...(and deeply into the occult). The following year, 1771, Adam decided to found a secret society aimed at "transforming" the human race...His first name for the proposed order, The Perfectibilists, suggests that he borrowed from the Cathars a gnostic religion that flourished in Europe for four hundred years...Adam fashioned his order in the form of (what else?) A pyramid. (In 1776, it was called the Order of the Illuminati).

The Illuminati was an off-shoot of the Freemasons. That is, the Illuminati had initiation rites, handshakes, signs, oaths and so forth much like the Masons. It was financed from behind the scenes by Mayer Amschel Rothschild (Fed, CFR, Round Table), and its purpose was to infiltrate all governments with its own agents, take over those governments and promote wars and revolutions throughout the world. It was conceived for violence and has been the major contributor to violent revolution in the world from the day of its organization, May 1, 1776, until now.

The Illuminati did not originate from nothing, but sprang from the philosophical ideas promulgated by Rosseau, Voltaire, Diderot and others of the Paris Academy around the middle of the 18th century. The so-called "age of reason" promoted by these philosophers was in reality a broad based hatred of Christianity and the hold it had on the monarchies of Europe. They formed a fraternity dedicated to the destruction of the Church called the "Philosophes."

For the bulk of the history of the Illuminati and its philosophical beginnings, here is a quotation from The New American "Conspiracy" Issue, 1997 edition p.32:

> Voltaire's influence over King Frederick of Prussia and the publication of Dierot's *Encyclopédie,* beginning in 1751, testified to the Philosophes' early success. The conspirators hoped that the *Encyclopédie* would become a standard reference source wherein every literate person would seek knowledge on all subjects and thus receive propaganda against civil order and the Christian reli-

gion. Its publication caused the influence of this group to grow rapidly.

Voltaire bore an implacable hatred of all religions, of all monarchs, and of all morality derived from religious belief. He was obsessed with a fiendish desire for the total destruction of all three. He ended all his letters with the battle, cry, "Let us crush the wretch! Crush the wretch!" The "wretch" to whom he referred, of course, is Christ and His Church. Christians, said Voltaire, are "beings exceedingly injurious, fanatics, thieves, dupes, imposters...enemies of the human race." In the war against Christianity, according to Voltaire, "It is necessary to lie like a devil, not timidly and for a time, but boldly and always."

Weishaupt planned for the Order to maintain publicly the image of a charitable and philanthropic organization. It was this image which attracted so many German educators and Protestant clergymen to the Order. When they joined they were convinced that the goal of the Order was the purest form of Christianity, to make of all mankind "one happy and prosperous family." Once enlisted as novices or "Minervals" in the Order, those who were prepared for deeper commitment were allowed to advance to the rank of Iluminatus Minor, where they were told that the only obstruction to the Order's goal of universal happiness was the power being held by the religious and governmental institutions of the world. Accordingly, the leaders of these institutions—monarchs (or future monarchs) and clergymen—had either to be brought under the control of the Order or destroyed. If such a prospect frightened the new Illuminatus Minor, he was kept inactive at this level until his ethical concepts were altered.

...After the candidate had proven his absolute devotion to the secrets of the Order, he was allowed to enter the top-level circle of initiates as an Illuminatus Major, just below the position of Rex help by Weishaupt. By now, all conventional idealism had been purged from the candidate and he was told about the real objectives of the Order: rule of the world, to be accomplished after the destruction of all existing governments and religions. He was now required to take an oath which bound his every thought and action, and his fate, to the administration of his superiors in the Order.

But Weishaupt did not simply rely on the sincerity of his disciples. He set up an elaborate spy network so that all members would constantly be checking on the loyalty of each other. The secret police of the Order killed anyone who tried to inform the authorities about the conspiracy. This band was know as the "Insinuating Brethren" and had as its insignia an all-seeing eye...Weishaupt, who had been raised and educated by the Jesuits before rebelling against them, adopted much of the organizational system of the Jesuits for his Order.

...The original writings of the Order included detailed instructions for fomenting hatred and bloodshed between different racial, religious, and ethnic groups and even between the sexes. The idea of promoting hatred between children and their parents was introduced. There were even instructions about the kinds of buildings to be burned in urban insurrections. In short, virtually every tactic employed by 20th-century subversives was planned and written down by Adam Weishaupt over 200 years ago.

It was not until the summer of 1782 that the Order really began to grow in power and influence outside Bavaria. Having already contemplated the possibility of infiltrating the free masonic bodies of Western Europe and them taking control of them, Weishaupt and his brilliant disciple, Baron Adolf von Knigge,...at last had their chance. During that summer, leaders and delegates of the continental European Freemason lodges met in a congress held in Wilhelmsbad. Acting as Weishaupt's agent, von Knigge joined them and offered enticing promises of the secrets that the Illuminati had to offer. Von Knigge persuaded many of the German and French delegates to join Weishaupt's movement, and they extended the influence of the Order into their individual lodges. The two leaders of German Freemasonry, Duke Ferdinand of Brunswick and Prince Karl of Hesse, joined the Order, thus bringing the whole of German freemasonry under the control of the Illuminati. (They later dominated all of European Freemasonry).

The Conspiracy Issue continues by saying that a French count, Honoré Gabriel Mirabeau, took Illuminism to France and succeeded in recruiting most of the characters who later formed the backbone of the French Revolution. (Yes, the French Revolution of the late 1700's was started by the Illuminati. That's something you never heard in history class). The Duke of Orléans helped create the Jacobin Club houses in Paris which mobilized the most radical subversives of the impending revolution. But then something happened to almost destroy the Illuminati. To continue with the story from Conspiracy Issue:

> The discovery of the (French Revolution) plot was literally providential: A courier sent from Frankfurt to Paris in 1785 was killed by a bolt of lightning. On his body were found incriminating papers about the Order and the name of Xavier Zwack. Zwack's home in Landshut was raided by the Elector's (of Bavaria) police and his copy of Weishaupt's writings was taken. The Elector publicly outlawed the Order and closed many of the free masonic lodges known to be under its control. The elector also sent printed copies of the Order's writings to all of the important monarchs in Europe. It was from copies of the Order's writings the Abbé Barruel in France and the eminent Professor John Robison in England gathered the information contained in their important books—Barruel's *Memoirs* (*Illustrating the History of Jacobism*), and Robison's *Proofs of a Conspiracy*.

The Illuminati never went out of existence but just went underground, split up into other organizations, changed names, and continued with the same agenda of war and revolution. The former members who formed other organizations even kept their secret handshakes, signs, names and other Illuminati rituals in each of the groups that survived. Today these other groups, even though they have different names, still refer to themselves as the Illuminati.

As a matter of fact, the original Illuminati had a seal made in May of 1776. It consisted of an unfinished pyramid with an all—seeing eye for the capstone. It also had the words, "Annuit Coeptis" (Announcing the conception of) and "Novus Ordo Seclorum" (The new order of the ages). Then it had the Roman Numerals for 1776 at the bottom of the pyramid. That's right. The original seal of the Illuminati happens to be the reverse side of the seal of the United States of America, as seen on all one dollar bills! How can anyone think that the Illuminati "disappeared?" They are as alive today as they were when they came into being in 1776. What the Illuminati evolved into will surprise you.

After fomenting so much trouble, the French Revolution turned on those who were responsible and Illuminists themselves began to get the guillotine. Robespierre, an Illuminist, himself got the blade. Before his death, however, he had plans to exterminate about 15 million Frenchmen. Although that plan was never fully implemented, about 300,000 French citizens were killed.

After the Bavarian suppression and the failure of the French Revolution, the Illuminati went into hiding. The most important thing to remember about them is that they never died out. They became chamaeleons. They started new organizations with new names, but each had the same goals of infiltration and revolution against all governments and the desire to exterminate all religions. Also, each succeeding organization had the same (or nearly so) signs, tokens, penalties, oaths and rituals of the original Illuminati. So whatever name these organizations call themselves today, the Illuminati still exists in them. It is important to know their names today, so I will give a partial list of the important groups.

▪ The German Union. Started by Baron von Knigge, it controlled the book publishing business in Prussia.

▪ The Tungenbund. This was started in 1810, after things settled down. This was a direct descendant of The Order.

• Jacobin Clubs. Started in France during the French Revolution. Sublimes Maitres Parfaits (Sublime Perfect Masters). Started by Filippo Michele Buonarroti.

▪ Société des Saisons (Society of the Seasons). Started by Louis Auguste Blanqui. He and Buonarroti joined their groups together to form the next one called:

▪ The League of the Just. Ready to have the hairs on the back of your neck stand up? The League commissioned Karl Marx, no less, to write the Communist Manifesto (through Frederick Engels). After publication of the Manifesto, the League of the Just changed its name to the *Communist League*. That's right. Has all the revolution and subversion you've just read about somehow seemed familiar? The Communist movement of the twentieth century was and is controlled from the top by the Illuminati. That's true even to this day. The Politburo of Russia, today, still get together and have their handshakes, signs, tokens and penalties of old, just like the Illuminati they replaced. They still believe in revolution, hatred, warfare and destruction of all religions. That's the real reason communist countries celebrate May Day every year. Because that is the day (May 1) in history that the Illuminati was founded in 1776. It's the same in all Communist nations. I will reveal more about this under the heading, Hegelian Dialectics.

For that reason, don't be fooled into thinking that Communism is dead because of *glasnost* or *perestroika*. The Communists, including Gorbachev, still believe they will take over the world with their own brand of the New World Order. The members of the world-wide conspiracy think that they control Communism, or at least are able to influence it, but the Communists think differently. It's kind of like trying to control a tiger by putting a leash around its neck. The Frankenstein monster of Communism created by the international conspiracy could easily turn on them. For that reason, I think there is an excellent chance that Communism could attack the West and start World War Three.

▪ The Thule Society, a secret German society started by the Illuminati. Very influential.

▪ The Skull and Bones. Originally a fraternal organization of Yale University, it was taken over by the Thule Society to recruit the best and brightest of Yale University youth into the Illuminati through gradual indoctrination. Those that received the brainwashing favorably were given status in the Illuminati. The same can be said for the Rhodes Scholarships. Former President Bush was a member of the Skull and Bones, and President Clinton was a Rhodes Scholar.

▪ The Club of Rome. One of the most powerful secret societies in the world. They control the papacy of Roman Catholicism. More about them in the next chapter.

▪ Fabian Socialism.

▪ Anarchism.

Still, there is one more group that needs to be mentioned. The Executive Committee of the Council on Foreign Relations is made up of Illuminists. To be more specific, when a person is inducted into the Executive Committee, he or she is taken to a small, semi-concealed room located in the United Nations building called the Meditation Room. In that room is an altar and at one end of the room is a mural with the all-seeing eye. There he or she is given all the handshakes, oaths and rituals of the highest level (Rex) of the Order of the Illuminati.

Hegelian Dialectics
or, "What the heck is that?"

In the Foreword is found the analogy that the world is in a great Punch and Judy show. Seemingly different organizations, political philosophies, economies and nations are all directed from behind the scenes and are secretly helping the overall effort to integrate the world into a one-world-government. Now we'll find out why. Hegelian dialectics describes the plan the Illuminati uses to achieve their NWO dream.

To portray Hegelian dialectics, I quote from The Cutting Edge radio program, with David Bay, a show entitled "Thesis x Antithesis=Synthesis":

> Time Magazine, May 25, 1992, "A Chat With The Gorbachev's", p.51. "Nothing about Mikhail Gorbachev's triumphal two-week tour of the U.S. suggested that he was a politician removed from power...Though his visit to the U.S. was ostensibly to raise funds and make contacts for...the Gorbachev Foundation, it also eased him smoothly into the rarefied ranks of senior statesmen whose pronouncements are expected to reverberate around the globe. His theme is a corollary of his own perestroika: the whole world is in need of change and reorientation...Gorbachev would not be drawn into an admission that socialist theory had failed or that Communism was dead. **"An alternative between capitalism and communism is in the offing..."**

> Most of you are probably shaking your head in bewilderment at this news article, not realizing that it contains one of the greatest admissions in the history of the modern world! Any student of the Illuminist conspiracy to bring about the New World Order, however, would immediately know what Gorbachev meant when he stated that "an alternative between capitalism and communism is in the offing [immediate future].

> As we consider Gorbachev's statement carefully, we see that he has told us there are three (3) systems of government, two presently constituted and one to come. He specifically mentions Communism and Capitalism as being presently established in the world, but states that a third, as yet unnamed, government is coming that will be neither Communist nor Capitalist.

What possibly can he be referring to? To understand, we must go back in history, to May 1, 1776, the day that Adam Weishaupt... formed his occult group, which he named The Masters of the Illuminati...They had a definite Plan to overthrow all religious and civil institutions and governments, replacing them with a brand new global government, a system which Weishaupt called, The New World Order.

What were the specific plans of this New World Order? Nesta Webster, writing in her book, "World Revolution", listed the following six (6) goals:

1. Abolition of Monarchy and all ordered Government.
2. Abolition of Private Property.
3. Abolition of Inheritance.
4. Abolition of Patriotism.
5. Abolition of the family (i.e., of marriage and all morality, and the institution of the communal education of children).
6. Abolition of all religion. (Page 22)

To achieve this plan, Weishaupt understood that he needed super-natural power, if he was going to successfully destroy Western Civilization, which was religiously Christian. Therefore, Weishaupt established his Masters of the Illuminati with an **occult base**!

...Weishaupt envisioned totally overthrowing all governments and replacing them with his global system. He aimed his Plan against the Western Governments of Europe, because they were estab-lished according to Judeo-Christian principles...Weishaupt saw two religious enemies, Roman Catholicism and the burgeoning Protestant Movement.

Here is the problem in a nutshell, from Weishaupt's viewpoint. He wanted badly to destroy the Western governments, replacing them with one new global government, called the New World Order. But, how do you get from point A to point B? How does one thoroughly, gradually *change every single aspect* of every Western nation, moving them from freedom into slavery, without the citizens of these countries finding out your Plan, and forcing their governments to attack and destroy you?...

Weishaupt lacked only one element in his grand Plan to establish his New World Order: a tactical Battle Plan that would clearly specify how he was to proceed overthrowing all the established governments in the Western World. 1823, a German professor named Hegel provided that formula, that specific battle plan. Hegel, a social philosopher, proposed that societies were governed by the following formula:

The existence of one type of government or society, named **Thesis**, would provoke the appearance of the opposite of that type of government of society, which Hegel named **Antithesis**.

Thesis and Antithesis would naturally begin to battle one another, since they were exactly opposite systems and, therefore, would see matters differently.

If Thesis and Antithesis battled each other for a long period of time, with neither side annihilating the other, that battling would result in both sides changing for a hybrid system of government and society, which Hegel called **Synthesis**.

A constant battling, or threat of battling, was the key. Hegel theorized that "Conflict brings about change, and planned conflict would bring about planned change." This theory swept through Europe, on college campuses, sparking many a debate! After awhile, student's fascination with this theory died down, but the Illuminati, with Freemasonry now thoroughly involved in the leadership in the New World Order Plan, now had their formula to achieve their goals!

Let us now define these terms as they relate to Weishaupt's Plan:

▪ **Thesis**—is the original system dominating Europe in the late 1700's. This system was economically Private Enterprise, politically either Monarchy or Democracy, and religiously Judeo-Christian.

■ **Anti-Thesis**—is the opposite system to Thesis, which, theoretically, by battling Thesis for an extended period of time, would produce a new system, called Synthesis. The major problem is that no truly opposite system to Thesis existed in 1776.

So, what can you do when no truly opposite system has "spontaneously" sprung up? If I were in charge of executing the New World Order Plan, and I believed in Hegel's theory, I suppose **I would sit down to create and exactly opposite system to Thesis...**

The radio broadcast then continued to state that in 1848 the "League of Twelve Just Men" of the Illuminati financed Karl Marx to write the Communist Manifesto. Then the League changed its name to the Communist League. A more perfect opposite system to Thesis could not be found. To return to the Broadcast:

Communism was economically State-owned and State-planned, and religiously Atheistic, and politically a dictatorship. A more complete opposite to Thesis could not have been made possible, even if it were planned that way, which, of course, it was.

■ **Synthesis**—is the new, hybrid system produced by constant battling between Thesis and Anti-Thesis is planned to be economically Fascist, where the means of production and the distribution of goods are privately held, but the government dictates how much is produced and how many companies can produce the same type product. Synthesis was **planned to be religiously Satanic**, which is the hybrid between the Judeo-Christian Thesis and the Atheistic Anti-Thesis. This new system, hypothetically called Synthesis, has always had a title. It has always been know as the **New World Order...**

As an aside, in order to understand the connection between

western capitalists and the Communist movement, read the book, *Wall Street and the Bolshevik Revolution* by Anthony Sutton. Also, read *Wall Street and the Rise of Hitler* by the same author. These books will manifest the truth of what I am about to tell you, which has already been hinted at. That is, American and European international bankers **financed both the Bolshevik revolution and the Nazi movement**. There were a number of reasons why, but mostly it was Hegelian Dialectics of Thesis v. Antithesis =Synthesis. (Punch and Judy controlled by the same puppeteer).

As for the Nazis, one important reason for financing Hitler was to see if the economic theory of Fascism was feasible. Would it really work if it were used in a society? The conspirators really wanted to know, because they planned on making fascism the economic basis of the NWO. So they financed Hitler with the marching orders to make Germany a Fascist State. Actually, the idea worked out spectacularly. Germany was transformed from a destroyed nation, racked by runaway inflation after WWI into a super-power that almost won WWII against the might of the United States. They conspirators knew they were on to something then.

Back to the radio broadcast:

Now back to the early part of this century. The number one requirement for this concept (i.e., Thesis v. Antithesis=Synthesis) to work was for the government of a large nation to be overthrown and replaced by this Anti-Thesis government, Communism. Since the United States of America was the unquestioned leader of the system of Thesis (Capitalism), it was absolutely necessary for the new Anti-Thesis (Communism) to be lead by a nation who was similarly endowed with land-mass, population, and natural resources. New World Oder planners decided, in the early 1900's, that this nation was to be Russia. Thus, western monies flowed early and continuously to Lenin to achieve the overthrow of the Russian Czars...Nesta Webster shows the Illuminati working through the German General Staff to Support Lenin in his revolution. Once Communism was in power, western monies, credits, and political support kept Communism from collapsing from its basic inefficiencies and flaws.

Once Russia was Communist, the next phase of the plan was introduced. This phase calls for the threat of conflict between America and Russia, with no side militarily defeating the other. Thus, after WWII, with Russia being built up as a superpower because of WWII aid, the peoples of the world were subjected to one crisis after another between America and Russia. As a result of 40+ years of planned conflict between Thesis (America) and Anti-Thesis (Russia), the time has now come for the planned merger into the new Synthesis, the New World Order. All along, **the leaders of Communism have been participants in the Plan to create the New World Order. They have been loyal soldiers to this cause, along with Western Capitalists and Western political leaders.** Gorbachev's statement clearly reveals the truth of this scenario...

This is why world events are like a giant Punch and Judy show. We have been the unwitting supporting cast of a huge, costly and deadly world-wide production. All major world historical events for the past two hundred years, including but not limited to wars and depressions, have been deliberately caused. Here is another quotation about the formation of Communism:

In *The New York Journal-American* (Feb. 3, 1949) one will read:

Today it is estimated even by Jacob's grandson, John Schiff, a prominent member of New York society, that the old man (Jacob Schiff was an International Banker) sank about $20,000,000 for the final triumph of Bolshevism in Russia. Other New York banking firms also contributed.

Secret Records Revealed
op cit, (28) Comment added.

Lest there be any holdouts who think that the internationalists

115

don't control Communism, here is an unusually candid remark:

> In (Bruce) Lockhart's *British Agent* (1933), he will write about (Raymond) Robins:

> Although a rich man himself, he was an anti-capitalist...Hitherto, his two heroes had been [Teddy] Roosevelt and Cecil Rhodes. Now Lenin captured his imagination...Robins was the only man whom Lenin was always willing to see and who ever succeeded in imposing his own personality on the unemotional Bolshevik leader...I returned from our interview to our flat to find an urgent message from Robins requesting me to come to see him at once...When I arrived, he had just finished telephoning Lenin. He had delivered his ultimatum [about Saalkind, Assistant Commissar for Foreign Affairs]...Then the telephone rang and Robins picked up the receiver. **Lenin had capitulated. Saalkind was dismissed from his post.**
>
> *Secret Records Revealed,*
> op cit, (31,32)

There is a reason for relating the history of Communism and how it was financed by capitalists. The idea of creating the enemies you need in order to grab power is not new, and one of the best examples in history occurred with the Triumvirate of Crassus, Pompeii and Julius Caesar:

> In 70 BC, an ambitious minor politician and extremely wealthy man, Marcus Licineus Crassus, wanted to rule Rome. Just to give you an idea of what sort of man Crassus really was, he is credited with invention of the fire brigade. But in Crassus' version, his fire-fighting slaves would race to the scene of a burning building whereupon Crassus would offer to buy it on the spot for a tiny fraction of it's worth. If the owner sold, Crassus' slaves would put out the fire. It the owner refused to sell, Crassus allowed the building to burn to the ground. By means of this device, Crassus eventually came to be the largest single private landholder in Rome, and used

some of his wealth to help back Julius Caesar against Cicero.

In 70 BC, Rome was still a Republic, which placed very strict limits on what Rulers could do, and more importantly NOT do. But Crassus had no intentions of enduring such limits to his personal power, and contrived a plan.

Crassus seized upon the slave revolt led by Spartacus in order to strike terror into the hearts of Rome, whose garrison Spartacus had already defeated in battle. But Spartacus had no intention of marching on Rome itself, a move he knew to be suicidal. Spartacus and his band wanted nothing to do with the Roman empire and had planned from the start merely to loot enough money from their former owners in the Italian countryside to hire a mercenary fleet in which to sail to freedom.

Sailing away was the last thing Crassus wanted Spartacus to do. He needed a convenient enemy with which to terrorize Rome itself for his personal political gain. So Crassus bribed the mercenary fleet to sail without Spartacus, then positioned two Roman legions in such a way that Spartacus had no choice but to march on Rome.

Terrified of the impending arrival of the much-feared army of gladiators, Rome declared Crassus Praetor. Crassus then crushed Spartacus' army and even though Pompeii took the credit, Crassus was elected Consul of Rome the following year.

With this maneuver, the Romans surrendered their Republican form of government. Soon would follow the first Triumvirate, consisting of Crassus, Pompeii, and Julius Caesar, followed by the reign of the god-like Emperors of Rome.

The Romans were hoaxed into surrendering their Republic, and accepting the rule of Emperors.
"Fake Terrorism—The Road To Dictatorship"
by Michael Rivero
Sightings.com

12/24/99

Because of the above article, it is possible the conspirators may do the same thing with us. That is, they could create an enemy, brainwash us into thinking that they need extraordinary powers not granted by the Constitution to defeat this 'enemy,' then once the 'enemy' is vanquished, brainwash us again into thinking that they need to perpetuate their new found control over us in order to defeat future 'enemies.' Look out for it.

The insiders also use it in other Punch and Judy shows called, Republican vs. Democrat and Conservative vs. Liberal. Hegelian Dialectics used in the domestic political arena in the United States is not exactly the same as is used in the Capitalism vs. Communism Punch and Judy show, because the conspirators are not trying to create a synthesis from the Republican vs. Democrat or Conservative vs. Liberal sideshow. But these political Punch and Judy shows are similar in the fact that domestic politics in the United States are definitely controlled from behind the scenes, like Western Democracies and Communism are controlled in the international arena.

The cabalists gradually assumed oversight of both of the major political parties, at least on the national level. Both the Republican and Democratic parties are owned by them. That's why many Americans have become disenchanted with the whole political process. They feel that no matter who is elected from either party, things seem to continue the same, the country continues down the same road and the parties are no longer responsive to the people but to "moneyed interests." Truer words were never spoken. Because of that sense, most people, while not knowing exactly what is going on, feel a loss of identity with either party. They feel in their gut that something is not right in politics but can't identify what it is or why they feel that way.

It's my Party and I'll Cry if I Want to...

The above caption comes from a popular rock and roll tune from the fifties. It could very well pertain to the common voter today, lamenting the fact that he no longer feels that his political party is responsive to his wishes. And well he should cry. To illustrate how the political parties and the election process in general were gradually sabotaged over the years, read the following:

The candidate-selection process is the means by which elective offices are filled in the United States. It is a process that is often called "political," but it is more preoccupied with individual ambition and image-building than it is with substantive issues. **It is a process in which most politicians develop binding ties to one or another clique with the power elite** while professing to speak for "the people..."

It is precisely because the candidate-selection process has become increasingly individualistic over the past several decades, and therefore dependent on name recognition and personal image, that it can be in good part dominated by members of the ruling class through the relatively simple and direct means of large campaign contributions. In the guise of fat cats and money raisers, the same men who direct corporations and take part in policy groups (like the Council on Foreign Relations) play a central role in the careers of most politicians who advance beyond the local level or state legislatures in states of any size or consequence: "Recruitment of elective elites remains closely associated, especially for the more important offices in the larger states, with the candidates' wealth or access to large campaign contributions."

Although reliable data were hard to come by in the past, the role of big money in major elections has been known to the political scientists who study campaign finance for some time, both through systematic studies and dramatic examples...

...it was left for the 1972 election to reveal the full scope of large campaign donations. New disclosure laws passed in 1971, combined with the uncovering of various scandals, including

Watergate, led to more complete information on campaign financing than ever had been available in the past. The results were stunning. The number of people known to have given $500 or more soared from 15,000 in 1968, when reporting laws were still lax, to 51,000 in 1972. Those known to have contributed $10,000 or over rose from 424 to 1,250. The donations of the $10,000-and-over givers were awesome—these 1,250 individuals gave $51.3 million to national-level candidates. This figure compares rather impressively with the $8.5 million which organized labor donated to all presidential and congressional candidates in 1972, and to the $10.5 million which McGovern netted from 600,000 people in his widely publicized direct mail solicitations in 1971 and 1972...

Large campaign donors are often hard to distinguish in their outlooks, whatever their political party...**Indeed, many of the largest donors give to both parties**. In 1972, for example, 36% of the $10,000-and-over donors gave to candidates of both political parties. Most of these split-givers were contributing to the presidential campaign of one party and a senatorial or House campaign of the other, but there were also **14 such donors who gave to both Nixon and McGovern. Whatever the motivation for these split gifts, they help give members of the power elite access to both political parties.**

In addition to the donations provided directly to candidates, wealthy individuals also support both parties through their contributions to the numerous political action committees of specific corporations and general business organizations. When all of these direct and indirect gifts are combined, **the power elite can be seen to provide the great bulk of the financial support to both parties at the national level**, far outspending the unions and middle-status liberals within the Democrats, and the mélange of physicians, dentists, engineers, real-estate operators and other white-collar conservatives within the right wing of the Republican Party...

The central role played by heavy money is a constant strain on the legitimacy of the electoral system. **It contributes to cynicism about politics and to a widespread belief that politicians are corrupt and easily bought...**
The Powers That Be
Processes of Ruling Class Domination in America
by G. William Domhoff
excerpts from 129-148

The book, *The Powers That Be,* is a sociological study of political power in America. The author, G. William Domhoff, was a professor of psychology and sociology at the University of California, Santa Cruz. The book is fascinating because it was written from the detached point of view of an empirical sociological study, not from a biased political view. It is *The Powers That Be,* by G. William Domhoff, Vintage Books, Jan. 1979.

But domination of the political parties through political financial contributions is not the only way the insiders control the political process. They also control it through the national political conventions, and to a lesser extent, the state political conventions. In support of this, read the following:

In pigment and chromosome, the 1980 Democratic Convention was nearly perfect...The Democratic National Committee proudly documented the diversity of the spectacle. Their figures showed that 15% of the 3,381 delegates were black, 49% were women and 11% were under 30...

Yet something was wrong. It was not in the statistics or the cosmetics. Reporters ran into it almost immediately whenever they began talking to delegates...All over the convention floor, the situation was the same: an inordinate number of the delegates seemed to be part of, or somehow plugged into the government at some level...

The best data it turned out were complied by CBS. They unlimbered their computer for TIME and went at the figures again. The earlier suspicions were confirmed—**40.3% of the delegates to the Democratic National Convention were public office-holders or government employees in some capacity. (Only 7% of the general population is employed by government at all levels). And the figure, some experts point out, does not reflect the number of other delegates who are dependent on Big Government spending, though they may work in the private sector.**

Austin Ranney, senior political scholar to the American Enterprise Institute, finds immense irony in this development. "One of the great reasons for reform from the very beginning was to get away from patronage, so delegates would not be beholden to the old bosses," he says. Ranney now fears that all of the electoral reforms have not prevented the beholden of a different kind from entering through a "back door" of the convention. Since there are no longer power centers like Chicago's late Mayor Richard Daly, and only 69 senators, Governors and members of the House were delegates this year, **the new "boss" is Big Government, and in most instances the trail leads back to Washington and the Administration.**

The Democratic Party seems to be forming itself like another part of the federal bureaucracy. In Ranney's view, a Kennedy revolt (Ted Kennedy tried to challenge Jimmy Carter for the presidential nomination, but it fizzled) of 400 or 500 delegates never materialized in part **because too many of the people on the floor had a personal stake in spending programs Jimmy Carter had fostered for states and localities.**

That network of elected officials, civil servants, their consultants and contractors looks alarmingly like a talent bank for preserving the political power of the incumbent President.

"Delegates from Big Brother"
TIME, Sept. 1, 1980, (13)

This is an example of what may be termed stacking the deck. And using indirect political pressure from the Government to control national political nominating conventions of both the Republican and Democratic parties happens all the time. Somehow or other, the insiders can always control the national conventions. But what about the state nominating conventions? Surely they are beyond the control of the conspirators.

As a matter of conjecture, in many cases, the insiders don't control the state conventions. In other cases, they do. Their influence, to some extent, is counterbalanced by the increased power of the vote of the individual, on the local or state level. You see, the power of the vote of the individual is indirectly proportional to the level of government for whom he or she votes. That is, the greater the level of government voted for, the lesser the power of the individual voter. Conversely, the smaller the level of government, the greater is the voter's power. To demonstrate that point, consider a national general election wherein the electorate is voting for the President, and 90 million votes are cast. One individual vote is therefore 1/90,000,000th of the total. But in a small city election for mayor that has 500 votes cast, one vote is 1/500th of the total.

Neither vote may seem like there is much power associated with it, but one vote in the small city election with only 500 votes cast has as much elective power as 180,000 votes in the national election cited above! So it is easier for people to control their local politicians and local party officials than national ones. Nevertheless, through the influence of the media, and through control of the national party, the state party nominating conventions are often controlled, or at least influenced to some degree, albeit indirectly, by the insiders. Do not discount their ability to impact the local scene.

Another aspect of the political scene must be addressed here. That is, everybody has heard of the political "left" and "right," of "conservative" as well as "liberal" Republicans and Democrats. Each of the above designations make people think that there is a diversity of opinion amongst the citizenry in this country, thereby fostering the idea that we really have a plurality of ideas.

Conservatism and liberalism are indeed different concepts, but they were taken over by members of the conspiracy. That is, both "conservative Republican" and "liberal Democrat" national leaders, such as Newt Gingrich and Ted Kennedy, are part of the international conspiracy. These two, along with others, use both "conservative" and "liberal"ideas to further promote one-world government.

Boy, is that radical! But contemplate this: No matter which side occupies the White House, be it a "conservative" or "liberal," Democrat or Republican, neither ideology actually addresses some very germane questions, such as: "Why do we have the Federal Reserve at all, since it never existed for almost one hundred years of our nation's history, and we did very well without it?" Or, "Why do we have the Council on Foreign Relations when it never existed before 1921 and America was better off before?"

Think about that for awhile. When was the last time you ever heard a conservative or liberal politician of national prominence ask such questions? When did you hear Gingrich, Gore, Clinton, Kemp, Bradley, Bush, Reagan, Carter, Nixon, Humphrey, Johnson or Eisenhower ever, ever, ever ask for the removal of the Fed, or at least its audit? In which Presidential debate did the question of dismissing the CFR ever come up? Isn't this a pluralistic society? Don't we have majority rule? The Fed and the CFR represent rule by the moneyed few.

These questions are legitimate—Why do we need the Fed? All we do is become more indebted to it, day by day. Our government used to issue interest-free National Bank Notes, not interest charged Federal Reserve Notes. And yet, not one—be they conservative or liberal—dares to ask such charged questions these days. Could it be because they're not supposed to ask such revealing questions? Could it be because the presidential candidates are part of a show?

Not only that, the difference between the two ideologies seems more muddled when one bears in mind the fruits of each ideology. That is, suppose that we had a liberal Democratic congress and president, as when Johnson was President. Then America wound up with heavy spending for social programs, thus becoming more indebted to the Fed. And, in truth, the Congress during Johnson's administration greatly increased the national debt.

But, oh, you say, the conservatives are so much better. They advocate fiscal responsibility. So let's suppose now that we had a majority congress of conservative Republicans and president, like under Reagan. At that time the congress stopped funding many social programs, and started funding more national defense programs, thus becoming more indebted to the Fed, just like with Johnson. The result was the same, no matter who was in charge. But isn't the general perception that conservatives are fiscally responsible, while liberals aren't? The national debt increased both under Reagan and Johnson. Are you beginning to see what is really going on?

Another example comes from local Utah politics. Governor Matheson, a liberal, believed in the goodness of big government, so was in favor of raising taxes on Utahns. He wanted increased government control over everything. But the majority of Utahns were conservative and wouldn't stand for increased taxes. So Matheson never dared to propose a substantial tax increase during his term as Governor of Utah. The next Governor after him was Bangerter, a conservative. He believed in limited government, and promised not to raise taxes. However, under Bangerter, Utah realized the greatest single state tax increase in its history, pushed through the legislature by none other than "fiscally conservative" Governor Bangerter. He did, as a conservative, what Mattheson never dared to do as a liberal. So why is it that these seemingly different men always end up doing the same thing, despite their labels?

The same thing could be said for the debate about the war in Vietnam, which Johnson, as a presidential candidate, opposed but his opponent, Goldwater, supported. During the 1964 presidential campaign, Johnson was portrayed as the voice of "peace" while Goldwater was the voice of "war," the labels put on them by the news media. But after Johnson won the election, he then turned around and did the same thing that Goldwater promised to do, had HE won. That is, Johnson, the voice of "peace," escalated the war.

The argument could go on and on, like when the "anti-communist" Nixon won over Humphrey in 1968, then proceeded to make detente with communist China, or when Carter, the "outsider," deliberately promised, if elected, not to appoint "insiders" to his cabinet (i.e., members of the Council on Foreign Relations), then promptly did so as soon as the election was over. It goes on and on. Bush said, "Read my lips, no new taxes," then raised them a year after being elected.

As an excellent example of saying one thing then doing another, Clinton, without approval of Congress, recently created a pilot program in four states, at a cost of $68 million that would empower the government to pay unemployment benefits to parents who stay home with their kids.

Joseph Farrah in a column entitled, The Helping Hand of Government (Dec. 3, 1999) shows up this program for the lie that it is:

> In other words, it's a way of taxing employers again for a new program without going through all the constitutional hassles of creating another tax.
>
> People who promote such schemes do so not because they are compassionate for the poor or, as President Clinton suggests, because "families are our most important natural resource." They do so because it empowers government rather than free individuals. It's a trap...
>
> ...Yes, it is our best interests as a society if one parent stays home to rear children. That has always been the case. Remember, though, it was Clinton's political philosophy that persuaded Americans years ago that kids would turn out just as well if they were raised in day-care centers—particularly government day-care

centers...Yet we're supposed to believe these geniuses have seen the light and have a new magical solution for us that just happens, once again, to empower government over the individual again...

Government, through heavy taxation, has created the need for both parents to enter the workforce. Now government, which created the problem in the first place, comes up with a plan to solve the problem, which, in reality will only worsen it.

Shouldn't we stop looking to government to put band-aids on injuries it has inflicted? Wouldn't it be better if one parent had the option of staying home to take care of kids because a single income was enough to support a family? That's the way it used to be in America. That's the way it ought to be. That's the way it can be again if we get government off our backs and out of our pockets. (He also proposed the elimination of the income tax as a means of allowing the one-paycheck family to exist again).

In other words, President Clinton, while mouthing praise on the family unit, started a program that will help destroy it. You see, more taxes on employers will drive more and more employers out of business, or force employees to accept smaller paychecks to make up for the increased taxation. Either way, the family is hurt by this program of taxing employers for unemployment benefits to spouses who wish to remain at home. This program has the overall effect of making individuals more dependent on government. When people are more dependent on government, they can more easily be compelled, or herded, into a one-world-government.

As a matter of fact, one of the candidates for president in the recent election freely admitted that the two parties were basically the same:

Bush said it himself with this line: "During the fall campaign (Election 2000), we differed about the details of these proposals, but **there was remarkable consensus about the important issues before us: excellent schools, retirement and health security, tax relief, a strong military, a more civil society.**"

He's right about that. There was consensus during the campaign. It was a political campaign more about personalities than policies. And the more I hear from Bush, the harder it is to tell him apart from Gore—on the issues, that is.

"The Honeymoon's Over"
by Joseph Farah
Article for World Net Daily
Dec. 14, 2000

And finally, here is what Russia, our so called enemy, thinks about the 2000 election:

In sharp contrast to statements made two days earlier, Moscow is now expressing confidence that "whatever the outcome" of the **U.S. presidential elections, U.S. foreign policy "will follow the same pattern" as with previous administrations**, according to official sources.

"Moscow OK 'whatever the outcome'"
by I.J. Troy Westerman
Article for World Net Daily
Oct. 24, 2000

To sum up the debate between conservative vs. liberal philosophies, the bottom line is that the national leaders who classify themselves as liberal or conservative use those labels to promote greater government influence in our lives, not less. That is the ultimate goal of the conspirators. In truth, the debate between the "conservatives" and "liberals," Republicans and Democrats is a Punch and Judy show all over again.

It is true that the conspirators can use the liberal side of the political argument to create a "Big Brother" government more easily than with the conservative side. It has been said that being a liberal politician is like driving toward the edge of a cliff at 100 miles an hour while a conservative politician drives toward the cliff at 40 miles and hour. For that reason, the news media is programmed to push the liberal side more, but make no mistake about it, the top conservatives and the top liberals, the Republicans and Democrats in this country do not represent the common people but the people with money.

As was said before, the overall direction of America as well as the world is toward the New World Order and it matters not one whit whether the leaders who accomplish this goal are conservative or liberal, Democrat or Republican. Therefore, it is the author's considered opinion that the reader should not vote for either the Republican or Democratic presidential candidates in future elections. They are bought and paid for by multinational corporations, no matter what they profess. There are many "third party" candidates who are honest and will actually represent the people. They should be sought after.

More Quotes on the Republican vs Democrat Punch and Judy issue:

The argument that the two parties should represent opposed ideals and policies, one, perhaps, of the Right and the other of the Left, is a foolish idea acceptable only to doctrinaire and academic thinkers. **Instead, the two parties should almost be identical, so that the American people can "throw the rascals out" at any election without leading to any profound or extensive shifts in policy. The policies that are vital and necessary for America are no longer subjects of significant disagreement but are disputable only in details of procedure, priority, or method...**

But either party in office becomes in time corrupt, tired, unenterprising, and vigorless. Then it should be possible to replace it, every four years if necessary, by the other party, which will be none of these things **but will still pursue, with new vigor, approximately the same basic policies.**

Tragedy and Hope, op cit, (1247—1248)

Hegelian Dialectics has been a useful philosophical tool for the Illuminati. Next we will discuss the apex of the conspiracy hierarchy.

Chapter 7

"Only three hundred men, each of whom knows all others, govern the
fate of Europe. They select their successors from their own
entourage. These men have the means in their hands of
putting an end to the form of State which they find unreasonable."
—Walter Rathenau, financial advisor to the Rothschilds,
quoted in the Wiener Press, December 24, 1921.
He was assassinated exactly six months later, on June 24, 1922.

The Committee of 300

Now we come to the "creme de la creme," as it were, of the hierarchy of conspiratorial groups. There are other groups, but not much
is known about them. However, a small amount of information can be
shared. The council of thirteen, for instance, is the Grand Druid
Council, or the highest ranking witches in the world. The Council of 33
includes the thirty-three highest ranked Masons. Other councils have
their own spheres of influence, or control.

The Committee of 300 coordinates the actions of other groups and
acts as a clearing house, disseminating information among their
members, displaying progress reports in different areas, funding
different groups and finalizing all strategy and tactics in bringing
about their goal of one world government.

This organization has been called different things by different
people. Many heads of foreign governments call them "The
Magicians," Stalin referred to them as "The Dark Forces," President
Eisenhower was perhaps closest to the truth when he called them "The
Military-Industrial Complex." They refer to themselves as "The
Olympians," meaning that they think of themselves as gods on earth.

The membership of this group consists of members and directors of the CFR, TLC, Round Table and Illuminati plus members of groups not yet named. Also, there is a class of people on the Committee that, at first glance, one would not normally associate with the conspiracy. The aristocracy of Europe, with a heavy emphasis on England, is on the Committee. Yes, the Royal Family of England is represented. And all this time the Queen of England was portrayed as the family matriarch of a rich but powerless monarchy, the vestige of an institution that outgrew its usefulness.

But the truth is more consistent with the basest of human nature in that once having tasted power, rulers don't want to give it up. Those aristocracies *seemed* to abdicate their powers, about 150 years ago, but only on the surface. In reality, they are more powerful than ever behind the scenes. The funny thing is, that the same time the European and English aristocracies were being phased out of power, so to speak, is about the time the Committee of 300 came into being, around the 1840's. What a coincidence!

Mention shall be made of other secret occult groups that you may never have heard of before, whose members have a place on the Committee. Some of them are: the Mumma Group, the Order of the Skull and Bones, Cultus Diabolicus, the Circle of Initiates, the Nine Unknown Men, Lucis Trust (formerly Lucifer Trust), British Quator Coronati, Italian P2 Masonry, the Order of St. John of Jerusalem, the Club of Rome, the Black Nobility of Europe, etc. Many members have a position with multiple groups.

The information on the Committee comes from the book, *Conspirator's Hierarchy: The Story of the Committee of 300* by Dr. John Coleman. He tells us about their goals:

> What are the goals of the secret elite group, the inheritors of illuminism...? This elite group that also calls itself the OLYMPIANS...absolutely believe they have been charged with implementing the following by divine right:

> 1. A One World Government—New World Order with a unified

church and monetary system under their direction.

2. The utter destruction of all national identity and national pride. (That means the destruction of the Constitution of the United States, and to the system of government that it establishes).

3. The destruction of religion and more especially the Christian religion, with one exception, their own creation mentioned above.

4. Control of each and every person through means of mind control and what Brzezinski calls "technotronics" which would create human-like robots and a system of terror besides which Felix Dzerzinski's Red Terror will look like children at play.

5. An end to all industrialization and the production of nuclear generated electric power in what they call "the post-industrial zero-growth society." Exempted are the computer and service industries. United States industries that remain will be exported to countries such as Mexico where abundant slave labor is available. Unemployables in the wake of industrial destruction will either become opium-heroin and or cocaine addicts, or become statistics in the elimination process...

6. Legalization of drugs and pornography.

7. Depopulation of large cities according to the trial run carried out by the Pol Pot regime in Cambodia...

8. Suppression of all scientific development except for those deemed beneficial by the Committee. Especially targeted is nuclear energy for peaceful purposes. Particularly hated are the fusion experiments presently being scorned and ridiculed by the Committee and its jackals of the press...

9. Cause by means of limited wars in the advanced countries, and by means of starvation and diseases in Third World countries, the death of 3 billion people, people they call "useless eaters." The Committee of 300 commissioned Cyrus Vance to write a paper on this subject of how best to bring about such genocide. The paper

was produced under the title the "Global 2000 Report" and was accepted and approved for action by President Carter, for and on behalf of the U.S. Government, and accepted by Edwin Muskie, then Secretary of State. Under the terms of the Global 2000 Report, the population of the United States is to be reduced by 100 million by the year 2050.

10. To weaken the moral fiber of the nation and to demoralize workers in the labor class by creating mass unemployment. As jobs dwindle due to the post industrial zero growth policies introduced by the Club of Rome, (a powerful group directly under their control) demoralized and discouraged workers will resort to alcohol and drugs. The youth of the land will be encouraged by means of rock music and drugs to rebel against the status quo, thus undermining and eventually destroying the family unit. In this regard The Committee of 300 commissioned Tavistock Institute (a think tank owned by them) to prepare a blueprint as to how this could be achieved. Tavistock directed Stanford Research to under- take the work under the direction of Professor Willis Harmon. This work later became known as "The Aquarian Conspiracy."

The tremendous evil of this work can't be overstated. If you wish to look up the reference yourself, it is officially known as Stanford's Charles F. Kettering Foundation's "CHANGING IMAGES OF MAN" under Stanford official reference "Contract Number URH (489)-2150 Policy Research Report Number 4/4/74, prepared by the SRI (Stanford Research Institute) Center for the Study of Social Policy, Director Willis Harmon."

The report, covering 319 pages, was written by 14 new age scientists under the supervision of Tavistock and 23 top controllers including B.F. Skinner, Margaret Meade, Ervin Lazlo and Sir Geoffrey Vickers...

A book was written based on "THE CHANGING IMAGES OF MAN" called, *The Aquarian Conspiracy* which covers most of the report. Specifically, the report wanted to program America in a new moral direction. The conspirators wanted to deliberately and gradually push America into accepting drugs, free sex, violence, murder, homosexuality, pornography, abortion on demand and every kind of evil they could think of. Their ultimate goal was to destroy the family unit. The "Olympians" knew it would take time. But their goal is gradually coming true, as we can see how the family unit is indeed dying in our generation. Single parent families are almost as common now as two parent families.

One of the most pernicious ways these insiders found to accomplish this goal was to promote hard rock bands that promoted drugs and free sex. The Beatles was the first among many that they promoted. This report, THE CHANGING IMAGES OF MAN, more than anything else, has changed America forever. Another part of the report planned to actually promote crimes and misdemeanors in high places, thereby discouraging the electorate and promoting apathy in our democratic republic. This cultivated disregard of the law by those in power has come to fruition in the Clinton administration, but make no mistake about it, Clinton is not the first to engage in sexual misconduct. Nor in criminal conduct. To quote from the book by John Coleman:

> Our once proud Republic of the United States of America became no more than a series of criminal front organizations, which history shows is always the start of totalitarianism. This is the stage of permanent alteration we are at in America...We live in a throw away society, programmed not to last. We do not flinch at the 4 million homeless nor the 30 million jobless, nor the 15 million babies murdered thus far. They are "throw-aways" of the Age of Aquarius...

> Who can deny that with the huge increase in drug usage— "crack" making thousands of instant new addicts each day—the shocking rise in the murder of infants each day, (aborticide),...the open

acceptance of homosexuality and lesbianism whose "rights" are protected by more and more laws each year, the terrible plague we call "AIDS" washing over our towns and cities, the total failure of our education system, the stunning increase in the divorce rate, a murder rate that shocks the rest of the world...satanic serial killings, the disappearance of thousands of young children, snatched off our streets by perverts, a virtual tidal wave of pornography accompanied by "permissiveness" on our television screens—who can deny that this nation is in crisis, which we are not addressing nor from which we are turning away.

All this is because of the planned changes deliberately implemented by the Committee of 300 through the report, "THE CHANGING IMAGES OF MAN."

11. To keep people everywhere from deciding their own destinies by means of one created crisis after another and then "managing" such crises. This will confuse and demoralize the population to the extent where faced with too many choices, **apathy on a massive scale will result...**

12. To introduce new cults and continue to boost those already functioning which includes rock "music" gangsters such as the filthy, degenerate Mick Jagger's "Rolling Stones"...and all of the Tavistock created "rock" groups which began with "The Beatles."

A time out is in order here. This particular goal of the Committee, plus no.10 above, is compared to an experience of Elder Gene R. Cook of the 1st Quorum of the Seventies of the LDS Church. He gave a talk at Ricks College in 1989 called The Eternal Nature of the Law of Chastity. He was giving young people a few suggestions on how to create a chaste and virtuous environment. One of the suggestions was about the influence music has on chastity and virtue:

Select Wholesome Music. Sometimes young people have a feeling that the music they listen to doesn't have anything to do with chastity. And yet, as I've had opportunity to interview many youth in varying countries throughout the world, I've found that this is just not so. I believe, without any doubt, that there is music of the Lord...It ought not surprise us that the devil has his own music as well. That kind of music is found throughout the world and has a great impact upon young people especially.

Let me try to bring this principle alive by relating a true story that happened with an individual of whom you probably have heard. How many of you have heard of Mick Jagger?...Well, you might be surprised to know that I had about 2-_ hours with him on an airplane and it was quite an experience...

Mr. Jagger and I were on a flight that originated in Mexico and were headed, I believe, to either Houston or Dallas...a man came and sat down by me...I offered a silent prayer as I often do when I try to talk to people about the Church...After the prayer, I said something like, "My name is Gene Cook, I'm a member of the Church of Jesus Christ of Latter-day Saints. What's your name?" And he said, "My name is Mick Jagger."...And then he opened up the magazine he was reading and pointed to his picture and said, "This is me."...

What I'm going to say is, in no way, speaking evil of Mick Jagger himself. Please understand that. I'm not speaking evil of the man, but I am of what he represents because it is wrong. It is of the devil himself, in my opinion...

After we visited back and forth a minute or two about what we were doing and all, I finally said something like, "You know, Mick, I have a question for you that I'd like you to answer for me." He said, "Well, I'll be glad to try." Then I said to him, "I have opportunity to be with young people in many different places around the world, and some of them have told me that the kind of music you and others like you sing has no effect on them, that it's okay, and that it doesn't affect them adversely in any way. Then other young people have told me very honestly that your kind of music has a real effect on them for evil and that it affects them in a very bad way. You've been in this business for a very long time, Mick. I'd like to know your opinion. What do you think is the impact of your music on the young people?"

This is a direct quote, brothers and sisters. He said, **"Our music is calculated to drive the kids to sex."** Those were his exact words...He quickly added, "Well, it's not my fault what they do. That's up to them. I'm just making a lot of money."

Then he told me he'd been in Mexico making a video...He told me this was a great day for them because now instead of just having audio where they could portray some of what they wanted to about sex and all, they now had videos and could have the people both hear it and see it portrayed. He said this would have much more impact on the youth...

As I said, we talked for a couple of hours. Let me just share a few things that happened because it teaches the importance of what we are discussing with respect to music. He told me that he was not married but that he had three children and was proud of it...He told me that it didn't matter what you did in life, that you could take whatever you wanted, and that you could do whatever you wanted. **He said there were no commandments, there was no God, and nothing really mattered...**(this is reminiscent of what Korihor said in the Book of Mormon. Read Alma 30:13-18.)

...He told me he believed in evolution and that he also believed he had descended from a monkey...He told me the importance, in his view, of freeing up the youth. He felt that they ought to be able to do whatever they wanted in spite of their parents. He said that parents were inhibiting them too much and controlling things...It was truly astounding to me. He told me **he was thankful the family, as an entity, was being destroyed.** And I gathered from what he was saying that he was doing his best to help that along. (Then he said disparaging things about the Mormons and the Book of Mormon.)

I finally bore my testimony to him and said something like, "My friend, the lie is not in the Book of Mormon. The lie is in you. And I bear witness to you in the name of the Lord that if you don't turn your life around, you'll be going to hell"...I bore a very fervent testimony to him and told him that I would be a witness (before God) that I had at least given him "the word."

From the talk, <u>The Eternal Nature of the Law of Chastity</u>
by Elder Gene Cook

Here is the plain evidence that Mick Jagger, by his own admission, using The Rolling Stones, seek the destruction of the youth and the family unit. As goals No.10 and 12 of the Committee said, this and other rock groups are part of a planned conspiracy called the Aquarian Conspiracy. That plan didn't just "evolve." Music, videos, movies, television, MTV, books and magazines are openly promoting drugs, sex, violence, homosexuality, murder, theft, pornography and every other idea that will destroy society by destroying the family, which is its basic unit. All these things are part of an overall plan.

These negative values are purposely displayed and promoted by the owners as part of the plan. That does not mean that there is nothing good on T.V. or other forms of the media, but that the *overall* direction is a scripted downward spiral. Again, we are being purposefully and subtly led down paths we would certainly reject if we knew that these things were deliberately being foisted upon us.

13. To press for the spread of religious cults such as the Moslem Brotherhood, Moslem fundamentalism, the Sikhs...It is worth noting that the late Ayatollah Khomeini was a creation of British Intelligence Military Intelligence 6, commonly known as MI6...

14. To export "religious liberation" ideas around the world so as to undermine all existing religions but more especially the Christian religion...

15. To cause a total collapse of the world's economies and engender

total political chaos.

This part of their scheme is chilling. It has not yet come to fruition, but it will in short order. That is one of the reasons the Lord, through his servants the prophets, have warned us about the necessity of procuring a year's supply of food, money, fuel and clothing. We will discuss that in a later chapter.

16. To take control of all Foreign and domestic policies of the United States.

17. To give the fullest support to supranational institutions such as the United Nations (UN), the International Monetary Fund (IMF), the Bank of International Settlements (BIS), the World Court and, as far as possible, make local institutions of lesser effect by gradually phasing them out or bringing them under the mantle of the United Nations.

18. Penetrate and subvert all governments, and work from within them to destroy the sovereign integrity of nations represented by them.

19. Organize a world-wide terrorist apparatus and negotiate with terrorists whenever terrorist activities take place...

20. Take control of education in America with the intent and purpose of utterly and completely destroying it.

American Education has been slowly deteriorating over the last forty years or more, so again we have another amazing coincidence. And there is evidence to support the idea of the destruction of education, as evidenced from this news report from World Net Daily:

Charlotte Thomson Iserbyt's new book, *The Deliberate Dumbing Down of America,* is without a doubt one of the most important publishing events in the annals of American education in the last hundred years...

...Iserbyt's has done what no one else wanted or could do. She has put together the most formidable and practical compilation of documentation describing the **well-planned "deliberate dumbing down" of American children by their education system.** Anyone who has had any lingering hope that what the educators have been doing is a result of error, accident, or stupidity will be shocked by the way American social engineers have systematically gone about destroying the intellect of millions of American children **for the purpose of leading the American people into a socialist world government controlled by behavioral and social scientists.**

This mammoth book is the size of a large city phone book: 462 pages of documentation, 205 pages of appendices, and a 48-page Index. The documentation is "A Chronological Paper Trail" which starts with the Sowing of the Seeds in the late 18th and 19th centuries, proceeds to The Turning of the Tides, then to The Troubling Thirties, The Fomentation of the Forties and Fifties, the Sick Sixties, The Serious Seventies, The "Effective" Eighties, and finally, The Noxious Nineties. The educators and social engineers indict themselves with their own words.

Iserbyt decided to compile this book because, as a "resister" to what is going on in American education, she was being constantly told that she was taking things out of context. The book, she writes, "was put together primarily to satisfy my own need to see the various components which led to the dumbing down of the United States of America assembled in chronological order—in writing. Even I, who had observed these weird activities taking place at all levels of government, **was reluctant to accept a malicious intent behind each individual, chronological activity or innovation, unless I could connect it with other, similar activities taking place at other times."**

And that is what this book does. **It connects educators, social engineers, planners, government grants, federal and** state agencies, billion-dollar foundations, think tanks, universities, research projects, policy organizations, etc., showing how they have worked together to advance an agenda that will change America from a free republic to a socialist state.

What is so mind boggling is that all of this is being financed by American people themselves through their own taxes. **In other words, the American people are underwriting the destruction of their own freedom and way of life by lavishly financing through federal and state grants the very social scientists who are undermining our national sovereignty and preparing our children to become the dumbed-down vassals of the new world order.**

One of the interesting insights revealed by these documents is **how the social engineers use a deliberately created education "crisis" to move their agenda forward by offering radical reforms that are sold to the public as fixing the crisis—which they never do. The new reforms simply set the stage for the next crisis, which provides the pretext for the next move forward.** This is the dialectical process at work, a process our behavioral engineers have learned to use very effectively.

By Samuel L. Blumenfeld
©1999 WorldNetDaily.com
12-16-99

That book says it all. It would make a great reference book for the reader. Education in the United States for the last few decades has changed into a front for humanism, atheism and deliberately created stupidity. Buy the book and find out for yourselves.

So these are the major goals of the Committee. Want to see the result if they have their way? What comes next is a perfect description of the New World Order. Again, from Dr. Coleman's book:

...Summarized, the intent and purpose of the Committee of 300 is to bring to pass the following conditions: a One World Government and one-unit monetary system under permanent non-elected hereditary oligarchists who self select from among their numbers in the form of a feudal system as it was in the Middle Ages. In this One World entity, population will be limited by restrictions on the number of children per family, diseases, wars, famines, until 1 billion people who are useful to the ruling class, in areas which will be strictly and clearly defined, remain as the total world population.

There will be no middle class, only rulers and servants. All laws will be uniform under a legal system of world courts practicing the same unified code of laws, backed up by a One World Government police force and a One World unified military to enforce laws in all former countries where no national boundaries shall exist. The system will be on the basis of a welfare state; those who are obedient and subservient to the One World Government will be rewarded with the means to live; those who are rebellious will simply be starved to death or be declared outlaws, thus a target for anyone who wishes to kill them. Privately owned firearms or weapons of any kind will be prohibited.

Only one religion will be allowed and that will be in the form of a One World Government Church,...Satanism, Luciferianism and Witchcraft shall be recognized as legitimate One World Government curricula with no private or church schools. All Christian churches...will be a thing of the past in the One World Government.

To induce a state where there is no individual freedom or any concept of liberty surviving, there shall be no such thing as republicanism, sovereignty or rights residing with the people. National pride and racial identity shall be stamped out and in the transition phase it shall be subject to severe penalties to even mention one's racial origin.

Each person shall be fully indoctrinated that he or she is a creature of the One World Government with an identification number clearly marked on their person so as to be readily accessible, which identifying number shall be in the master file of the NATO computer in Brussels, Belgium, subject to instant retrieval by any agency of the One World Government at any time. The master files of the CIA, FBI, state and local police agencies, IRS, FEMA (and) Social Security shall be vastly expanded and form the basis of personal records of all individuals in the United States.

Marriage shall be outlawed and there shall be no family life as we know it. Children will be removed from their parents at an early age and brought up by wards as state property. Such an experiment was carried out in East Germany under Erich Honnecker when children were taken away from parents considered by the state to be disloyal citizens. Women will be degraded through the continued process of "women's liberation" movements. Free sex shall be mandatory.

...Self-abortion shall be taught and practiced after two children are born to a woman; such records shall be contained in the personal file of each woman in the One World Government's regional computers. If a woman falls pregnant after she has previously given birth to two children, she shall be forcibly removed to an abortion clinic for such an abortion and sterilization to be carried out.

Pornography shall be promoted and be compulsory showing in every theater of cinema, including homosexual and lesbian pornography. The use of "recreational" drugs shall be compulsory, with each person allotted drug quotas which can be purchased at One World Government stores throughout the world. Mind control drugs will be expanded and usage become compulsory. Such mind control drugs shall be given in food and/or water supplies without the knowledge and/or consent of the people. Drug bars shall be set up...where the slave-class shall be able to spend their free time. In this manner the non-elite masses will be reduced to the level...of controlled animals with no will of their own and easily regimented and controlled.

The economic system shall be based upon the ruling oligarchical class allowing just enough foods and services to be produced to keep the mass slave labor camps going. All wealth shall be aggregated in the hands of the elite members of the Committee of 300. Each individual shall be indoctrinated to understand that he or she is totally dependent upon the state for survival. The world shall be ruled by Committee of 300 Executive Decrees which become instant law. Boris Yeltsin is using Committee of 300 decrees to impose the Committee's will on Russia as a trial run. Courts of punishment and not courts of justice shall exist.

Industry is to be totally destroyed along with nuclear powered energy systems. Only the Committee of 300 members and the elitists shall have the right to any of the earth's resources. Agriculture shall be solely in the hands of the Committee of 300 with food production strictly controlled. As these measures begin to take effect, large populations in the cities shall be forcibly removed to remote areas and those who refuse to go shall be exterminated in the manner of the One World Government experiment carried out by Pol Pot in Cambodia.

Euthanasia for the terminally ill and the aged shall be compulsory. No cities shall be larger than a predetermined number as described in the work of Kalgeri...

At least 4 billion "useless eaters" shall be eliminated by the year 2050 by means of limited wars, organized epidemics of fatal rapid-acting diseases and starvation. Energy, food and water shall be kept at subsistence levels for the non-elite...until the world's population reaches a manageable level of 1 billion, of which 500 million

144

will consist of Chinese and Japanese races, selected because they are people who have been regimented for centuries and who are accustomed to obeying authority without question.

From time to time there shall be artificially contrived food and water shortages and medical care to remind the masses that their very existence depends on the goodwill of the Committee of 300.

...No central bank save the Bank of international Settlements and the World Bank shall be allowed to operate. Private banks will be outlawed. Remuneration for work performed shall be under a uniform predetermined scale throughout the One World Government. There shall be no wage disputes allowed, nor any diversion from the standard uniform scales of pay laid down by the One World Government. Those who break the law will be instantly executed.

This is the New World Order. The whole scenario sounds like something out of 1984 or from the movie THX-1138. It almost sounds too incredible to be believed. Certainly if the general populace knew what was going on, they would fight to the last man to prevent the NWO. But that also was taken into account. Read the following quotation:

...when the struggle seems to be drifting definitely towards a world social democracy, there may still be very great delays and disappointments before it becomes an efficient and beneficent world system. **Countless people...will hate the new world order...and will die protesting against it**. When we attempt to evaluate its promise, we have to bear in mind **the distress of a generation or so of malcontents**, many of them quite gallant and graceful-looking people.

H.G.Wells, in his book,
The New World Order, 1939.

Here's another one:

We are not going to achieve a New World Order without paying for it **in blood** as well as in words and money.

Arthur Schlesinger, Jr.

in *Foreign Affairs* (July/August 1995)

After President Bush used the term "New World Order" in some of his speeches around 1990, at the same time Gorbachev was mentioning the same thing, many people became concerned. They started to investigate and ask questions of Bush about that term. Some editorial cartoons began to appear that were unkind to the New World Order. And King Hussein of Jordan spoke out against the New World Order army that trounced Iraq in Operation Desert Storm. Because of the negative comments that began to surface, the insiders stopped using the term, "New Wold Order." That is, they still use it in their secret meetings, but to the public they now use the term "Globalization." It means exactly the same thing as the New World Order, but is a more generalized term and the public doesn't have such a negative reaction to it as they do with the NWO.

To get an inside glimpse of what is really going on these days, you will occasionally hear the term "Globalization," a "Global Economy," and other similar terms. They arise in news broadcasts, PBS specials and on Meet the Press and so forth. When you hear these terms, mentally substitute the expression "New World Order" and see if a different intellectual interpretation of what is being said comes to mind. When I try this mental exercise, it can sometimes be scary. They are talking about the NWO all the time, right out in the open, by the simple ruse of just using a different term. This is another example of how they hide in plain sight.

What has become of us? Where did we lose the way? We have lost a precious thing over the last fifty years. We have lost a national identity or conscience. We (or the majority) have lost our collective souls, or in other words, our innocence. The founding fathers knew something that we don't know today. They knew that a society or nation has a collective conscience. They knew that collective conscience could be good or bad. But a nation itself doesn't have a soul or spirit. That is, when a person dies, the soul lives on. But when a nation dies, it having no soul doesn't live on. When a nation is dead, it's dead. They also believed that the person may be judged by God either here in this life or on the other side but since a nation has no soul, it can't be judged the same way.

Because of that fact, our forefathers surmised that if the collective conscience of a nation became evil or at least pleasure seeking to the exclusion of everything else, since the nation couldn't be judged beyond the veil, the only time it could be judged is when it is still in existence. And down through the ages, God has judged evil nations by destroying them when their collective consciences became vile enough to justify it. So a pertinent question to ask is, Are we there? Will we be destroyed also? We will if we don't repent.

The Committee of 300 has numerous front organizations that carry out its orders. Two of the most important organizations are as follows:

TAVISTOCK INSTITUTE

Purpose: It is the largest brainwashing institution in the world, centered in Sussex University, England. It not only controls what the worlds news media shoves down our throats, but conducts mind control experiments to transform humans into mindless robots. The importance of this tremendously powerful think tank cannot be overstated. Whenever the conspirators want us to swallow some of their lies, they commission the Tavistock Institute to find some way, (i.e., do a policy study on how to brainwash the masses), to accomplish that specific task. As already stated, The Aquarian Conspiracy to destroy the morals of the youth with drugs, and to destroy the family as the basis of society, is one example of their handiwork. Again, the Tavistock Institute is a very important and powerful brainwashing think tank.

ECONOMIC COMMITTEE OF THE NORTH ATLANTIC INSTITUTE

Officials: Founder Robert Hutchins on the Committee of 300, Harry Ashmore, Frank Kelly and a large group of "Fellows."

Purpose: To spread ideas that will bring on social reforms of the liberal kind with democracy as an ideology. One of its activities is to draft a new constitution for the U. S. which will be strongly monarchical and socialistic as found in Denmark.

The center is an "Olympian" stronghold. Located in Santa Barbara, it is housed in what is affectionately called "the Parthenon." Former Representative John Rarick called it "an outfit loaded with Communists." By 1973 work on a new United States Constitution was in its thirty-fifth draft which proposes an amendment guaranteeing "environmental right," the thrust of which is to reduce the industrial base of the U.S. to a mere whisper of what it was in 1969. In other words, this institution is carrying out Club of Rome zero-growth post-industrial policies laid down by the Committee of 300.

There are many more organizations founded and run by the Committee of 300 and other groups that work with it. Just to name a few more, there is the Systems Development Corporation, which is trying to bring into place a nation wide system of complete and total information database about each and every individual in the country; medical, financial, criminal, and personal. There is the Mount Pelerin Society, The Hoover Institution, (originally an anti-communist think tank that was taken over) and the Heritage Foundation (a conservative think tank also under their domination).

...I get by with a little help from my friends...

Before leaving the subject of the Committee of 300, there is one other aspect of it that must be discussed. The above title to this section comes from a Beatles song. The "friends" referred to in the lyrics is drugs, and it is and has been controlled from the beginning by the Committee of 300 and its front organizations, for instance, the Columbian family cartels and the American and Italian Mafia. Let me reiterate this. The Royal Family of England (through the Committee) has been the ultimate movers and shakers in the drug trade for about 300 years. Read on and learn something else you were never told about on "Meet the Press."

The history of the Committee's hand in the drug trade began with, of all things, the British East India Company, or BEIC. At first, they were a legitimate trading company, specializing in trading tea from India to England. They had other concerns, such as trading British manufactured goods for Beaver pelts and other animal skins from the New World. They were governed by a "Council of 300" which held the stock in the company. And guess who had a finger in that pie? The British Aristocracy held the majority of the stock in the BEIC. As a matter of fact, they created the BEIC in the first place to conduct trade with their world—wide colonial empire. Many have heard of the famous British Tea Clippers that ran the tea from India to England. And as far as it goes, the tea trade existed, and was profitable for the BEIC.

But soon it became apparent that there was a commodity on the market that promised to be much more lucrative than all the other enterprises of the BEIC (and indeed, all the industry of the whole of Britain put together). That commodity was opium. They found that they could get people hooked on the stuff and make them users for the rest of their lives, totally dependent on the drug that they would supply. Instead of being concerned about the fact that they were destroying the character and the souls of their fellow men, they were ecstatic at the prospect of such vast amounts of money that could be made. But since it did not hurt them in the least to actually trade in human flesh, (yes, they were also in the slave trade), they thought nothing about exploiting everyone they came in contact with through opium.

The information about the drug trade also comes from the book, *Conspirators' Hierarchy: The Story of the Committee of 300*. It is scattered around the book, so the story will be paraphrased rather than quoted from here on.

At first, the BEIC tried to introduce opium to the masses of England. To that end, the first opium shipments came to England from Bengal in 1683, carried by the same Tea Clippers. To quote: "...Opium was brought to England as a test, an experiment, to see whether the common folk of England, the yeomen and the lower classes, could be induced into taking the drug. It was what we could call today 'test marketing' of a new product. But the sturdy yeomen and the much derided 'lower classes' were made of stern stuff, and the test marketing experiment was a total flop. The 'lower classes' of British society firmly rejected opium smoking."

Although disappointed, the BEIC did not give up. "The plutocrats and oligarchists in high society in London began casting about for a market that would not be so resistant, so unbending. They found such a market in China..."

The Chinese peasants were a downtrodden class of people. They were subjects of the Emperor and had absolutely no rights whatsoever. Chinese Royalty treated their subjects rather like cannon fodder. The peasants died for their Emperor in wars or public work projects such as the Great Wall or the Forbidden City. They truly lead miserable lives. It was into this atmosphere that the BEIC found ready and willing subjects for opium.

The BEIC sold the opium by using what we would call pushers today. But back then, it was an organization called the China Inland Mission. Ostensibly it was a "Christian" missionary society trying to win converts to Christ in China, but in reality, was just pushers. And they acted like pushers do today. The first samples were always free, to get the peasants hooked. They even showed them how to smoke the stuff. Of course, the British Royal Family sanctioned all this.

This went on for about a hundred years before the Chinese Government got wind of what was afoot. In 1729 they passed the first laws against smoking opium. The Committee began a series of running battles with China, not willing to give up their lucrative trade, and defeated them with superior technology at every turn.

American super rich families were in on it too, in the mid 1800's. They helped the drug trade and got filthy rich as a result. Chinese coolies imported to America ostensibly were here to help build the railroad going east but were really here pushing dope on the American people. The coolies came as indentured servants, and when their contracts were up, they stayed in San Francisco and introduced opium to over 100,000 Americans. That, along with the Chinese junkies, made for a very lucrative American market for the stuff.

Did you ever ask yourself, "Why didn't they use the American Negro to help build the railroads?" After all, their labor was just as cheap, there were plenty of them who needed work after having just been emancipated by the Civil War, and they were already here, as opposed to the coolie which was imported from half way around the world. They were better workers, stronger and more adapted to the climate than the emaciated coolies strung out on opium. They also understood English, while most of the coolies didn't. There were many reasons as to why blacks were better suited to the task. But the reason they weren't recruited is that they needed the coolie to introduce dope to the continent. Blacks at the time were not into opium at all.

Back in China, things finally came to a head in the early 1900's with the war known as the Boxer Rebellion. We were told as students in school that the Boxer Rebellion was an attempt by China to rid itself of all Western influence and that Britain and the West were merely defending their legitimate interests. That is a whitewash of the truth. China was trying to get rid of the opium trade once and for all, and the Committee (through the British Parliament) was trying to force it down China's throat. China started the war by using her army to destroy tons of opium lying in warehouses in the city of Shanghai. Then they sank many British ships in the harbor. The Committee used that as a pretext for declaring war on China. The British citizen never knew the real reason for the war, but he blindly went to fight and die for the Crown. The typical Brit was used by the Committee to push opium down China's throat through war, but he was never told that. It was called a "patriotic" war.

Unfortunately, the Chinese were outgunned. They didn't have the modern technology Britain had and were defeated. They were forced to sign the Treaty of Tientsin, which allowed British ships unfettered access to all Chinese ports and were not permitted to tax, regulate or prohibit the opium trade in any way. To the Chinese, this was a very bitter pill to swallow, but they had no choice. Later, though, they became partners with the Committee in drugs. When the Communists took over China in 1949, Mao—Tse Tung had to agree not to interfere with the trade and in return was given some of the profits, as his predecessors were. The same holds true today. I'll bet that not one in a thousand heard this version of history before. But it is the truth.

Today, if you hear of a big drug bust, it is never the Committee that is busted, but independents who try to muscle in on the profits. The Committee has eyes and ears all over the world, and when they hear of someone else trying to smuggle dope, they tip off the DEA so as to get rid of the competition. They always have the inside track. A lot of their smuggled drugs come through diplomatic pouches, which are exempt from customs searches. They are good at what they do.

The insatiable greed of these people, who are willing to destroy lives and souls for money, reminds me of a very prophetic statement in the scriptures. In DC 89:4 it reads:

> Behold, verily, thus saith the Lord unto you: In consequence of evils which do and **will exist** in the hearts of **conspiring men** in the last days, I have warned you, and **forewarn** you, by giving unto you this word of wisdom by revelation...

It is true that Section 89 of the Doctrine and Covenants talks only about the evils of coffee, tea, tobacco and alcohol. Illegal drugs, as we know them today, are not mentioned. We know that even though drugs such as opium were available back then, they were nowhere near the problem they are today. They simply were a world away from the mostly New England founders of the Church in the 1830's. But the

Lord knew that if He gave us a warning about tea, coffee, alcohol and tobacco, we would be able to use our God given logical minds and extrapolate, through deduction, that habit forming drugs should also be one of the items frowned upon in the Word of Wisdom.

But it is amazing that Joseph Smith knew, only through revelation, that there were evil men who would try to get people hooked on different forms of substance abuse. It is interesting to note that in the past, tobacco companies tried to hook service men on tobacco the same way pushers try to hook people on drugs. That is, during WWI, WWII and thereafter, big tobacco gave away free packs of cigarettes to armed service personnel, just like pushers do with dope today. They passed out free first samples for years. After getting service personnel hooked, they then had to pay for cigarettes. They knew very well the addictive nature of nicotine, even way back then, despite their denials.

There is more information on the Committee of 300. To read more on the British Royal Family and drugs, read Rowntree's book, *The imperial Drug Trade*. It is really an eye-opener.

The next chapter involves the official religion of the NWO.

Chapter 8

The men the American people admire most extravagantly are the most daring liars. The men they detest most violently are those who try to tell them the truth.

—H.L. Mencken

The New World Order Religion

There is within each man, an innate desire to know if there is a grand scheme to the universe; and if there is, what is man's place in that scheme. That desire can be described as a religious yearning, which yearning is deep and strikes at the core of man's whole being. There is nothing more profoundly motivating in all of man's endeavors throughout history. It is also the reason that man throughout the ages has embodied or materialized that grand scheme of the universe into a supreme being called God, Allah or some other deity. The yearning or desire to believe in a god who is the primal cause of everything is universal to all mortal beings and that very longing is described in the Doctrine and Covenants as the Spirit of Jesus Christ.

For the word of the Lord is truth, and whatsoever is truth is light, and whatsoever is light is Spirit, even the Spirit of Jesus Christ.

And the Spirit giveth light to every man that cometh into the world; and the Spirit enlighteneth every man through the world, that hearkeneth to the voice of the Spirit.

And every one that hearkeneth to the voice of the Spirit **cometh unto God, even the Father.**

Doctrine and Covenants 84:45—47

See also Moroni 7:16,17

The Spirit of Jesus Christ urges and inspires man to believe in God and his Son. It enlightens them as to the truth, as long as men respond to those urgings. If they do not, the devil tries to focus that innate urging down other paths, at the same time fulfilling the universal yearning to believe in a 'god.' That is exemplified in the scriptures. In Alma 21:5-11, it talks of the Amalekites and Amulonites who had rejected the true Gospel, nevertheless, they still built synagogues and attempted to worship God to the best of their understanding.

The logical question is: If they rejected the Gospel, why did they try to replace it with something else? Why not just carry on their lives without any religion at all? Can't they be just as happy without believing in anything? Apparently not. Again, the desire to believe in a god of some kind is deep and universal. When the Amalekites rejected the truth, they also rejected the urgings of the Spirit of Christ that they once had. Then the devil filled that vacuum with his own urgings to worship a god, but not the true God.

At first, Satan tries to get men to worship anything or believe in any doctrine other than the Gospel. In Alma chapter 21, Satan tried to make the Amalekites believe in the doctrine of the Nehors. But there are many other doctrines he tries to sell. That is why there is such a diversity of churches throughout the world. See Alma 31 for another example of the devil leading the Zoramites astray after another false doctrine.

But that approach does not fully satisfy Satan. He doesn't want to lead people into the worship of just any old doctrine that comes along. The attempt to get them to worship the 'god(s) of nature,' for example, is one step away from the truth, but not the final solution as to who Satan wants people to worship. There is one and only one object of worship that he, ultimately, tries to impose on mankind. Let us see examples of that in the scriptures.

And it came to pass that when Moses had said these words, behold, Satan came tempting him, saying: Moses, son of man, **worship me...**

And again Moses said: I will not cease to call upon God, I have other things to inquire of him: for his glory has been upon me, wherefore I can judge between him and thee. Depart hence, Satan.

And now, when Moses had said these words, Satan cries with a loud voice, and ranted upon the earth, and commanded, saying: **I am the Only Begotten, worship me**.

And it came to pass that Moses began to fear exceedingly; and as he began to fear, he saw the bitterness of hell. Nevertheless, calling upon God, he received strength, and he commanded, saying: Depart from me, Satan, for this one God only will I worship, which is the God of glory.

And now Satan began to tremble, and the earth shook; and Moses received strength, and called upon God, saying: In the name of the Only Begotten, depart hence, Satan.

And it came to pass that Satan cried with a loud voice, with weeping, and wailing, and gnashing of teeth; and he departed hence, even from the presence of Moses, that he beheld him not.
Moses 1:12,18-22

Again, in Matt. 4:8-10, recounts one of the temptations of Christ wherein Satan offered Christ the kingdoms of the world if Christ would fall down and worship Satan. Another example is found in the book of Moses 4:1-4 wherein Lucifer tried to take God's glory and power for himself in the pre-mortal existence by offering to save all men. These scriptural evidences point to one conclusion; that Satan wants mankind to worship him and him only. That has always been his supreme goal.

Satan has not changed over the ages. He is still the same, opposed to God and his Son, Jesus Christ. That is why he is called "The Adversary." Everything he tries to do is in opposition to what God implements. To take that thought one step further, one may say that the devil does not act of his own accord, he only reacts to God's initiatives. That is why when Adam and Eve were created, Satan did nothing to them until God initiated an action and gave them the command-ment not to partake of the Tree of Knowledge of Good and Evil. Only then did Satan react and tempt Adam and Eve to go contrary to God's command. It's almost like he was obeying a law of physics, that for every action there is an equal but opposite reaction. The point being that the reaction cannot occur of its own volition, but only in opposi-tion to an action. The action, however, may be initiated of its own accord.

The ability for something to act through its own volition was mentioned by Lehi in 2 Nephi:

> And now, my sons, I speak unto you these things for your profit and learning; for there is a God, and he hath created all things, both the heavens and the earth, and all things that are, both **things to act** and things to be acted upon.
>
> 2 Nephi 2:14

The ability for something to act of its own will or volition has another name. It is called intelligence. And things that are acted upon are called inanimate matter. In fact, intelligence and matter are the only two things that have existed for all eternity. That is substantiated in DC 93:29, 33. So if Satan cannot act of his own accord, then we may say that he has no intelligence. For, according to verse 29, intelligence is the "light of truth." Since Satan has no light (he is the Prince of Darkness) or truth (the Father of all lies), then he cannot have intelli-gence.

But to reiterate, Satan wants men to worship him and him only. He has always wanted that. He will always want that. He will not change, for what he wants is always in opposition to what God wants, which is that men worship God. So we must ask ourselves a pertinent question: What does Satan want men to do today? Has he lost the desire to have men worship him? No. Never. *He won't because he will only react in an opposite direction to what God desires.* So if we look at the world in our day, we should be able to see evidence of his desire for men to worship him (Satan). Devil worship is called by the scriptures the

Church of the Devil.

Now let's see the evidence for this "church" in the scriptures. In 2 Nephi 14:10,11, Nephi talks about the two and only two churches in the last days. He wrote:

> And he said unto me: Behold there are save two churches only; the one is the church of the Lamb of God, and the other is the church of the devil; wherefore, whoso belongeth not to the church of the Lamb of God belongeth to that great church, which is the mother of abominations; and she is the whore of all the earth.

> And it came to pass that I looked and beheld the whore of all the earth, and she sat upon many waters; **and she had dominion over all the earth, among all nations, kindreds, tongues, and people.**

Doesn't that sound similar to what President Benson said in General Conference in October of 1988?

Secret combinations lusting for power, gain, and glory are flourishing. A secret combination that **seeks to overthrow the freedom of all lands, nations and countries is increasing its evil influence and control over America and the entire world.**

Ensign, Nov. 1988, (86)

Since dominion is a synonym for control, basically what President Benson and 2 Nephi 14 are talking about is the same thing. We have seen how the latter-day conspiracy controls politics, media, economics and education. Now let's see how they control religion.

As we do so, it is important to understand a very basic concept. That is, the conspirators are not atheists, by any stretch of the imagination. They eagerly adopt and foster the philosophy of atheism in its various forms, i.e., humanism, existentialism, relativism, the theory of evolution, materialism, et al, as a tool to weaken the religions of the world but they themselves are deeply committed to a belief in supernatural beings. Taking this idea one step further, the conspirators practice a religion, complete with doctrines, rituals and trappings.

Sometime in the future, this religion will be imposed on the world, by force if necessary, for that is how Satan acts, to the exclusion of all other religions, especially Christianity. The insiders hate Christianity and its downfall is their greatest desire.

Now what I have to say from here on is not easy to discuss. If the world were good and kind, then the worship of Lucifer would not exist. But the world is not good and kind. It is mostly inhabited by telestial people. They are people that God loves and wants to save, but He will not interfere with their agency. So as we talk about devil worship, we must understand that the practitioners are still children of God who have been deceived. We need to pray for them and love them, no matter what they think of God or those who worship Him.

Also, talking about the worship of Satan is spiritually depressing. But pray to God to help you see the world the way it is, without being overcome by its evil. It is important to know things the way they are, for that is truth and we are to pursue truth in our eternal progression. DC 93:24 states: "And truth is knowledge of things as they are, and as they were, and as they are to come." Unfortunately, the knowledge of things as they are in these latter days is not all sweetness and light. But it is part of this real, telestial world. We need to know about evil without participating in it. To come to a knowledge of all things is an important part of our journey to godhood. Pray to understand evil and love those who participate in it, but also pray to be delivered from evil. So here goes.

The official religion of the NWO is Luciferianism. That's correct. They believe in and worship Lucifer. In support of that, read this statement:

> "Lucifer comes to give us the final gift of wholeness. If we accept it then he is free and we are free. That is the Luciferic initiation. It is one that many people now, and in the days ahead, will be facing, for it is an initiation into the New Age."
>
> *Reflections on the Christ* by David Spangler
> Findhorn Publications, 1977 (45)

Now, who is David Spangler? Nobody in particular. He is merely the Director of Planetary Initiative for the United Nations. He belongs to the new age movement. And the new age movement is a deception to point mankind towards the worship of Lucifer. In support of that, read what the founder of the new age movement has to say about Lucifer.

"Lucifer represents... Life... Thought... Progress... Civilization... Liberty... Independence. Lucifer is the Logos... the Serpent, the Savior."

The Secret Doctrine
by Helena Petrovna Blavatsky
p.171, 225, 255 (Vol II)

The new age movement is in on the conspiracy, and the conspirators believe that Lucifer is a good god, and the god we worship is evil. In their minds, Lucifer never fell from heaven and is not Satan! Incredible, but that is their position. But should the thought that Lucifer being worshiped by the secret combination of the last days be a surprise to the LDS mind? We have already seen how the devil will always try to establish his church among men, so as to be in opposition to God. That places an ominous responsibility on everyone to be able to discern between the two.

Each of us must come to the understanding that there are, indeed, two churches only and make our choice. The guidance of the Holy Spirit in this subject is of supreme importance. I'm sure that not one Latter—day Saint would intentionally choose to be involved in the church of the devil if he or she knew what it was. Most LDS people know that in these last days, Satan is gaining enormous power here on the earth and that the world will see a great clash between God and Lucifer prior to the Second Coming of the Savior.

From prophecy both ancient and modern, we learn that there will be great wars, plagues, natural catastrophes, famine, drugs, murders, rapes, pornography, homosexuality, hatred, abortions, the anti—Christ, and devastations of a global nature. All these abominations will destroy the bodies and souls of all those who practice these evils. And the church of the devil will be in the forefront in trying to get all humanity to pursue every evil.

There are those who believe that the church of the devil cited in the scripture above refers to the Roman Catholic Church. But I think the scripture is not so narrowly defined as that. In order to precisely define the term "church of the devil," we need to first define the word "church" as used in this scripture. Here is one possibility. A church could be defined as: **An organization that worships or adores a supernatural being, has a defined set of tenets or beliefs, and practices prescribed rites or ordinances.** Perhaps there is a better definition out there, but this will do for the purposes of this book.

To reiterate, a church worships a supernatural being, has defined beliefs and rites. But what if the organization in question does all the above but is classified as political or financial instead of religious in nature? Does it still count as a church? The answer is yes, because they worship a god. And we shall see examples of political, financial, religious and fraternal organizations that worship Lucifer and have defined beliefs and rites. Perhaps this is a radical idea for some readers. If so, think and pray about it. The author will give evidence to establish this fact. But what will the Lord do with us if we in ignorance become a member of an organization that worships Lucifer, (though we're not aware of that) but still belong to and think of ourselves as members of, the Lord's church?

Perhaps His judgment of us will depend on the intent or the desires of our hearts (DC, Sec. 137), but in any case it is extremely risky to be involved with the devil, even if we have been innocently deceived. So the importance of discerning just what is the church of the devil and who could be in its membership is paramount. We cannot afford to be misled on this point.

Now let's put that definition back into the scripture. There are two "churches", one of God and one of the devil. So the church of God worships God and has a defined set of beliefs and ordinances that come from God. Therefore, the church of the devil will worship the devil, and also has a set of beliefs and ordinances that come from the devil.

Using that definition, the church of the devil does indeed exist here on earth, and is much more widespread than most people think. Again, while there is only one organization that is the true church of God, there are many organizations, not necessarily churches, that belong to the church of the devil. These all have distinct beliefs, sometimes contradictory to other organizations in the church of the devil, but all worship Lucifer, Satan or the devil.

Here an important detail must be discussed. Those who worship the devil in the various organizations that make up the church of the devil **are those in power over these organizations**. That point is crucial to proceed beyond here. The author is not inferring that **all** members of the organizations of the G.A.(Great and Abominable church of the devil) worship Satan. Almost never do the rank and file members of a given group know that Lucifer is being worshiped by their leaders. That is one of the reasons it is vitally important to know which organizations belong to the church of the devil and which do not.

Now, armed with above definition, let's examine many organizations around the world and see if they belong to the "church of the devil."

In a former chapter in was mentioned that in order to be inducted into the Executive Committee of the Council on Foreign Relations required that the person go into the Meditation Room of the U.N. building and take the oaths, handshakes, signs and penalties of the highest level (Rex) of the Order of the Illuminati. Then they take a covenant of loyalty to Lucifer. That evidence comes from the book, *Secret Societies/New World Order* by Milton William Cooper. So that makes the CFR a part of the church of the devil, even though the Council on Foreign Relations is not, per se, a religious organization at all but is a semi-secret *political* organization. The members of the

Executive Committee of the CFR are the only members of the CFR that are inducted into the worship of Lucifer. And so, this is a word of caution to all who are members of the Council on Foreign Relations to GET OUT OF IT. It is one of the organizations of the church of the devil.

Now why would the devil try to exclude himself from worship by the masses of the organizations he controls? Why doesn't he reveal himself to all of them, or even to the world at large? Why not go public with his claims that he is the true "God of this world" and let people choose openly between himself and the Christian God? Why so much secrecy?

The answer to that, of course, is that all mortals have *already* made their choice between God and Lucifer, and that was done in the pre-mortal existence. All mortals on this earth who now live, or who have ever lived, already rejected Lucifer and his plan for mankind. (Moses 4: 1-4, Revelations 12:3,4; 7-9). We didn't accept him then and came to earth to live according to the plan that God has set forth.

For that reason, mortals instinctively know to reject Satan here on earth if they know what he is really like. The Spirit of Christ is a guiding spirit inside all of humanity that helps them to cling to good and reject evil once both sides are fairly and accurately portrayed. Because we rejected him once, Satan and his angels have nursed a long and bitter hatred of all mortals. He wants to destroy all souls who rejected him in the beginning. Especially those who were active in promoting God's plan.

Lucifer is also worshiped at the top levels of other political organizations controlled by the conspiracy. That includes the Tri-Lateral Commission, the Bilderbergers, the Royal Institute for International Affairs, the Round Table Group, the Club of Rome, the Skull and Bones, the Thule Society, the World Council of Churches, the Illuminati and many other groups. To be more specific, the Boards of Directors, the Executive Committees, the Ruling Bodies or whatever they may be called for these various organizations are all actively engaged, albeit in secret, in the worship of Lucifer. So the same admonition is given to all the honest in heart who are included the above named groups: GET OUT OF THEM. They are dangerous.

As long as we're mentioning groups that worship Lucifer, it almost goes without saying to include witchcraft and Satanism. The masses initiated into the outer court are told that witchcraft is an old polytheistic religion that worships the "gods" of nature. They are told that they can get in touch with "spirit guides" (a.k.a. evil spirits) that will speak to their minds and guide them to "higher levels of consciousness." These evil spirits also help fulfill spells that are cast. So if someone in witchcraft tells you that they can make spells come to pass, believe it. They are telling the truth.

It must be stressed that these spells come from the power of Satan, and are no match compared to the power of the Priesthood of God, which ultimately controls the very forces of nature itself. Satan's power is a lame imitation of God's power. Those who keep the covenants found in the Church of Jesus Christ may be protected from Satan's power, no matter what temptations or deceptions he strews in their way.

The leaders of witchcraft are called the Council of Thirteen, or Grand Druid Council. And again, they take similar oaths, covenants, signs, tokens and penalties that are taken by the Illuminati, and are told the greater secrets of witchcraft. That is, of course, that Lucifer is their god and Jesus is an imposter. As a matter of fact, witchcraft is the religion of the Illuminati. And the Golden Dawn coven is the personal coven of the Rothschilds.

Freemasonry

Freemasonry, as already noted, began in its modern form in 1717 but their signs, tokens, penalties and oaths have been in existence for a very long time. Before them, the Knights Templar in the middle ages had the same rites. The Gnostics practiced these rites before that. The

Masons claim that their rites came from the builders of the temple of Solomon.

Freemasonry professes to be a fraternal organization, (not religious), bent on benefitting mankind through good works and virtuous living. The author talked at length to a dedicated 32° Mason, also LDS, who is actively engaged in politics, and the earnestness of his belief that Masonry is nothing more than a benevolent organization was apparent. He stated more than once that nothing about Masonry is contrary to any teachings of the Gospel. He was proud of his association with this group. Indeed, the Masons do perform many charitable deeds.

To demonstrate that fact, when Dr. W. Cleon Skousen was Chief of Police of Salt Lake City, the local Freemason lodge was one of his biggest supporters. They used their influence to help him rid the city of prostitution during Skousen's tenure. The prostitutes were organized enough that they had circuits of several western cities. Salt Lake was on circuit #2. They would stay in one city for six weeks then go on to another city on the circuit before they were recognized by the local police. With the help of the local Masons, among others, they made it necessary for the prostitutes to cross Salt Lake City off circuit #2. So Freemasonry does indeed do good works.

There are many LDS who are dedicated Masons. For this reason, it is hard to say anything negative about Freemasonry. The good feelings that many have for it makes it all the harder to bring up the results of a lifetime of study about Freemasonry, along with other secret societies. The author wishes from the bottom of his heart that those involved in Freemasonry look at the evidences provided and honestly ask God if there is something of truth in what is presented here. Let the spirit be your guide.

The common members do good works for humanity. They honestly pursue truth, beauty, noble aspirations, charity, etc. But these lofty ideals, though honourably pursued by the rank and file, are used by the leaders of Masonry as a shield to hide evil. Let me be very specific here and please do not be offended, for no offense is intended.

The Freemasons started out as a secret fraternity dedicated to the pursuit of truth and uplifting mankind through teaching morality and charitable good works. Let there be no doubt as to the truth of that statement. But over time they were infiltrated and subverted by Luciferians (the Illuminati).

The Luciferians took control but kept the good works and public charity of the Freemasons as an ongoing public relations shield to cloak what they were doing in secret. That's how they hide in plain sight. And today, what are they doing in secret? They 1— worship Lucifer and 2— try to infiltrate positions of power in government, business, education, media, foundations, labor and even religion to further their idea of one world government.

Let us examine the evidence for the worship of Lucifer in Freemasonry. There are definite confessions to that by prominent Masons, written down in some of their most pre-eminent books. One of them, *Morals and Dogma of the Ancient and Accepted Scottish Rite of Freemasonry*, by Albert Pike, is given to each adept upon achieving the 32°. It is not the Mason's 'Bible' but is very important to them. Read this paragraph praising Lucifer and judge for yourself:

> "Lucifer, the Light-bearer! Strange and mysterious name to give to the Spirit of Darkness! Lucifer, the son of the morning! Is it he who bears the Light, and with it's splendors intolerable blinds feeble, sensual or selfish Souls? Doubt it not!"
> *Morals and Dogma*, (321)

Lucifer bears Light that blinds feeble souls? That's different from what I learned in the Gospel. Lucifer is the Prince of Darkness because he spreads doubt, confusion and lies. He is not a personage of light but of darkness. He doesn't illuminate but blinds all that listen to him. And the above quotation is only a precursor to others. Here is another, again from *Morals and Dogma*:

...To retain the rays of Light still remaining among his Eons, and ever tending to escape and return, by concentrating them, **the Prince of Darkness**, with their consent, **made Adam**, whose soul was of the Divine Light, contributed by the Eons, and his body of matter, so that he belonged to both Empires, that of Light and that of Darkness. To prevent the light from escaping at once, **the Demons forbade Adam to eat the fruit of "knowledge of good and evil,"** by which he would have known the Empire of Light and that of Darkness. He obeyed; **an Angel of Light induced him to transgress, and gave him the means of victory;** but the **Demons** created Eve, who seduced him into an act of Sensualism, that enfeebled him, and bound him anew in the bonds of matter. This is repeated in the case of every man that lives.

Morals and Dogma, (566-567)

To understand what was just said, it is necessary to know how Satan talks. When he declares a doctrine, it is always *the exact opposite of the Gospel view*. That is how one can distinguish between the ideas of men, which tend to go off on tangents from the truth, and the doctrines of Satan, which are always 180° opposite of the truth. Knowing that, let's look at that passage again. When it talks of the Prince of Darkness creating Adam, that means the God we worship. Again, the Demons who forbade Adam from eating the fruit of the "knowledge of good and evil," are in reality God and Jesus Christ. And the Angel of Light who induced Adam to transgress is of course, Satan, the Prince of Darkness.

But it gets better. Later on the same page it gives this remarkable statement:

"Satan is the son and lord of matter; and the secondary angels and demons, children of matter. **Satan created and governs the visible world."**

ibid, (567)

Now, let's think about that. If you, dear reader, came across that last sentence in a book with no further comment, what would you think? It seems obvious that one would think that whoever said that believed in Satan as the Creator. This is not from an anti-Masonic source, but from one of the most respected Masons ever, Albert Pike. In fact, there is a statue of him in Washington D.C.

Let me give you some other quotations, with no other comment. Make up your own mind.

"We shall unleash the Nihilists and Atheists, and we shall provoke a formidable social cataclysm which in all its horror will show clearly to the nations the effects of absolute atheism, origin of savagery and of the most bloody turmoil. Then everywhere, the citizens, obliged to defend themselves against the world minority of revolutionaries, will exterminate those destroyers of civilization, and the multitude, disillusioned with Christianity, whose deistic spirits will be from that moment without compass, anxious for an ideal, but without knowing where to render its adoration, **will receive the pure doctrine of Lucifer, brought finally out in the public view**, a manifestation which will result from the general reactionary movement **which will follow the destruction of Christianity and atheism,** both conquered and exterminated at the same time."

Illustrious Albert Pike 33°

Letter 15 August 1871

Addressed to Grand Master Guiseppie Mazzini 33°

Archives British Museum, London, England

Another:

"When the Mason learns that the Key to the warrior on the block is the proper application of the dynamo of living power, he has learned the Mystery of his Craft. The seething energies of Lucifer are in his hands and before he may step onward and upward, he must prove his ability to properly apply this energy."

Illustrious Manley Palmer Hall 33°,

The Lost Keys of Freemasonry, (48)

Another:

"What is more absurd and more impious than to attribute the name of Lucifer to the devil, that is, to personified evil. **The intellectual Lucifer is the spirit of intelligence and love; it is the paraclete, it is the Holy Spirit, while the physical Lucifer is the great agent of universal magnetism.**"

Brother Eliphas Levi,
The Mysteries of Magic, (428)

So what is one to conclude? These are not anti-Masonic quotations, they are Masonic! Even so, if Masons read this and still choose to believe that Lucifer is not worshiped by their leadership, I can't say as I blame them. It is hard to believe, even for me. It's hard for any normal minded Christian to think of such evil as being so organized and entrenched as Luciferianism.

One of the Masonic objections to the idea of Lucifer being worshiped by them goes like this: If Masonic leaders practice Luciferianism, why did George Washington, other founding fathers, Joseph Smith, Brigham Young and other presidents of the Church belong to it? Wouldn't the Holy Ghost warn them about the Satanic activities of this fraternity? Therefore, Masonry must be okay if these spiritual men had no objections to it.

The answer is that at the time these men were members of Freemasonry, there was no worship of Lucifer being practiced. At least, in American Freemasonry. Let us take some time here to go over the history of European and American Freemasonry.

As already mentioned, Freemasonry opened its first lodge in England in 1717. At first, it was a beneficial fraternal order as already described. In 1776, the Illuminati was formed by a former Mason, Adam Weishaupt, who borrowed the form and function of the Order of the Illuminati from Masonic and Jesuit sources. He also was an occultist, who worshiped the devil and introduced Luciferianism into the Illuminati. The Illuminati was formed to destroy civilization, especially Christianity, and spread revolution. That was already conveyed in chapter six. He desired to infiltrate European Freemasonry to subject it to his Order.

To repeat the information found in Chapter six, in 1782, at the Masonic Congress held at Wilhelmsbad, Germany, the Illuminati gained ascendency over the Masonic lodges of Europe by enlisting the aid of the heads of the lodges of Germany, France and Italy. At the same time, Weishaupt formed a financial alliance with the Rothschilds to give the Order the money needed to carry out its plans. (Nesta Webster, *World Revolution*, p.20, and Count Egon Caesar Corti, *The Rise of the House of Rothschild*, Boston: Western Islands, 1972, p.ix). The Illuminization of European Freemasonry was testified to by George Washington himself in various letters he wrote. He warned his friends against the influence of the Illuminati.

In those days, world-wide Freemasonry was not united under one head or council. American Freemasonry was apart from European Freemasonry and was organized into two factions, the Southern Jurisdiction, headed in Charleston, S.C, and the Northern Jurisdiction, in Boston. However, the Northern group was established as an extension of the Southern group in 1813, so the Southern Jurisdiction heads all of the lodges in America.

In 1859, Albert Pike was elected to the position of Sovereign Grand Commander of the Southern Supreme Council (Mackey's *Encyclopedia of Freemasonry*, p. 564). That is analogous to being elected President of the U.S. He was its head until he died in 1891. In the 1860's, Giuseppe Mazzini, the Italian leader of European Illuminized Freemasonry, contacted Pike, inducted him into the Illuminati and made Pike the head of the Illuminati's activities in the United States. (Kirban, *Satan's Angels Exposed*, p. 157—158, and Ralph Epperson, *The Unseen Hand*, Tucson, Publius Press, 1985, p. 223).

Finally, on Sept. 20, 1870, a constitution was drafted by Pike and

Mazzini that established an ultra-secret governing body of world-wide Freemasonry, at Rome under Mazzini, with two other main centers, at Charleston and Berlin. At the same time, the constitution created a new super-rite for American Freemasonry. (Edith Starr Miller, *Occult Theocracy*, P. 207-208, 215). The headquarters for American Freemasonry was later moved to Washington D.C.

"Pike named the Order (super-rite) the New and Reformed Palladian Rite." Author Miller described it as Neo-Gnosticism, "teaching that the divinity is dual and that Lucifer is the equal of Adonay (old Hebrew name for God). (Ibid, 216-217). It is Lucifer who is worshiped within this Rite of Freemasonry."

The Rite was practiced only in Charleston, Berlin and Rome, (Kirban, op cit., p.159). When the Headquarters for the Southern Jurisdiction was moved to Washington D.C., the Rite went with it. The worship of Lucifer is now practiced in our nation's capitol, Washington D.C.

Mazzini wrote a letter to Pike on January 22, 1870, before the constitution was signed, and said:

"We must allow all the federations to continue just as they are, with their systems, their central authorities and their divers modes of correspondence between high grades of the same rite, organized as they are at present, **but we must create a supreme rite, which will remain unknown, to which we will call those Masons of high degree whom we shall select. With regard to their brothers in masonry, these men must be pledged to the strictest secrecy. Through this supreme rite, we will govern all Freemasonry which will become the one international centre, the more powerful because its direction will be unknown."**

Occult Theocracy, op cit, (208-209).

World-wide Freemasonry has been under the control of the Illuminati ever since. That is why George Washington and Joseph Smith detected no evil in Masonry, because there was no worship of

Lucifer in American Freemasonry when those men were associated with it.

The middle east has its own form of Masonry called the Ancient Arabic Order Nobles of the Mystic Shrine. It is the author's belief that they also worship Lucifer at the top. It was adopted by American Freemasonry and is known as the Shriners. Again, similar signs, tokens, oaths and covenants are taken. It started when a Mason named William J. Florence was initiated into an eastern "secret society" by an Arabian diplomat. (*Ancient Arabic Order Nobles of the Mystic Shrine: A Short History,* Shrine General Offices, Tampa, Fl., 4/85, p.3). So you see, the church of the devil prophesied about in the Book of Mormon is starting to look pretty big. The same admonition must be said to honest hearted Masons as were also said to the others earlier: Please GET OUT OF IT.

Next we come to the Rosicrucians, or the Society of the Rose Cross. They are a secret society much like the masons, but they assert that theirs began with the Egyptians. That may be true, but they still have similar tokens, handshakes and rites of the Masons. The God they worship is Ra, which is the Egyptian name of Lucifer. According to Mackey, (*Encyclopedia of Freemasonry,*) the Templars, many of whom were destroyed in the 1200's, joined with the Rose Croix and laid low for over three hundred years. The two later merged with Freemasonry. That is why Masonry has orders (or levels) of the Rose Croix and the Templars.

There are other secret societies with their handshakes and all the same stuff as the Masons. These include, but are not limited to, the Thule Society, the Skull and Bones, the Nine Unknown Men, the Club of Rome, DeMolay and the Eastern Star. The last two are also associated with the Masons.

The Communist world movement was established when Karl Heinrich Marx joined an offshoot of the Illuminati called the League of the Just. After Marx wrote the Communist Manifesto, the League changed its name to the Communist League. (Kirban, op cit, p.157).

Mazzini, who established ties with Pike for the control of American Freemasonry, also was closely associated with Marx. (Miller, op cit, p. 219). Mazzini used Marx to subvert the Socialist Labour Movement (ibid, p.218). So obvious was the connection between Marx and Mazzini, the Illuminati head of Freemasonry, that the early Russian Revolutionaries called themselves Spartacusts, (after Adam Weishaupt's Illuminati pseudonym), before they were known as Bolsheviks and later as Communists. (Gerald Winrod, *Adam Weishaupt*, Clackamas, OR: Emissary Publications, 1937, p.48). Today, the leaders of Russia and China practice the same Illuminati handshakes, signs and tokens as their Illuminati forebearers. The funny thing is that the so-called atheists of the hierarchy of Communism actually believe in Lucifer.

And next there is Judaism. It is run from the top by the Cabala, and you guessed it, has comparable signs, tokens, rituals, and god as the others. It is probably the oldest of all the secret societies and there is evidence that other societies evolved from it. The people who were actively engaged in the crucifiction of Christ (i.e., Ananias and Caiphas, among others) were part of the Cabala, in the authors' opinion. The good people in the rank and file of the Jewish Religion have been duped but they are earnest in their desire to do good. But it is necessary to GET OUT OF IT.

Now, what about the Christian religions of the world? Some of them are part of the church of the devil and some aren't. Those that aren't part of the conspiracy are fairly easy to distinguish. They are, for the most part, small and poor and they are persecuted by the powers that be. That is, the conspirators use zoning laws, safety laws, environmental laws and the IRS to harass the small churches that do not belong to the church of the devil. These tend to be small fundamentalist churches that have little power or influence. The main stream churches like the Methodists, Presbyterians or Episcopalians are controlled at the top by the conspiracy. And because of that, are never persecuted with zoning laws like the little ones. John Todd Collins, who was converted from witchcraft said that many pastors and ministers were actually bought off to preach a "liberal" type of theology. From his own words:

...Now I spent several hours trying to think of a Christian church that I could go to and ask questions of that we didn't own the minister of. Now, that may seem kinda strange to you, but as an ex-Grand Druid it's not strange at all. Much that you see in churches that you just think is liberalism is pay-off-ism. I'll go over that more simple: They've taken the money and rejected the Lord. It's kinda hard for a minister who's not sold to God to turn down half a million dollars that's laid down as a bribe.

And that can get even higher. In fact, ah, one church I know of got 8 million dollars in 2 years and another one got 10 million dollars in 1 year. So they can receive the money.

"Conversion from Witchcraft and the Illuminati"
by John Todd Collins

The hierarchy of the Roman Catholic Church is part of the conspiracy. For many years the Illuminati tried to infiltrate the Church but never succeeded in placing one of their own on the throne of St. Peter. Nubius, an illuminist writing in 1818, said that one goal of the Illuminati was:

...the complete annihilation of Catholicism, and even ultimately of Christianity. Were Christianity to survive, even upon the ruins of Rome, it would, a little later on, revive and live.

The Papacy has been for seventeen hundred years interwoven with the history of Italy. Italy can neither breathe nor move without the leave of the Supreme Pontiff...It is necessary to seek a remedy. Very well, a remedy is at hand. The Pope...will never enter into a secret society. It therefore becomes the duty of the secret societies to make the first advance to the Church and the Pope, with the object of conquering both.

They were not successful for many years in this goal. That is, until the 1960's. When Pope Paul VI ascended to the papacy, he was probably the first. Why is that? On October 4, 1965, Pope Paul VI addressed the United Nations. His speech contained liberal social progressive statements that many revolutionaries believe and none of the religious doctrines found so often in the old Catholic Church. After the speech, Pope Paul went to the Meditation Room in the United Nations building and was initiated into the Illuminati by the same signs, tokens, etc. that we have already heard about. Please re—read the quotation of Pope Paul VI at the end of Chapter 3. Paul's successors have all been part of the church of the devil. Pope John Paul the 2nd is also one of the conspirators, even though he professes to believe in Christ. In 1983 he issued a Papal Bull legalizing secret society membership for Roman Catholics. Up to that time, the Church had vociferously opposed such membership.

So we see that the church of the devil is quite wide spread. President Benson was truly inspired to say that this secret combination has control over America and the entire world. There are organizations not yet mentioned, such as the Jesuits, but the ones in this chapter are the most important. They all intermesh and cooperate with each other. If this is discouraging to read, let the Holy Ghost whisper peace to your heart. After all, according to the Book of Revelation, God wins, and will always win in a show down with the devil.

The next chapter talks about the anti-Christ.

Chapter 9

"...for that day shall not come, except there come a falling away first,
and that man of sin be revealed, the son of
perdition...so that he as God sitteth in the temple of God, shewing
himself that he is God."
-2 Thess. 2:3-4

Maitreya

Maitreya is the name of the Buddhist "Christ." Buddhism, along with Christianity, Islam, Judaism and most other major religions believe in a god or being who will return to earth in the last days. To Christians, it is the Christ. To Jews it's the Messiah. To Muslims it's the Imam Mahdi. To Hindus, it's Krishna and to Buddhism it's Maitreya. Each religion's Christ persona will come in a different way, for instance, Krishna and Maitreya will come as reincarnated beings while the Messiah will be born at Bethlehem, and Jesus will come in power as a resurrected God. But the general idea that they are to bring enlightenment and peace to the world are all commonplace.

In February of 1962 a child was born in the middle east. According to one source, his real name is Rahmat Ahmad, born into the Ahmadi sect of Muslims. In or around 1975, the Rothschild Banking family found out about him and began to bankroll him. Today he is called Lord Maitreya, or the Christ returned. In July of 1977 he moved into the Indian community of London, England and goes around the world lecturing and performing miracles. London is currently his headquarters, so to speak.

Maitreya seems to be perfectly possessed. That is, everything he does or says is the will of Lucifer, his master. He has no mind or will of his own. It has been said that He can speak all languages, can appear and disappear at will and has great Satanic powers. He has traveled around the earth, and could be fulfilling a scripture in the Doctrine and Covenants:

> And again, verily I say unto you, that the Son of Man cometh not in the form of a woman, neither of a man traveling on the earth. (DC 49:22)

The press has not reported about Maitreya to a great extent, although they know of his existence. In fact, many of the owners of the media who are "in" on the conspiracy have met him, along with many of the political leaders of the world. George Bush Sr. and Mikhail Gorbachev met him in 1989 on a U.S. battleship off Malta. Maitreya has attended the planning meetings of the World Economic Council, the World Trade Organization, the Bilderbergers and others. He is crucially intertwined with the planning for the NWO. The reason is that Maitreya will not only appear as the Christ in the future, he will, at the same time put an end to a pre-orchestrated war in the middle east and terminate a world-wide economic depression, both events caused by the insiders in the first place. By bringing peace and prosperity he will more easily be able to persuade us that he truly is the Christ. That kind of coordination and foresight requires precise planning to pull it off.

Maitreya has been discreetly displayed before the world at specific times and places by the media but for the most part, left alone. The reason is that when he finally is announced to the world it will be as the "Christ returned." That will be the "Day of Declaration," or what may be termed a coming out party. Then the media will be told to advertise him in a conspicuous manner. They will follow their orders and lavish Maitreya with attention.

According to the plan, the "Day of Declaration" will be carefully scripted and cosmologically speaking, very entertaining. Maitreya and his followers will use both technology and the powers of the devil in staging an elaborate hoax. Without going into details, Maitreya will try to make the world believe that he is Christ returning by using world-wide images and sounds speaking to all people simultaneously, each in his own language. The conspirators may even be able to create earthquakes to fulfill scripture. That is, Maitreya may appear on the Mount of Olives at the time of a great earthquake, simulating what the real Christ does when He comes again. It will be very impressive.

The artificial creation of earthquakes may be hard to believe, but U.S. Secretary of Defense, William Cohen, doesn't think so:

> Others (terrorists) are engaging even in an eco-type of terrorism, whereby they can **alter the climate, set off earthquakes, volcanoes** remotely through the use of electromagnetic waves...So there are plenty of ingenious minds out there that are at work finding ways in which they can wreak terror upon other nations...**It's real**, and that's the reason why we have to intensify our (counter terrorism) efforts.
>
> Secretary of Defense William Cohen
> DoD News Briefing,
> Q&A at the Conference on Terrorism, Weapons of Mass Destruction, and U.S. Strategy,
> University of Georgia, Athens,
> April 28, 1997

The following quotation also reinforces the idea of great delusions being perpetuated at this time:

> ...there will be no neutrals in the approaching battle. I say again, that God the Highest of all will make bare his arm in the eyes of all nations. And the heavens even will be rent, and the lighting down of His power will be felt by all nations. But this is not all. **Satan also will be revealed**. He has made some manifestations of his power in different periods of the world, but never before has there been such an array of numbers on his side, never before such a consolidation of armies and rulers, **never before has there been such an imposing and overwhelming exhibition of miracles as Satan will shortly make manifest**... He it is that will head the opposition against God and **be allowed a much longer chain than before**. And such will be the greatness of his

power, that it will seem to many that he is entirely loose. He will be so far unshackled and unchained that his power will deceive all nations, even the world. And the elect will barely escape the power of his sorceries, enchantment, and miracles! And even God himself, the true God, will **contribute to put means and instruments in his (Satan's) way and at hand for his use, so that he can have a full trial of his strength and cunning, with all deceivableness of unrighteousness in them that perish...**

Being Prince of the power of the air, (Eph. 2:2) he understands **aeronautic and steam navigation, and he can compose and combine the various elements, through the co-operation of them that believe in him, with far more than human skill.**

The Coming Crisis
How to Meet It
Reprinted from the Millenial Star
Issue of April 30, 1853
pp.5-7

Also, one of the tricks of Satan in the last days will be the ability for Maitreya to project his voice around the whole earth at one time, so that everyone will be able to hear him simultaneously. Perhaps the followers of Maitreya will use the following device to do that:

US PATENT 4,858,612 — HEARING DEVICE.

A method and apparatus for simulation of hearing in mammals by introduction of a plurality of microwaves into the region of the auditory cortex is shown and described.

A microphone is used to transform sound signals into electrical signals which are in turn analyzed and processed to provide controls for generating a plurality of microwave signals at different frequencies. The multifrequency microwaves are then applied to the brain in the region of the auditory complex. By this method sounds are perceived by the mammal which are representative of the original sound received by the microphone.

In other words, this device can transform sound waves into electrical signals which are turned into microwaves which can be beamed around the world and are picked up by the auditory complex of the brain directly and transformed back into a perception of sound by the listener.

Those in witchcraft, Satanism and new agers who "channel" all have spirits that literally speak to them. They call them "spirit guides," but Latter-day Saints really know them as evil spirits. With one acclaim, the spirit guides (demons) of these people are telling them about Maitreya and have been doing so for years. They have known for a long time that their leader, the anti-Christ, is about to come upon the scene and they are waiting in great anticipation for that event.

There is something else that must be discussed before going on with the next subject. The International Bankers, knowingly or unknowingly, are maybe fulfilling Biblical prophecy with a project they are bankrolling called the Maitreya Project.

In Bodhgaya, India many years ago, the Indian Prince who would become the original Buddha underwent an enlightenment around 500 BC. Ever after, Bodhgaya has remained a holy city for Buddhists worldwide. Now the Rothschilds want to build a statue of Buddha in that city. But it's not just any statue. It will be the only statue of Buddha in the world specifically called the Maitreya Buddha, dedicated to the anti-Christ, Maitreya. It will be 500 feet tall, or about three times the size of the Statue of Liberty. It will even be slightly taller than the great pyramid of Kufu. It will be built to stand for a thousand years, according to the plans of the architects. The Bankers are sparing no expense in its construction. They plan for it to be completed in 2005. It also has pneumatic systems (for movement) and auditory systems (for sound). The question arises, is this in fulfillment of prophecy, specifically Revelation 13:14,15? Read it and decide for yourself.

I've Got You Under My Skin

What comes next is a treatment of the future of money, and what the International Bankers plan on doing. As you read, you will understand the heading to this section, which comes from a popular tune.

First of all, let's look at a well known scripture.

And he causeth all, both small and great, rich and poor, free and bond, to receive a mark in their right hand, or in their foreheads: And that no man might buy or sell, save he that had the mark, or the name of the beast, or the number of his name. Here is wisdom. Let him that hath understanding count the number of the beast: for it is the number of a man; and his number is six hundred threescore and six.

Revelation 13:16-18

This enigmatic scripture seems to be saying that in our day, people will receive a "mark" in their right hands or in their foreheads that will enable them to buy and sell things. Those who don't have the mark can't. Also, there seems to be a number associated with the "mark" which is connected to the beast or the number of its (his) name. The number is 666. But it's important to remember that the scripture says that the mark will be "in" their hands or foreheads, not "on" their hands or foreheads. That will be explained later.

This one scripture has caused more debate, probably, than any other that we have. Various people used to declare their interpretation of what it meant. In the middle ages, people used gematria (the practice of adding up the numbers in a name or title) to add up the letters in the names of kings or popes to come up with the number 666. It has been ascribed to various people at various times and still is, today, the subject of much debate.

The scripture has two possible interpretations. One '666' is the number of a man. The other '666' will be the number of a mark in the hand or forehead. For the first interpretation, we must look at the mitre or papal cap of the Pope of Rome. Supposedly, there was, at one time, an inscription on his mitre cap that read in Latin, "Vicarius Filii Dei." In English that means, "The Vicar (or representative) of the Son of God." That inscription was removed years ago from the papal mitres because people were using gematria to prove that the Pope was the Beast. But numerous Catholic publications over the years and official historical documents prove that the Pope was referred to as the Vicar of the Son of God. The Popes also referred to themselves by the same title, as did the masses of the Church. When one takes out all the roman numerals and adds them up, if you haven't already guessed by now, you have this:

VICARIUS; V=5, I=1, C=100, I=1, U(formerly the same as V)=5

Total= 112
FILII;   I=1, L=50, I=1, I=1   Total= 53
DEI;   D=500, I=1   Total= 501
                                             666

Now, the Pope is not the beast nor anti-Christ. The Latin inscription is there to fulfill a prophecy in the future. That means that the true anti—Christ will wear the mitre that contains the aforementioned inscription at some time in the future. In fact, he will be given the papal mitre by the Pope himself and when that happens, the 666 will be there on the head of the anti-Christ for all to see.

For the second interpretation of the scripture, let's do an object lesson. Procure any grocery item from your cupboard. Look at the UPC bar code. If you look carefully at the bar code itself, you'll see two small thin parallel lines stick down below the other lines at the beginning, the middle and the end of the code. These are called the separators. They were invented by the engineers to separate the bar code message into two parts, the first half and the second half. So the lines in front and in the middle tell the bar code reader, "In between the lines is the first half of the message," and the lines in the middle and on the end tell the reader, "In between these lines are the second half of the message." That, quite frankly, is their only function. The two halves of the message itself give the name of the product and its price.

The UPC bar codes were invented to speed up check out lines and minimize mistakes made by cashiers. They do a marvelous job of that. They are an example of how wonderful modern technology can be.

They are found worldwide, and not just in grocery stores, because they have proven to be a great labor saving device.

There is a tape recording of a man who was one of the engineers to develop the UPC bar codes. He said that when they were trying to design a system to speed up checkout lines in the grocery stores, they had to both invent the bar code reader and the bar codes themselves to do the job faster. They had to decide how the message should be displayed to the reader so that it would recognize that it was receiving a message. In order to do that, they arbitrarily decided on a certain number that would separate the bar code message in two parts. If you're ahead of the game, you will already have guessed which number the engineers chose.

That's right. The number they decided on was 6. So the two thin lines at the beginning of the code is the number 6, in the middle is the number 6 again, and on the end, you see the number six yet again. 6-6-6. The number 6 is the separator used on all codes. Yes, the number 666 is on all items that are bought or sold that use the UPC bar codes. And that includes just about everything. There are not many products that don't use them.

A representation of a typical bar code is given here as an illustration:

All of the marks, or bars, are associated with numbers at the bottom, except the marks at the first, middle, and end. Notice the marks for the number "6" are " ". And these marks are the same marks at the first, in the middle and at the end!

Here the other numbers are removed.

The number "666" is hidden in every UPC bar code!

(*If you don't believe it, get a bar code and look at it!*)

Now, you may say: "Just because the UPC bar codes have a 6-6-6 imbedded in them doesn't mean that those codes are the mark of the beast described by John in Revelations 13.That could just be a coincidence. Besides, the scripture says that the mark will be in the right hand or in the forehead of the customer, not on the product." True enough, it does say that, doesn't it?

But the International Bankers have a master plan for the future of money that is both scary and all inclusive. There are two steps to this plan. Step 1. Slowly, over the years, convert the world to a cashless society. That has been a hard sell for them, because mankind has always been enamored with the idea of having cash in one's pocket. We just like our society that way. But they have made inroads. The use of credit cards and automatic deposit are two small steps in that direction.

Another step along the path to a cashless society is the use of Club Cards and Savings Cards. According to Katherine Albrecht, these cards are a deception. The stores use them to garner information about store customers such as the SSN, driver's license numbers, birth dates, etc. along with their buying habits. The real intention of the cards is to get customers used to using them, then later to transpose them into smart cards. If food shortages occur (which will be pre—engineered), then those with smart cards will be given preference. We have already seen the introduction of smart cards on TV. Then a total collapse of the financial system will occur, and society will go truly cashless, which will be step 2.

Step 2. They eventually want to eliminate all cards together and place microchip implants under the skin on the right hand or forehead. These chips will have the person's social security number and a code for their country of origin. The numbers will be separated by, you guessed it, the ubiquitous 6-6-6 of UPC fame. The numbers under the skin will replace all checking account numbers, ATM numbers, credit card numbers and all other financial codes or PINS. The money system will thus be streamlined.

Then a person can go to the store and buy whatever he wants without cash, checks or credit cards. The UPC code on the product will be compared with the code embedded in the skin of the buyer and the appropriate purchase amount will electronically be deducted from the person's bank account. Money will disappear. For a better treatise on this, read the article <u>Warning: 666 is Coming</u>! by Terry Watkins. Search for it on the internet.

The arguments in favor of this arrangement will be presented as follows:

1.   The drug problem will go away. How can one sell drugs if no cash is involved? The one good thing about cash (but bad for the bankers) is that it is anonymous. Money transactions based on cash can't identify people because cash can't be traced. Therefore, cash gives the drug dealers a hay day. They can deal drugs with impunity because cash has no electronic trail.

2.   Efficiency and safety. If <u>all</u> one's financial needs can be met with just one number, and one will always have that number with them (because you always carry your right hand or your head around with you), you'll never have to worry about forgetting passwords, never be without electronic cash, and never be burdened with security concerns like someone using your credit card, forging your checks or stealing your money.

To be sure, those reasons, on the surface, are very compelling. And that is just how they will present the idea of a cashless society to us. But there is one great big reason to be against it, which more than destroys all the good reasons to support it. And that reason is: control.

Let's think about that for a minute. If there were no cash money, then there would be no privacy. All your financial transactions would be recorded. For instance, everything you bought, when and where you bought it, would be known by someone else. If or when you went to a restaurant, movie, bar, visited your doctor or lawyer or even contributed money to your church would be known by the rulers. All investments, retirement plans and every other financial transaction you would ever engage in would be known. There would be absolutely no privacy.

But if invasion of privacy were the only concern against the idea of a cashless society, that would be a piece of cake compared to the other reason. Suppose that we didn't have a benign government. And human nature being self—centered as it is, that is certainly a possibility. (D&C 121:39). Suppose that the government decided to take a dislike to you, for whatever reason. Perhaps they think you are not a very forward thinking person, or even don't seem to like the government and speak against it. All the government has to do is go to its master computer and invalidate the social security number under your skin, then you wouldn't be able to live at all. Since all financial transactions are conducted using the number under your skin, you could literally starve to death. No reader would validate your number, and you couldn't buy or sell anything. In other words, total control. An effective way to quell dissent. Control is what it's all about. They, the conspirators, could literally mold the masses to think the way they want them to think. The objectives of control in the book "1984" by George Orwell could not be achieved more perfectly. Here's another quote along these lines:

> Give me control over a man's economic actions, and hence over his means of survival, and except for a few occasional heroes, I'll promise to deliver to you men who think and write and behave as I want them to.
>
> Benjamine A. Rooge

Does that sound scary? It should. But for those who think that this is just so much imagination run wild, I offer this quotation from an article in Time Magazine. The article talks about large banking mergers and what the banks want to do about finances in the future. One paragraph talks hypothetically about what you could do if you had a daughter in college, and wanted to send her money. It goes like this:

> For starters, you can send the money over the Internet encoded in an E-mail instead of sending a check. This saves you the trouble of balancing the checkbook at the end of the month, and it gives you the option of transferring the money from wherever you want:

mutual fund, money market, even an old—fashioned checking account. Your daughter can store the money any way she wants—on her laptop, on a debit card, **even (in the not too distant future) on a chip implanted under her skin...**

> Time Magazine, April 27, 1998
> cover story, "The Big Bank Theory."
> By Joshua Cooper Ramo

If you need more convincing, then examine U.S. Patent # 709471. Check it out for yourself.

The future is now and they will start this soon. They are already trying it out on pets. I'm sure you've heard about the chips implanted under the skin of pets so that their masters can be located if the pet is lost. It seems innocent, but it is just a precursor to trying it on humans. The next step will be to try it on convicts, then the general population.

We'll see the day when the mass media, along with the financial community tries to sell us on the idea of replacing cash altogether with a chip implant. When that happens, try to be prepared for it by refusing the implant and having cash, gold, and rations stocked up for at least a year and especially get out of debt. The prophets have been telling us this for many years, it's time that we listened and obeyed.

After Maitreya's "Day of Declaration," the Pope of the Catholic Church will hand to Maitreya his mitre with the name "Vicarius Filii Dei," because the Pope is "in" on the conspiracy. He, along with all religious leaders of the world controlled by the conspirators will acknowledge Maitreya as the Christ, thus uniting the churches under him. Most of the masses of all these religions will unite in the worship of the Anti-Christ Maitreya, because the populace trust that their respective religious leaders are acting in the name of God. The same goes for the Buddhists and Hindus.

The next quotation consists of a set of notes by David Bay, a Baptist preacher who was invited to a secret seminar of the Theosophical Society in Massachusetts wherein they boldly explained how the NWO would unfold. Bay was allowed to attend through the influence of a friend who deserted the Theosophical Society in his heart, but was still considered a member by the leadership. This friend (the name was anonymous) was allowed to bring a friend (Bay), to attend these lectures on the future.

Sometime between 1985-2010, the following scenario will unfold, depending on the right set of circumstances:

Moslem and Jewish areas in Jerusalem will be combined with Christian to create the **New Jerusalem Covenant**.

All religions will convene to celebrate three religious festivals simultaneously.

> 1. Festival of Goodwill
> 2. Festival of Easter
> 3. Festival of Wesak (Celebrates birth of Buddha).

The celebration of these three combined Festivals will create the New World Order Religion and will be the spiritual equivalent to the political United Nations.

Then, and only then will it be possible to build a combination Temple/Church/Mosque in Jerusalem.

The impetus toward this type of settlement is made possible only because of a general fear of war. This fear of war <u>must be maintained</u> until the desired political and religious changes have been instituted. (Punch and Judy again).

Possible and Probable Events in the Future
Seminar by Bill Lambert, Director–New England District
The Theosophical Society
Boston, Massachusetts, 8-18-91
Notes by David Bay

It's not good to feel fear, so pray until the fear leaves you. This is just to remind us of what is really going on in this world. So that naturally brings up the following question, "What should one do to prepare?" That is the subject of the next chapter.

Chapter 10

The Times, They are a-Changin'

As you know, there is nothing in this world as constant as change. In this day and age, change seems to be the only thing one can count on. Unfortunately, the world isn't changing for the better. The world is getting sicker, both physically and spiritually. A person with spiritual eyes can see the sickness of the world, and how hard Satan is trying to deceive all of us. Satan will try his hardest in the next few years to deceive as many as possible for, as Revelation 12:12 says: ...for the devil is come down unto you, having great wrath, because he knoweth that he hath but a short time. With the assurance of the Gospel, however, the meek follower of Christ can navigate through the last days successfully.

This chapter is about preparing for the final tribulations of the last days. The ideas expressed by the author are helpful but are neither all-inclusive nor the final definitive word on preparation for the last days. If any advice given in this chapter should inadvertently vary from what the Prophet says, follow the advice of the Prophet of the Church of Jesus Christ of Latter-Day Saints. His is the final word on this subject.

I tell you these things because of your prayers; wherefore, treasure up wisdom in your bosoms, lest the wickedness of men reveal these things unto you by their wickedness, in a manner which shall speak in your ears with a voice louder than that which shall shake the earth; **but if ye are prepared ye shall not fear.** (DC 38:30).

The above quotation doesn't mean that faithful Latter-day Saints are immune from trials, or even from laying down their lives for the Gospel's sake, or as a consequence of some natural disaster or plague that God allows to happen in the last days. The scripture means that if one is prepared in all things, then even laying one's life down for the Gospel is not to be feared.

One of the enduring truths we know is that this life is but one stage of our eternal existence. We know that how or when we die is not as important as how we live. If we live righteously, through our own volition, and know through the spirit that we are acceptable to God, then the knowledge that God loves us makes the thought of dying less fearful. Keeping that in mind, what we do here should be in preparation for the life to come. And that brings us to the first step:

> *Become spiritually prepared. The first thing, before any other preparation, is to become prepared from within. Spiritual preparation acts like an anchor to the soul so that no matter what happens, one can accept anything that comes through the comfort and assurance of the Holy Ghost.

This preparation is found in the doctrines of the gospel. It was preached from the beginning of the Church until this day. So much has been revealed to us that it would be re-inventing the wheel to repeat all that has been said. For instruction on spiritual preparedness, practice the virtues of love, forgiveness and patience given as wise counsel from talks given by the Brethren and from the Standard Works. Attend the prescribed meetings of the Church. Follow the teachings found therein. The importance of following this advice cannot be overstated. That, in the end, is the best single protection to live in the last days. Only the knowledge that God loves us, which comes from living His commandments, will save us when all else fails.

Having said that, still there are certain commandments which, if followed, contain promises that apply specifically to spiritual preparedness in the last days.

1. The law of tithing. D&C 64:23,24 states:

> Behold, now it is called today until the coming of the Son of Man, and verily it is a day of sacrifice, and a day for the tithing of my

people; **for he that is tithed shall not be burned at his coming.**

For after today cometh the burning—this is speaking after the manner of the Lord—for verily I say, tomorrow all the proud and they that do wickedly shall be as stubble; and I will burn them up, for I an the Lord of Hosts; and I will not spare any that remain in Babylon.

The Lord in the last days will build up his Kingdom on the earth. It needs money, time and effort for it to succeed. Those who sacrifice willingly through tithing are actively helping to build that Kingdom. And one of the rewards is that they will not be burned up with the wicked. What a blessing. It is not the only blessing of tithe paying, but it pertains specifically to the last days.

The Lord seems to be saying that the willingness to pay tithing is one characteristic of a true saint. That is one way to tell the difference between those who live in Babylon(i.e. the world) and those who don't. That's one of the hardest things to heed about the Gospel. That is, the voluntary giving of one-tenth of one's annual increase. After all, the world puts ample emphasis on acquiring possessions, and the subsequent lie that possessions equates to happiness. It is a real sacrifice for a person new to the church to learn that the things of this world (money, fame, power) are not as important as the things of the spirit. The spirit of generosity with regards to tithing is perhaps one of the greatest signals to God that we are not "of the world."

Those who have formal membership in the church and don't pay tithing, for whatever reason, are risking not only their spiritual future in the afterlife, but also their physical lives here. It is hoped that all who read this book and fulfil the above mentioned conditions get the attitude of humility and start paying their tithing. Above all, remember that tithing must be given ungrudgingly. (Moroni 7:6-11).

2. The Word of Wisdom. DC 89:4, 21 says:

Behold, verily, thus saith the Lord unto you: In consequence of evils and designs which do and will exist in the hearts of **conspiring men in the last days**, I have warned you, and forewarn you, by giving unto you this word of wisdom by revelation—

And I, the Lord, give unto them a promise, that the **destroying angel shall pass by them**, as the children of Israel, and not slay them. Amen.

We can see how that statement has prophetically been fulfilled. Many people have been destroyed body and soul by the influence of tobacco, drugs and alcohol. These substances enslave, destroy health and cause those so enslaved to commit crimes. But perhaps the most far reaching effect of substance abuse is not what happens in mortality, but what happens to the abuser beyond the grave.

The various kinds of enslaving substances are part of the mortal experience. But the spirit in man can also be enslaved, along with the body. That is, the spirit itself can crave drugs. So what happens when the person dies? The same spirit which craved the substance in life will also crave it in death. But since drugs belong to the physical world only, the cravings the spirit has will intensify after death but never be satisfied. It is such a sad thing to see people who can't function without constantly thinking about their next "fix," whether it be drugs, alcohol, tobacco or even caffeine. How wise Father was in giving us this revelation to help us become free.

3. Live so as to be able to be worthy of giving and receiving Priesthood blessings. Why is that important to living in the last days? Actually, there are many facets to that question the answers to which could take a lengthy explanation. But this treatise will only deal with one reason. And that is so that we can bless our homes as places of refuge from the sins and iniquities of the world. That will be of prime importance in the last days. Read these words from President Howard W. Hunter:

I promise you **in the name of the Lord** whose servant I am that God will always protect and care for his people. We will have our difficulties the way every generation and people have had difficulties. But with the gospel of Jesus Christ, you have every hope and promise and reassurance.

The Lord has power over his Saints and will always **prepare places of peace, defense, and safety for his people.** When we have faith in God we can hope for a better world—for us personally, and for all mankind.

Howard W. Hunter, "An Anchor to the Souls of Men."
Ensign Magazine, Oct. 1993, pp. 72—73

Consider the following scripture along with Br. Hunter's statement:

And there shall be men standing in that generation, that shall not pass until they shall see an overflowing scourge; for a desolating sickness shall cover the land.

But my disciples shall stand in holy places, and shall not be moved; but among the wicked, men shall lift up their voices and curse God and die.

DC 45:31,32

There is a connection between the statement of Pres. Hunter and the above scripture. That is, the holy places described in the 45th section of the Doctrine and Covenants is the same as the places of peace, defense and safety as stated by Br. Hunter. Let's take it one step further. President Benson, in referring to DC 45:31,32 has said that the holy places referred to in DC 45 are the *temples, chapels and homes of* the saints. They are specifically designated as such. Now take that definition and apply it to the following scripture:

And the Lord will create upon every **dwelling place** of mount Zion, and upon her **assemblies, a cloud and smoke by day, and the shining of a flaming fire by night: for upon all the glory shall be a defence.**

And there shall be a **tabernacle** for a shadow in the daytime from the heat, **and for a place of refuge**, and for a covert from storm and from rain.

Isaiah 4:5,6

That scripture is talking about the last days. Mount Zion specifically refers to the Church of Jesus Christ in the last days. Now, what is a dwelling place? Is it not a home? And what is an assembly? Is it not a church house or stake center? Do we not assemble in these places to worship? And is not the tabernacle spoken of a reference to the temple? That is what it was called in Moses's day. The scripture seems to say that the homes, chapels/stake centers and temples of the last days, that are dedicated and set apart as places of refuge, (the temples are set apart for that exact purpose), and wherein are found saints who are trying to live the gospel, will actually be protected by a "cloud and smoke by day, and the shining of a flaming fire by night..." when the storms of war, famine, plague, crime, natural disaster and anarchy threaten to destroy all the earth.

Which brings us full circle, that we should bless our homes, using the authority of the priesthood that we hold, as places of refuge from the sins and iniquities of the world. And then we should so live the gospel so as to be worthy of receiving that blessing. Then our homes may indeed be blessed and protected as Isaiah said.

4. Strengthen your families. That was the main theme of a proclamation to the world issued in 1995 by the First Presidency of the LDS Church. Here are excerpts:

We, the First Presidency and the Council of the Twelve Apostles, of the Church of Jesus Christ of Latter-Day Saints, solemnly proclaim that marriage between a man and a woman is ordained of God and that the family is central to the Creator's plan for the eternal destiny of His children...

The family is ordained of God. Marriage between an man and woman is essential to His eternal plan. Children are entitled to birth within the bonds of matrimony, and to be reared by a father and a mother who honor marital vows with complete fidelity...

We warn that individuals who violate covenants of chastity, who abuse spouse or offspring, or who fail to fulfill family responsibilities will one day stand accountable before God. **Further, we warn that the disintegration of the family unit will bring upon the individuals, communities and nations the calamities foretold by ancient and modern prophets.**

We call upon responsible citizens and officers of government everywhere to promote those measures designed to maintain and strengthen the family as the fundamental unit of society.

First Presidency Proclamation to the World

1995.

Remember the Aquarian Conspiracy? The persons who participate in it are responsible, in large part, for the disintegration of our families in these last days. That, along with the destruction of moral values and the promotion of drugs and violence is destroying society right before our eyes. Only a return to moral responsibility, the elevation of the family, and ultimately the voluntary acceptance of the Gospel of the Lord Jesus Christ in its fulness by the peoples of the world will save us from the destructions prophesied. We must do all we can to bring the world to Christ, in order to be cleansed from the sins and iniquities of this generation.

5. Become worthy to enter the temples of the Lord. That is of great significance. Contemplate this talk given by Elder Vaughn J. Featherstone:

The season of the world before us will be like no other in the history of mankind. Satan has unleased every evil, every scheme, every blatant, vile perversion ever know to man in any generation. Just as this is the dispensation of the fulness of times, so it is also the **dispensation of the fulness of evil.** We and our wives and husbands, our children, and our members must find safety. **There is no safety in the world; wealth cannot provide it,**

enforcement agencies cannot assure it, membership in this Church alone cannot bring it.

As the evil night darkens this generation, we must come to the temple for light and safety. In our temples we find quiet, sacred havens where the storm cannot penetrate to us. **There are hosts of unseen sentinels watching over and guarding our temples. Angels attend every door...**

Before the Savior comes the world will darken. **There will come a period of time where even the elect will lose hope if they do not come to the temples. The world will be so filled with evil that the righteous will only feel secure within these walls.** They will long to bring their children here for safety sake...

There will be greater hosts of unseen beings in the temple. Prophets of old as well as those in this dispensation will visit the temples. Those who attend will feel their strength and feel their companionship. We will not be alone in our temples.

Our garments worn as instructed will clothe us in a manner as protective as temple walls. The covenants and ordinances will fill us with faith as a living fire.

In a day of desolating sickness, scorched earth, barren wastes, sickening plagues, disease, destruction, and death, we as a people will rest in the shade of trees, we will drink from the cooling fountains. We will be as fair as the sun and clear as the moon.

The Savior will come and will honor his people. Those who are spared and prepared will be a temple loving people. They will know him. They will cry out, "Blessed be the name of he that cometh in the name of the Lord, thou art my God and I will bless thee, thou art my God and I will exalt thee."

Our children will bow down at this feet and worship him as the

196

Lord of Lords, the King of Kings. **They will bathe his feet with their tears and he will weep and bless them for having suffered through the greatest trials ever known to man.** His bowels will be filled with compassion and his heart will swell wide as eternity and he will love them. He will bring peace that will last a thousand years and they will receive their reward to dwell with Him...

Great blessings are promised to those who so live the Gospel that they can go to the temple. This talk is remarkable in its pledges of protection. He seems to be saying that those who don't live so as to be able to attend the temples may not make it through the last days.

6. Be willing to sacrifice to defend freedom. That may be required of us in days to come. Apostle Benson said this in 1977:

...Yes, we are fast approaching that moment prophecied (sic) by Joseph Smith: "Even this nation will be on the very verge of crumbling to pieces and tumbling to the ground, and when the Constitution is upon the brink of ruin, this people will be the staff upon which the nation shall lean, and they shall bear the Constitution away from the very verge of destruction." (Joseph Smith, July 1840, Church Historian's Office: Salt Lake City.)

Will we be prepared? Will we be among those who will "bear the Constitution away from the very verge of destruction?" If you desire to be numbered among those who will, here are some things you must do:

A. You must be righteous and moral. Live the gospel principles—all of them. You have no right to expect a higher degree of morality from those who represent you than what you are. In the final analysis, people generally get the kind of government they deserve. That means we "forsake (our) sins,...wicked ways, the pride of (our) hearts, and ...covetousness, and all detestable things." You will not design to receive what you have not earned by your own labor. Government owes you nothing. You owe a debt to preserve what preceding generations made possible for you. You will keep the laws of the land, for in Lincoln's words, "to violate the law is to trample on the blood of his father, and to tear the charter of his own and his children's liberty."

B. You must learn the principles of the Constitution to abide by its precepts. You were instructed by the First Presidency in 1973 "to begin now to reflect more intently on the meanings and importance of the Constitution, and of adherence to its principles." What have you done about this instruction? Have you read the Constitution, pondered it? Are you aware of its principles? Could you defend it? Can you recognize when a law is constitutionally unsound? **As a Church, we will not tell you how to do this, but we admonish you to do it.** Again to quote Lincoln: "Let (the Constitution) be taught in schools, in seminaries, and in colleges, let it be written in primers, in spelling books and in almanacs, let it be preached from the pulpit, proclaimed in legislative halls, and enforced in courts of justice. And, in short, let it become the political religion of the nation, and in particular, a reverence for the Constitution.

C. As a citizen of this republic, you cannot do your duty and be an idle spectator. It is vital that you follow this counsel from the Lord: "Wherefore, honest men and wise men should be sought for **diligently**, and good men and wise men ye should observe to uphold." (D&C 98:10.)

Do you note the qualities that the Lord demands in those who are to represent you? They must be good, wise, and honest. Some men may be honest and good, **but unwise in legislation they choose to support.** Others may possess wisdom, **but be dishonest and unvirtuous**. Be concerned in your desire and efforts to see men and women represent you who possess these qualities...

I have faith that the Constitution will be saved as prophecied by Joseph Smith. It will not be saved in Washington. It will be saved by enlightened members of this Church—men and women who will subscribe to and abide its principles.

...I testify that the God of heaven sent His choice spirits to lay the foundation of this government, **and He has sent other choice spirits—you—to preserve it.**

This is the land reserved for the establishment of Zion and the second coming of our Lord and Savior. When all events are finished and written, we will look back and see that "There's a Divinity that shaped our ends," that this and other crises which preceded the glorious event of Christ's return were foreknown to God. **Yes, we will see that He sent special spirits willing to give their blood to defend our freedoms.**

The Crises of our Constitution
by
President Ezra Taft Benson
Valley Central Area Special Interest Lecture Series
Harvard Ward, Salt Lake City, Utah
September 8, 1977

There is a wealth of information here for all to glean. But the time may well come when we will be asked to lay down our lives to defend our freedoms and liberties. Remember this statement by the Savior: "And all they who suffer persecution for my name, and endure in faith, though they are called to lay down their lives for my sake yet shall they partake of all this glory. Wherefore, fear not even unto death: for in this world your joy is not full, but in me your joy is full. Therefore, care not for the body, neither the life of the body; but care for the soul, and for the life of the soul." (D&C 101:35-37.)

Lastly, here is a quote from the Prophet Joseph Smith:

For a man to lay down his all, his character and reputation, his honor and applause, his good name among men, his houses, his lands, his brothers and sisters, his wife and children, and even his life—counting all things but filth and dross for the excellency of the knowledge of Jesus Christ—requires more than mere belief or supposition that he is doing the will of God; but actual knowledge, realizing that, when these sufferings are ended he will enter into eternal rest; and be a partaker of the glory of God...A religion that does not require the sacrifice of all things never has power sufficient to produce the faith necessary unto life and salvation; for, from the first existence of man, the faith necessary unto the enjoyment of life and salvation never could be obtained without the sacrifice of all earthly things. It was through this sacrifice, and this only that God has ordained that men should enjoy eternal life.

Joseph Smith
Lectures on Faith, p.58-60

7. Become aware of how glorious and inspired is the Constitution of the United States. To that end, read a copy of the book, "The Making of America" by W. Cleon Skousen. It explains the history of the Revolutionary War and the Constitutional Convention. Then it painstakingly explains each and every point of the Constitution so that the reader understands the real meaning and the thoughts of the founding fathers as they put their ideas into that document. The same thing can be said for the Federalist Papers. The Constitution of the United States is the word of the Lord to us on how to frame a government of and by men that will uphold, above all things, the principles of liberty and freedom; at the same time giving enough limited powers to a federal government to ensure that it will be able to perform its proper function in upholding those freedoms.

The day will come that a great decision will have to be made about the Constitution. This decision will affect the future of our form of government, and it may go something like this. The conspirators will manufacture some kind of national or international crisis, that will call for immediate and drastic action. Then they come to us as a wolf in sheep's clothing and say, "We will save you from this crisis, but it will be necessary for us to bypass the Constitution in order to do it. We promise you we will keep you from harm and will uphold the principles embodied in the Constitution, but we cannot help you unless we can make the decisions necessary without being bogged down by that cumbersome document." That is not a direct quote, of course, but it will embody sentiments similar to that, especially when it comes to the Second Amendment, the right to bear arms. Be aware of their machinations and not only resist all attempts to replace the Constitution, but use all your influence on others to do so.

Be especially wary of any attempts to destroy the second amendment of the Constitution. The right to bear arms is the last line of defense we have in upholding the Constitution. Be aware of the fact that the controversy over the second amendment is not about making society safer by taking away gun ownership. It is about control over your lives, and about the destruction of the Constitution. The Mormon pioneers had a unique viewpoint about gun control. It was this: If you had guns, you had control. This comes from the days of the persecutions of Missouri, which is analogous to us today.

That is, during the Missouri persecutions, the State Legislature decreed that both the Mormons and Missourians lay down their arms. The Mormons, believing in being subject to authority, did so but the Missouri mob did not. After the Mormons turned in their guns, the Missourians ran roughshod over the Mormons, killing, raping and stealing with impunity. The implication being that gun ownership helps maintain law and order, whereas lack of gun ownership actually increases crime. And believe it or not, that is true.

To prove that, all one has to do is look at Kennesaw Georgia. "Where?" you may ask. Kennesaw Georgia is a small town that actually has a lot to say about the propriety of gun ownership. If you have never heard about it, that is because the national news media have thrown a blanket of secrecy over it. They choose to ignore it in their frenzy to cast a negative view of gun ownership. But there is much to be said in favor of guns in the hands of law abiding citizens by looking at the case of Kennesaw.

On March 25, 1982, Kennesaw passed a city ordinance **requiring** heads of households, with a few exceptions, to keep at least one firearm in their homes. The city had a population increase of from 5,000 in 1980 to about 13,000 in 1996. The following statistics come from the New American magazine.

"After the law went into effect in 1982, crime against persons **plummeted** 74% compared to 1981, and fell **another 45%** in 1983 compared to 1982. And it has stayed impressively low. In addition to nearly non-existent homicide (murders have averaged a mere **0.19 per year**), the annual number of armed robberies, residential burglaries, commercial burglaries and rapes have averaged, respectively, 1.69, 31.63, 19.75 and 2.00 through 1998." There have been only three murders during this time: two with knives and only **one** with a firearm, that in 1997.

Kennesaw is a small town, but not so small as to make it statistically insignificant. It proves that ownership of guns, in the hands of responsible, law abiding citizens will actually help decrease crime and increase public safety. So why isn't the national news media out there, covering the story of Kennesaw? Like I said in chapter two, that's because they are neither objective nor unbiased. They want to create the impression that: 1. People are in favor of more gun control legislation, and 2. That gun ownership increases crime, thereby making it easier to promote the idea that gun ownership is not good for society, so let's get rid of guns.

"The strongest reason for the people to retain the right to keep and bear arms is, as a last resort, **to protect themselves against tyranny in their government.**"

Thomas Jefferson

"The right of the citizens to bear arms is just one more guarantee against arbitrary government, one more safeguard against a tyranny which now appears remote in America, **but which historically has proved to be always possible.**"

Sen. Hubert H. Humphrey

However, there is another safeguard built in our Constitution (among others) that has the conspiracy fit to be tied. That safeguard is embodied in the Constitution, Article III.2.3.

"The trial of all crimes, except in cases of impeachment, shall be by jury." This right cannot be overstated. Consider this quotation:

The Original American Common Law
Jury System.

Up until 1895 Americans enjoyed all of the powers of the original common law jury. This was a far more powerful instrument of justice than the jury system today. In fact, the Founders considered it the foremost defense in the American legal structure to protect the people against oppressive laws passed by the legislature or abusive judges deliberately misinterpreting the law.

The common law jury not only had power to "determine the facts, but it also had authority to determine the law." It could determine what the law meant and whether or not the jury considered it constitutional. The jury could even ignore the law if it felt it would cause an injustice if applied to the case at hand.

Under these circumstances the jury was allowed to hear the arguments of attorneys on both sides as to the meaning of the law and how it should be applied in that particular case.

Furthermore, although the judge interpreted the law for the jury, they **were not bound to accept his interpretation.** In other words, the interpretation of the judge was merely "advisory." The jury was free to reach its own conclusions as to just what the law required.

The power of the common law jury was stated by Chief Justice John Jay in the **first jury trial before the Supreme Court in 1794.** The case was entitled Georgia v. Brailsford (3 Dall. 1). This was a case in which the Supreme Court had original jurisdiction and therefore a jury was impaneled to determine both the law and the facts. In his instructions to the jury, Chief Justice Jay outlined the independent authority of the jury in those days:

"It may not be amiss, here, gentlemen, to remind you of the good old rule, that on questions of fact, it is the province of the jury, on questions of law it is the province of the court to decide. But it must be observed that by the same law, which recognizes the reasonable distribution of jurisdiction, *you have nevertheless a right to take upon yourselves to judge of both, and to determine the law as well as the fact controversy...*

Limitations on the Common Law Jury

It must be understood, of course, that a jury could not repeal a law, but if it thought the law was unconstitutional or oppressive in a particular case, the jury could return a verdict of "not guilty" on the basis of their opinion of the law.

At the same time, the jury could not use its interpretation of the law to injure anyone. In other words, while it had the power to interpret the law to prevent the government from taking a person's money, life, or property, it could not turn around and use its interpretation of the law to take any of these things away from him out of malice...

In spite of the clear statement of Chief Justice John Jay concerning the prerogatives of the common law jury...the courts have used a variety of methods to invade its turf. By using ironclad instructions to the jury they were beginning to straightjacket juries to an observable degree as early as 1852. Lysander Spooner pointed out the seriousness of this erosion of America's foremost security against government abuse:

"For more than six hundred years—that is, since Magna Carta, in 1215—there has been no dearer principle of English or American constitutional law, than that, in criminal cases, it is not only the right and duty of juries to judge what are the facts, what is the law, and what was the moral intent of the accused; *but that it is also their right, and their primary and paramount duty, to judge of the justice of the law, and to hold all laws invalid, that are, in their opinion, unjust or oppressive, and all persons guiltless in violating, or resisting the execution of, such laws.*

The pressure by the courts to deprive the jury of the right to find the law as well as the facts finally prevailed after the case of *Sparf v. U.S.* in 1895. From then on the strict instructions of the judges defined for the jury precisely what the judge considered the law to be, and the jury was left without an option in reaching its decision, regardless of how unjust or unconstitutional the jury might consider the law to be.

The Making of America
By W. Cleon Skousen
The National Center for Constitutional Studies 1985
excerpts from pp. 614-616

The right of trial by jury was designated by the Founders themselves as one of the greatest checks against the usurpation of power by the Government, and served as an example, once again, to show that the Founders considered the ultimate sovereignty lay with the people, not the government. The importance of keeping this tradition alive is very important.

There are other rights guaranteed us by the Constitution and we need to know what they are. Again let me reiterate to read *The Making of America* by W. Cleon Skousen.

8. Learn the signs of the times and the signs about the Second Coming of the Lord Jesus Christ. An especially good discourse on this subject was given by Joseph Fielding McConkie, Professor of ancient scripture at Brigham Young University:

Question: Will the Second Coming be in the year 2000?

Answer: Not according to Doctrine and Covenants 77. In his great apocalyptic vision, John the Revelator gives a prophetic description of the seven thousand years of earth's temporal history (see Revelation 5-10). While laboring on his translation of the Bible, Joseph Smith recorded a revelation explaining John's writings (see D&C 77). Both that revelation the revelation of John along with Doctrine and Covenants 88 affirm that earth's temporal history, contrary to all scientific theories, is confined to what John called seven seals, or seven thousand-year periods. It is generally though by Latter-day Saints that Christ will return at the beginning of the final, or seventh, thousand-year period. This idea may have given rise to the notion that he will come in the year 2000, based on the understanding that there were four thousand years from the fall of Adam to the birth of Christ (see the Chronology chart in the LDS Bible Dictionary, 635) and that we are approaching the year 2000 after the birth of Christ. Thus six thousand years of earth's temporal history will have been completed and the stage set for the seventh thousand-year period, or the time of Christ's millennial reign.

Yet, in the Doctrine and Covenants we read: "In the beginning of the seventh thousand years will the Lord God sanctify the earth, and complete the salvation of man, and judge all things, and shall redeem all things,...and the sounding of the trumpets of the seven angels are the preparing and finishing of his work, in the beginning of the seventh thousand **years...the preparing of the way before the time of his coming.**" (D&C 77:12). Rather that welcome Christ at this time, we are told, we will begin the preparations for his coming. The revelation, which takes the form of questions and answers, then asks, "When are the things to be accomplished, which are written in the 9th chapter of Revelation?" which describes the wars and plagues to be poured out during the seventh seal. The Lord answered, "They are to be accomplished **after** the opening of the seventh seal, **before** the coming of Christ. (D&C 77:13; emphasis added). Again we are told that the coming of Christ and the beginning of the seventh seal are not synonymous.

Question: How close are we to the Second Coming?

Answer: The question cannot be answered by turning to a calender. It can only be answered in terms of the events that have been prophesied to take place before Christ's return. After the coming forth of the Book of Mormon and the restoration of the gospel, the most important event to precede the Second Coming is the **declaration of the restored gospel throughout the nations of the earth** (see Joseph Smith-Matthew 1:31; Moses 7:62). John the Revelator promised that the massage of the restored gospel would go to "every nation, and kindred, and tongue, and people" through the Book of Mormon (Revelation 14:6; D&C 133:37). In a revelation to Joseph Smith, we are told that everyone will be privileged to hear the fulness of the gospel "in his own tongue, and in his own language" by legal administrators (D&C 90:11). Alma tells us that "the Lord doth grant unto all nations, of their own nation and tongue, to teach his word" (Alma 29:8). In describing the vision shown to him and his father, Nephi tells us that there will be congregations of the Saints "upon all the face of the earth" before Christ's return (1 Nephi 14:12). John the Revelator tells us that before that day, there will be those among "every kindred, and tongue, and people, and nation" who have found redemption through Christ and have been ordained "kings and priests" (Revelation 5:9-10), meaning they had received the fulness of temple blessings.

This chain of thought suggests not only that the restored gospel must be freely taught among the Arab nations, for example, but that it must be taught in their native tongues by Arabs who are legal administrators of the gospel. It further requires that there be Latter-day Saint congregations throughout all Arab nations and that there be those in their congregations who have received the fulness of temple blessings. Some considerable time will be necessary for such promises to be fulfilled. It also suggests that we have a considerable labor ahead of us and that missionary work is still in its infancy.

For the world the coming of Christ will, in the imagery of the scriptures, be as a thief in the night. They will be caught unaware. For the Latter-day Saints, however, that should not be the case. We have been given many prophetic signs of the times by which we are to know, if not the day land hour, surely the approximate time of the Lord's coming. For us the coming of Christ is to be as it is with the woman in travail, that is, the expectant mother in labor. Though the moment of birth is not known to her, the blessed event will neither be a surprise nor come too soon (see 1 Thessalonians 5:2-8; D&C 106:4-5). As we move closer to the time of the Second Coming, ours becomes a world increasingly "filled with all manner of lyings, and of deceits, and of mischiefs, and all manner of hypocrisy, and murders, and priestcrafts, and whoredoms, and of secret abominations" (3 Nephi 16:10). It will be , we are told, a day of false Christs, false prophets, and false doctrines. It will be a day in which the Prince of Darkness will gather his multitudes upon the face of the earth among all the nations of the Gentiles to fight against the Lamb of God. So evil will things become that our only promise of protection will be in keeping the sacred covenants we have made and in being "armed with righteousness and with the power of God" (1 Nephi 14:14).

For a more detailed consideration of the year 2000 and the Second Coming of Christ, see Answers: Straightforward Answers to Tough Gospel Questions by Joseph Fielding McConkie.

Another sign of the last days is the fulfillment of the parable of the Ten Virgins. Found in Matthew 25:1-13, it alludes to ten virgins waiting with their lamps to meet the bridegroom (Christ). Five were wise and five were foolish. Those who were foolish took no extra oil for their lamps. As they waited for the bridegroom, they all slumbered. Suddenly the call went out, "Behold, the bridegroom cometh; go ye out to meet him." At that time, the foolish virgins found out that the scant oil they brought was used up and begged some from the others. They were told that there wouldn't be enough for both the five wise and the five foolish, but "go ye rather to them that sell, and buy for yourselves." While they were gone, the bridegroom came and the five wise virgins went with him to the marriage. "And the doors were shut." The foolish virgins came and knocked on the door to be let in, but the bridegroom refused to let them in.

D&C 45:56-57 gives this explanation of that parable: "And at that day, when I shall come in my glory, shall the parable be fulfilled which I spake concerning the ten virgins. For they that are wise and have received the truth, and have taken the Holy Spirit for their guide, and have not been deceived—verily I say unto you, they shall not be hewn down and cast into the fire, buy shall abide the day."

That seems to mean that the oil the virgins had was in both receiving the truth, and taking the Holy Spirit for their guide. To receive the truth means to live it, meaning the gospel. That means that the good works we do for the gospel's sake can't be given to others. They are only credited, in the Justice of God, to the doer only. Thus, the wise virgins were not being selfish in refusing to share their oil. But how does one accumulate a lifetime of good works by living the gospel in the short time between the announcement of His coming and the actual arrival? To say nothing about letting Satan deceive one into thinking that the gospel isn't important or that it isn't needful to prepare every day of one's life for His coming. Those are the ones who have not taken the Holy Spirit for their guide.

The point being that the ten virgins talked about are the members of the church, and the church only. It means that the time will come that half of the membership of the Church of Jesus Christ of Latter-day Saints will not be spiritually prepared for the Second Coming and will lose membership in the Kingdom of God when He comes. They may even be destroyed in the flesh at that time.

There will come a time that the great secret combination of all the earth will turn against the church. That is borne out by the passage found in 1 Nephi 14:12-17. At that day, the persecution will be intense, but the promise of protection will also be there for those who keep their covenants in the gospel. We must be prepared to face it when it comes. That will be when the cream rises to the top, as they say. Exactly what kind of persecution, and how it comes to pass is unknown at this time, but it is hinted at in the following prophecy:

> I will relate the story of an open vision had by brother Stephen M. Farnsworth, of Pleasant Grove, Utah County, while he was residing in Nauvoo, previous to the death of the Prophets Joseph and Hyrum. Some may think and say, it was manufactured for this occasion. But there are many here under the sound of my voice who heard brother Farnsworth relate the vision years ago. I will tell it as correctly as my memory will allow me.

> In the spring of 1844, brother Farnsworth started out after dinner, to go to work on the Temple as usual. The sun shone brightly as he walked down Parley-street towards the place of his labour, when suddenly the sky became overcast, and a drizzling rain set in. He stood amazed, and saw a tumult and excitement among the people about the Temple, and a great excitement in the lower part of town. He wondered what it could mean. Presently he was told that the Saints had to leave Nauvoo and take a great journey to the west. So great was the journey that it seemed almost impossible for him to perform it. Now he could see numerous trains of covered waggons (sic) and teams crossing the Mississippi river, and bending their course westward as far as the eye could reach. He also hitched up and joined the trains, and the journey did not seem so arduous as he first anticipated. He saw the Twelve Apostles in the crowd; but saw neither Joseph nor Hyrum.

> They journeyed westward a great distance, and finally came to a place where they intended to locate. They stopped, and began to make improvements: but distress and starvation stared them in the face, and it really seemed to him that they must perish; but soon there began to be plenty of everything to eat, &c. This lasted quite a time: then there began to be scarcity again, and famine

seemed to prevail; yet he saw none die of starvation, yet great distress among the people. Then there began to be plenty again—enough to eat of everything desirable. The people all appeared in one place, with large, strong hoops around them in a body. The Twelve followed brother Brigham with mallets and fierce countenances, and vigorously drove those hoops upon the people until it did seem that they would be pinched to squeezed to death. Still they resolutely continued to drive the hoops. Dark clouds now began to arise, and a general gloom prevailed. The hoops were all the time being driven tighter and tighter.

About this time, an army of the enemy came into the neighborhood and offered protection to all who wished it. The darkness of the clouds, and their awfully-threatening aspect are now past description. The people burst those hoops and sallied out like a flock of sheep, and **more than one-half** of them went to the enemy for protection. The scene was so awfully frightful that he was just on the eve of flying himself, (that is, Br. Farnsworth) but a thought occurred to him to hold on a little longer. He did so. Dark, angry, and frightful were the clouds, indeed! Now is your hour and the power of darkness! Presently the cloud over the Saints burst, and light beamed upon them.

The clouds rolled off upon the enemy and those who had fled to them for protection; and oh! The scenes of death, lamentation, and mourning that occurred in the enemies' camp beggar all description. The burning wrath of earth, heaven, and hell, in fiery streams of molten lava seemed to leave not one alive to tell the tale. It did not stop here, but rolled throughout the United States, carrying the same desolation in its track...

...I have considerable confidence in this vision, for two reasons. First, brother Farnsworth is a correct man; his character is without spot or blemish. Secondly, this vision corresponds with a hundred and one other sacred things written in ancient and modern times. And I may add a third reason,—it has all been fulfilled to the very letter, so far as time would allow.

Orson Hyde
Journal of Discourses,
Vol. 5, pp. 142-145

Here is an interesting talk given by Elder Bruce R. McConkie of the Quorum of the Twelve, in the April 1980 conference. It is very prophetic about the last days. Here are some excerpts:

...We see the little stone cut from the mountain without hands beginning to roll forth toward that coming day when it shall smite the Babylonian image, break in pieces the kingdoms of men, and fill the whole earth (see Dan. 2:34-35).

We see the elders of the kingdom going forth to many nations, crying repentance, gathering Israel, and assembling the faithful in the tops of the mountains where stands the house of the Lord (see 2 Ne. 12:2).

We see converts and stakes and temples. Gifts and signs and miracles abound. The sick are healed and the dead are raised by the power of God, and the work of the Lord goes forward...

...But our joy and rejoicing is not in what lies below, not in our past—great and glorious as that is—but in our present and in our future.

Nor are the days of our greatest sorrows and our deepest suffering all behind us. They too lie ahead. We shall yet face greater perils, we shall yet be tested with more severe trials, and we shall yet weep more tears of sorrow than we have ever known before..

We see the Lord break down the barriers so that the world of Islam and the world of Communism can hear the message of the restoration; and we glory in the fact that Ishmael—as well as Jacob—shall have an inheritance in the eternal kingdom.

We see congregations of the covenant people worshiping the Lord in Moscow and Peking and Saigon. We see saints of the Most High raising their voices in Egypt and India and Africa...

...But the vision of the future is not all sweetness and light and peace. All that is yet to be shall go forward in the midst of greater evils and perils and desolations than have been known on earth at any time.

As the Saints prepare to meet their God, so those who are carnal and sensual and devilish prepare to face their doom...

We see evil forces everywhere uniting to destroy the family, to ridicule morality and decency, to glorify all that is lewd and base. We see wars and plagues and pestilence. Nations rise and fall. Blood and carnage and death are everywhere. **Gadianton robbers fill the judgment seats in many nations. An evil power seeks to overthrow the freedom of all nations and countries. Satan reigns in the hearts of men; it is the great day of his power...**

...amid it all, there are revelations and visions and prophecies. There are gifts and signs and miracles. There is a rich outpouring of the Holy Spirit of God.

Amid it all believing souls are born again, their souls are sanctified by the power of the Spirit, and they prepare themselves to dwell with God and Christ and holy beings in the eternal kingdom...

Truly the world is and will be in commotion, but the Zion of God will be unmoved. The wicked and ungodly shall be swept from the Church, and the little stone will continue to grow until it fills the whole earth.

The way ahead is dark and dreary and dreadful. **There will yet be martyrs;** the doors in Carthage shall again enclose the innocent. We have not been promised that the trials and evils of the world will entirely pass us by.

If we, as a people, keep the commandments of God; if we take the side of the Church on all issues, **both religious and political;** if we take the Holy Spirit for our guide; if we give heed to the words of the apostles and prophets who minister among us—then, from and eternal standpoint, all things will work together for our good.

Elder Bruce R. McConkie

The Coming Tests and Trials and Glory

Ensign Magazine, May 1980, p.71

—Become physically prepared. In a way, spiritual and physical preparedness are intertwined. If one is spiritually prepared, that will help engender the humility necessary to follow the advice the Brethren have given to be physical prepared. So the one gives birth to the other.

1. GET OUT OF DEBT. Many good people, even LDS who should know better, flirt with the danger of indebtedness. It is far more insidious than most realize in this day and age. It is one of the best ways the conspirators have of trying to enslave us.

Let me put it this way: Suppose an average family by the name of L. D. Saint had two mortgages on their house, four credit cards charged up to their respective limits, a small business loan and were in general living beyond their means. That scenario is not at all unusual in this day and age. Then suppose some economic depression or panic happened which caused the collapse of the international economy (Which, by the way, would be deliberately caused).

Then someone in authority, like the head of the Federal Reserve, goes on TV throughout the world and says that in order to bring financial sanity back to the world, (from a problem they created in the first place), the Fed would have to impose a system that requires everyone to receive a computer chip in their right hand or forehead that would take care of all financial transactions. And because the economic situation was so bad, everyone would be compelled to do it. If anyone resisted, all their loans would become immediately due and all the possessions they owed money on would be confiscated. They would even be barred from buying or selling anything. They could literally starve to death. Mr. Saint would either have to get this computer chip or lose his house, business and all possessions on which he had a loan. And if he also neglected to get a year's supply of food, it would almost be impossible for him to say "no" to the mark of the beast. That may sound like a fantasy, but those in control of world finances plan scenarios like that all the time.

Years ago, before the Federal Reserve System came into being, people of the United States generally had the attitude of saving up money to be able to buy what they wanted. That accomplished two things: 1. They were paid interest by their banks or savings and loan which increased their overall financial solvency, and 2. By paying on the spot, instead of taking out a loan, they avoided carrying and interest charges. How simple that is, yet how far away from today's thinking. We could, with reason, listen to and heed lessons from the past.

Debt is an extremely dangerous financial instrument to carry at this time in world history. All should do their utmost to get out of debt. For a sample of what the First Presidency thinks about it, read the First Presidency Message in the June Ensign of 1987, given by President Ezra Taft Benson.

2. Get a year's supply of food, water, clothing, fuel, money and all else that would be needful to be able to weather the threat of economic collapse, war, famine, plague, natural disasters, or even something as mundane as the loss of a job or death of the financial breadwinner. The Church, through the instrumentality of the Bishop's Storehouse, has and active interest in helping the members, or indeed anyone who has an interest in food storage to prepare themselves. They do this with dry pack canning facilities all over the United States and in some foreign countries. The cost is low compared to commercial dry pack canners, and the food lasts as long.

Using a food dehydrator is a good way to prepare vegetables, fruits and meats that last a long time. Also, buying canned goods in bulk from warehouse stores helps to diversify one's supply. As for water, a well is the best way to go. For those without one, 55 gallon drums are readily available. Water filters and filtration systems are important too. And don't forget first aid kits. It is suggested to have at least two weeks of water on hand, or fourteen gallons per person.

Fuel is also important. Coal, wood, gasoline, kerosene and propane are fuels that readily come to mind. Have at least enough to be enabled to cook your food. Those with fireplaces will have a better advantage than others as they also provide space heating. For those without a fireplace, a barbecue grill with propane bottles is a good substitute.

Lately, with the weather and the Y2K threat, there has been an upsurge in interest in food storage. Whether or not the Y2K problem is large or small, it is important to be prepared for this and other eventualities. The stake welfare specialist can help anyone who desires to start, or continue, in their quest to become prepared with a year's supply of food.

There are books that explain the details of food storage. Seek the best information you can that is more suited to your peculiar situation, then put that advice into action. Above all, **do not delay getting your food storage**. Because it is something that cannot be accumulated overnight, unless you are independently wealthy, it is important to start now. You may never get another chance. Also, you may need to have extra for your neighbors. We are under the commandment to always share with our neighbors. Use thoughtful prayer to help you in your decisions and God will point things out to you as you fulfill this responsibility.

Along those lines, a good supply of cash, gold and silver will help in the trials to come. Gold and silver have always been considered the money of last resort, meaning that they will have a definite value even when or if paper currency fails. The conspirators realize this, which is why they control most of the gold, silver, gems and other hard currency assets of the world. That is why most of the gold in Fort Knox (U.S. government) has been gradually transferred over the years to the

Federal Reserve Banks (private ownership).

In the coming years, an inflationary depression may come upon us. That occurs when, due to overprinting, the value of the currency approaches zero. This situation happened to Germany after WWI. For the first few years of the 1920's, the value of the German mark diminished until it was estimated that all German marks, added together, had the approximate value of one U.S. penny. There were literally trillions and trillions of marks printed. The reason behind the wild printing of marks had its roots in the ill—fated Treaty of Versailles which was forced upon Germany at the close of WWI. So a supply of money including gold and silver is important also.

The best way to start out with the acquisition of precious metals is to buy junk silver coins. Those are coins that were minted prior to 1965. After that date, the silver content was gradually reduced until there is none left now. Silver is at a low price and the gold/silver ratio is very high. That makes the ownership of silver very attractive right now. Gold and silver will always have value, no matter what happens to the rest of the economy. And the best way to store these coins is to rent private storage boxes.

It is critical to prepare food/water/fuel/money storage particularly because many in the church and most outside the church do not have a years supply. That sounds strange given the fact that we have been encouraged to acquire one, it being preached for many years. And yet it seems that the majority of Latter-day Saints, right now, **are not prepared** in this simple but important way.

Let us pass on to a patriotic theme. Just what is so great about the U.S. Constitution? How does one recognize constitutional principles in statements by candidates and when laws are passed? We will deal with those topics next.

Chapter 11

Whoever will introduce into public affairs the principles of
Christianity will change the face of the world. —Benjamin Franklin

...Where the Spirit of the Lord is, there is Liberty
2 Cor. 3:17

In an obscure Maryland history textbook printed in 1856 is a fascinating story about the father of our country, George Washington. This story is unknown by many nowadays, but was well known by most one hundred years ago. The founders of our country were inspired and preserved in their lives so that God could reveal to them His design for a government of men that held sacred human liberty and by that created the greatest nation in the history of the world.

The story starts with a young George Washington who fought on the side of the British in the French and Indian War that preceded the American Revolution by about twenty years or so. Washington, 23 years old and a major in the Virginia Militia, commanded a force of colonial soldiers under a British General named Braddock. There were about 300 Americans and 1,000 regular British troops. They were told to march to Fort Duquesne, later called Pittsburgh, and take it from the French.

On July 9th, 1755, about 8-10 miles from Fort Duquesne they were ambushed by about 300 French and Indians. It turned into a massacre. Most were killed. A little over 300 men survived. The problem was that the French and Indians fired from behind rocks and trees while Braddock insisted his men stand up in a line in the open and return fire. The estimate was that only about 30 French and Indians were killed. There was confusion, with some men deserting and others refusing to obey orders.

218

The amazing thing was that of all the officers, George Washington was the only officer not killed. He continued to shuffle back and forth with orders from Braddock and to ride back and forth behind the men to inspire them. He was in peril the whole time. In all, about sixty officers died but Washington never received a wound. Here is his version of the encounter, as written to his mother, Mary Washington:

> The General was wounded, of which he died three days after. Sir Peter Halket was killed in the field, where died many other brave officers. **I luckily escaped without a wound, though I had four bullets through my coat, and two horses shot under me.** Captains Orme and Morris, two of the aids-de-camp, were wounded early in the engagement, which rendered the duty harder upon me, as I was the only person then left to distribute the General's orders, which I was scarcely able to do, as I was not half recovered from a violent illness, that had confined me to my bed and a wagon for above ten days...
>
> Letter to Mary Washington,
dated July 18, 1755

It was a huge defeat but the story doesn't end there. Some fifteen years later, Washington was again in the vicinity when he heard that a local Indian chief wanted to talk to him. The chief came from a long distance just to meet Washington, which was slightly surprising, since Washington could not remember having befriended any Indians before. When they finally met, the chief said, "You don't know me, we never met face to face, but fifteen years ago we met in battle in this valley when Braddock was killed. I was over the Indians who fought the British here."

"We knew the value of killing the commanders so as to demoralize the troops, so I told my braves to shoot the officers first. After killing all we could see, you were the only one left. We all tried to bring you down, and I myself shot at you seventeen times but could not kill you. When I saw you couldn't be killed, I ordered my men to stop wasting powder and shot on you. I recently heard you were coming here and I had to arrive to see with my own eyes the man God would not let die." Add to that the fact that after the Revolutionary War, many men of means urged George Washington to declare himself King of America. He quietly refused, although he could have done so with almost unanimous public acceptance.

This, dear reader, is the caliber of man who we fondly call the Father of our country. You may have heard disparaging stories about him and the other founders, but you have to compare that to the following scripture: "And for this purpose have I established the Constitution of this land, by the hands of wise men whom I raised up unto this very purpose, and redeemed the land by the shedding of blood." (D&C 101:80)

They were wise and good men, inspired of God to give succeeding generations the precious gift of liberty. How we take that freedom for granted! How many people were and are willing to risk their very lives to have but a taste of the liberty that we drink to our fill on a daily basis. And another fact about the founding fathers is that they paid dearly, many of them, for having the courage to stand for liberty against the mightiest nation on earth at the time.

Here is an article from the BBC news dated July 3, 1999, eloquently manifesting the sacrifices of our founding fathers:

> This Sunday we'll celebrate Independence Day. But have you ever wondered what happened to the 56 men who signed the Declaration of Independence?
>
> Five signers were captured by the British as traitors, and tortured before they died. Twelve had their homes ransacked and burned. Two lost their sons serving in the Revolutionary Army, another had two sons captured.
>
> Nine of the 56 fought and died from wounds or hardships of the Revolutionary War.
>
> They signed and they pledged their lives, their fortunes, and their sacred honor. What kind of men were they?

Twenty-four were lawyers and jurists. Eleven were merchants, nine were farmers and large plantation owners, men of means, well educated. But they signed the Declaration of Independence knowing full well that the penalty would be death if they were captured.

Carter Braxton of Virginia, a wealthy planter and trader, saw his ships swept from the seas by the British Navy. He sold his home and properties to pay his debts, and died in rags.

Thomas McKeam was so hounded by the British that he was forced to move his family almost constantly. He served in the Congress without pay, and his family was kept in hiding. His possessions were taken from him, and poverty was his reward.

Vandals or soldiers looted the properties of Dillery, Hall, Clymer, Walton, Gwinnett, Heyward, Ruttledge and Middleton.

At the battle of Yorktown, Thomas Nelson, Jr., noted that the British General Cornwallis had taken over the Nelson home for his headquarters. He quietly urged General George Washington to open fire. The home was destroyed and Nelson died bankrupt.

Francis Lewis had his home and properties destroyed. The enemy jailed his wife, and she died within a few months.

John Hart was driven from his wife's bedside as she was dying. Their 13 children fled for their lives. His fields and his gristmill were laid to waste. For more than a year he lived in forests and caves, returning to his home to find his wife dead and his children vanished. A few weeks later he died from exhaustion and a broken heart.

Norris and Livingston suffered similar fates.

Such were the stories and sacrifices of the American Revolution. These were not wild eyed, rabble-rousing ruffians. They were soft-spoken men of means and education. They had security, but they valued liberty more. Standing tall, straight and unwavering, they pledged: "For the support of this declaration, with firm reliance on the protection of the divine providence, we mutually pledge to each other, our lives, our fortunes, and our sacred honor."

They gave you and me a free and independent America. The history books never told you a lot of what happened in the Revolutionary War. We didn't just fight the British. We were British subjects at the time and we fought our own government! Some of us take these liberties so much for granted...We shouldn't.

So, take a couple of minutes while enjoying your 4th of July holiday and silently thank these patriots. It's not much to ask for the price they paid...

We should thank God for the wonderful men He placed here to give us the gifts of liberty and freedom. They deserve our gratitude. The fact is that God has blessed us with an inspired Constitution that was given as a precursor to the restoration of the Gospel. We in the LDS community understand that for that idea has been preached from the pulpit since the beginning of the Church. Apparently the Lord wanted to establish a country that allowed freedom of worship so as to be able to bring forth the purity of the Gospel again, in relative freedom.

Read this quotation from a talk given by Elder Ezra Taft Benson:

> Following the drafting, the Constitution awaited ratification by the states. In 1787 three states ratified it. The next year, eight more followed; and on **April 6, 1789, forty-one years before the restoration of the Church, the Constitution of the United States went into operation as the basic law of the land** when the electoral college unanimously elected George Washington as the first president of the nation. **This date, I believe, is not accidental.**
>
> Harvard Ward, Salt Lake City, Utah
> September 8, 1977

The conspirators who want to destroy our Constitution try to downplay its divine nature. They desire us to believe that the founders were deists, for example, and not Christians. They try to convince us that the founders didn't go to church or that they didn't know their Bible. Another point we are to believe is that the founders erected a high wall of separation of church and state and intended not only that the government shouldn't foster any one religion, but also that religion not be allowed into government, especially the Christian religion.

The point being that if they can make us believe those lies, that might loosen our faith in the product of their collective intelligence, i.e., the Constitution. But the truth is that they were devoted Christians and knew their Bible well. In fact, they used the Bible in formulating the Constitution. And the separation of church and state, to the founders, had a different meaning than in the above paragraph.

Mull over the following quotations of our founding fathers, concerning Christianity in government and come to your own conclusion:

> Providence has given to our people the choice of their rulers and it is the duty as well as the privilege and interest of a Christian nation to select and prefer Christians for their rulers. —John Jay, first Chief Justice of the Supreme Court.

> ...reason and experience both forbid us to expect that national morality can prevail in exclusion of religious principle. —George Washington in his farewell address.

> The reason that Christianity is the best friend of government is because Christianity is the only religion that deals with the heart. —Thomas Jefferson (Meaning that Christianity was the only religion that prevented crime because all crime comes from the heart and if you have a religion that prevents feelings or thoughts of crime, you will never have to deal with the crime itself).

There are many others, but these will do. Not only did the founding fathers believe that Christianity was an integral part of the government they founded, but the Supreme Court reiterated that sentiment also, in decision after decision. Ponder these rulings:

In 1892, a case came before the Supreme Court of a religious body that contended that there should be complete separation of church and state, meaning that Christianity should be taken out of government. (Sound familiar? Like today's headlines?) In their decision, the Supreme Court listed 87 examples of statements made by the founding fathers of the deep connection between Christianity and the formation of our nation. Then the court said that they could have listed many more, but what they did list was enough to prove the point that the founders were deeply Christian and they meant for the nation to be Christian. Then they said the following:

> Our laws and our institutions must necessarily be based upon and embody the teachings of the Redeemer of mankind. It is impossible that it should be otherwise; and in this sense and to this extent our civilization and our institutions are emphatically Christian. —Church of the Holy Trinity v. United States, 1892.

Or how about the case of a school that advocated the teaching of morality without preaching a particular religion? The Supreme Court said this:

> The purest principles of morality are to be taught. Where are they to be found? ...Whoever searches for them must go to the source from which a Christian man derives his faith—the Bible. —Vidal v. Girard's Executors, 1844.

In 1811, a man who hated God and Jesus Christ began to publicly blaspheme their names. Not only did he say negative things about them, he printed and circulated his opinion. He was arrested for blasphemy and his case went all the way to the Supreme Court. Here's what they said:

> Whatever strikes at the root of Christianity tends manifestly to the dissolution of civil government. An attack on Jesus Christ is an attack on Christianity, and an attack on Christianity is an attack on the foundation of the government of the United States. — People v. Ruggles, 1811. (The man got three months in jail and a $500 fine.)

And what about the contention that there should be a wall of separation between church and state? The founders had a different view than the courts of today. In our day, the courts have ruled that not only should government stay out of religion, but that religion should stay out of government. That's why they ruled in Engel v. Vitale (June 25, 1962) that prayer should be taken out of public schools. In it, they said that the founding fathers intended for there to be a high wall of separation of church and state. The Supreme Court in 1962 cited a ruling made in 1947 (Everson v. Board of Education) in which the court quoted a letter written by Thomas Jefferson in 1802 that used the phrase "separation of church and state." But they used it out of context. Here is what Jefferson said, then we'll see what he really meant.

In Oct. 27, 1801 the Danbury Connecticut Baptist Association heard a rumor that the Congregationalist denomination was about to become the national religion of the United States and wrote to Thomas Jefferson with their concerns. The rumor, of course, was false and Jefferson returned a letter on Jan. 1, 1802 to assure the Danbury Baptists that they need not fear such an event from ever occurring.

The part of the letter quoted by the Supreme Court in 1947 was this: "I contemplate with sovereign reverence that act of the whole American people which declared that their legislature should 'make no law respecting an establishment of religion, or prohibiting the free exercise thereof,' thus building a wall of separation between church and State."

Now we must ask, did Jefferson mean? There are two interpretations on that statement. 1. That not only should the government stay out of religion, that is, to not sponsor a state religion, but that religion should also stay out of government, meaning no school prayer, bible reading, etc. (Complete separation doctrine).

And 2. That the separation of church and state is one—directional. That is, the government shouldn't promote one religion over others but that Christian teachings have a rightful place in government. (Partial separation doctrine).

Which way did Jefferson mean the phrase, "thus building a wall of separation between church and State?" Knowing what he really meant helps us to determine which course to take today, if we want to be faithful to the original intent of the Constitution. The Supreme Court in 1947 seemed to want to do just that, by quoting Jefferson in the first place.

So which way did he mean it? Well, we can determine what he really meant by examining both what he said elsewhere that sheds light on the issue of separation, as well as what he did while in public life. That is, his words and his actions may help clarify the situation. Let us examine two quotations that essentially say the same thing:

"In matters of religion, I have considered that its free exercise is placed by the constitution independent of the powers of the General [i.e., federal] Government. I have therefore undertaken, on no occasion to prescribe the religious exercises suited to it; but have left them, as the constitution found them, under the direction and discipline of State and Church authorities acknowledged by the several religious societies."

Jefferson's second inaugural address, March 4, 1805.

On January 23, 1808, Jefferson wrote in response to a letter received by the Rev. Samuel Miller, who requested him to declare a national day of thanksgiving and prayer:

"I consider the government of the United States as interdicted by the Constitution from intermeddling with religious institutions, their doctrines, discipline, or exercises. This results not only from the provisions that no law shall be made respecting the establishment or free exercise of religion [First Amendment], but from that also which reserves to the States the powers not delegated to the United States" [Tenth Amendment].

Certainly no power to prescribe any religious exercise, or to assume authority in religious discipline, has been delegated to the General [i.e., federal] Government. It must then rest with the States, as far as it can be in any human authority."

Jefferson is saying that the Federal Government has no power to legislate anything pertaining to religion because that was not granted to it by the First Amendment. Any religious questions may only be taken up by the states, because of the Tenth Amendment.

In the days of the founders, their view was that the Congress was the initiator of everything. That is, if the Congress passed a law, then the Executive Branch could carry out that law and the Supreme Court could rule on its constitutionality. But if the Congress passed no laws concerning religion, for example, then the Executive Branch couldn't execute the law nor could the Supreme Court rule on it. So what the Supreme Court did in the case of Engel v. Vitale in 1962 was a usurpation, for Congress never passed any kind of religious law on which the Court could rule.

So Jefferson thought that the Federal Government should just stay out of all religious questions. But there's more to this question than just quotes from Jefferson that repudiates the modern idea of total separation of church and state, but there's also something he did while President that really shows what he meant about Christianity in schools. While President of the United States, Thomas Jefferson was also made president of the Washington D.C. school system. As president of the school system he did something he never could have done as President of the country. Jefferson placed the Bible and Isaac Watt's hymnal in the system as the two primary reading texts! So from that we can see what Jefferson really meant by his "separation of church and state" quote.

Also, in the 1962 case, the Supreme Court quoted no precedents. Why is that important? Because normally, when the high court makes a decision, it must quote former court rulings as precedents so as to give their opinions legal weight. The court does it all the time. They rarely decide a case without quoting a precedent. But that's what happened in 1962. The court in 1962 cited zero precedents. They couldn't, except for the 1947 decision, which was misquoted.

And the funny thing about the 1947 decision was that the justices were influenced by the doctrines of William James, the father of modern psychology. James was opposed to religious principles in both government and education and sought a complete separation.

Please read from this article called "Separation of Church and State" by Charles A. Fuller, Jr. (July, 1992):

> (William) James, like Adolph Hitler, recognized the power of repetition in getting people to believe lies. He said, "There's nothing so absurd that if you repeat it often enough, people will believe it." Similarly, the Supreme Court and the mass media have used that technique so successfully that they have indoctrinated the bulk of the American people into believing the Constitution and the Founding Fathers favored removal of religion from both government and education. Nothing could be further from the truth, and in fact, one dissenting Supreme Court justice wrote in 1958 that "if this court doesn't stop talking about separation of church and state, someone's going to think it's part of the Constitution."

> ...Again, let me quote Thomas Jefferson, **six years** after his letter to the Danbury Baptists. Letter to Samuel Miller, Jan. 23, 1808: "I consider the government of the United States as interdicted by the Constitution from intermeddling with religious institutions, their doctrines, discipline, or exercises. This results not only from the provision of law that shall be made respecting the establishment or free exercise of religion, but from that also which reserves to the states the powers not delegated to the U.S. government [10th Amendment]. **Certainly no power to prescribe any religious exercise, or to assume authority in religious discipline, has been delegated to the general government. It must then rest with the states as far as it can be in any human authority.**"

> ...in order to destroy America and turn it into a socialist paradise, it is first necessary to destroy Christianity by eliminating the people's faith in God and replacing it with faith in government.

What better way to do this than to banish all references to God and Christianity in the public schools as the Supreme Court has done repeatedly? In 1962, our anti-American Supreme Court banned school prayer; in 1963 it outlawed Bible reading, and in 1980, it outlawed the posting of the Ten Commandments in schools where children could see them. The extreme danger which the absence of moral and religious instruction poses to a nation was well recognized by John Adams who wrote:

"We have no government armed in power capable of contending with human passions unbridled by morality and religion. Our Constitution was made only for a moral and religious people. It is wholly inadequate for the government of any other."

Here are excerpts from two other Supreme Court decisions:

June 17, 1963, Abington v. Schempp (outlawing Bible reading in schools): "if portions of the New Testament were read without explanation, they could be, and have been, psychologically harmful to the child." (Imagine things like "Do unto others as you would have them do unto you" as being psychologically harmful to children. If they listen to and practice such teachings, we wouldn't have the school violence we have today).

1980, Stove v. Graham, Kentucky (outlawing the passive display of the ten commandments in school): "If the posted copies of the Ten Commandments are to have any effect at all...it will be to induce schoolchildren to read, meditate upon...perhaps to venerate and obey the Commandments. **This is not a permissible objective**." (Here the court says that obeying the Commandments is not a permissible objective. Then are they saying that they really want schoolchildren to disobey the Commandments, like "Thou shalt not kill" or "Thou shalt not steal)?"

Lastly, the founders not only wanted Christian principles in government, they actually built our Constitution right out of the Bible! For instance, the most fundamental idea found in the Constitution is the idea the government will be divided into three separate branches, judicial, legislative and executive. That came from Isaiah 33:22:

> For the Lord is our judge, the Lord is our lawgiver, the Lord is our king; he will save us.

The idea for tax exemption for churches came from Ezra 7:24: "Also, we certify you, that touching any of the priests and Levites, singers, porters, Nethinims, of ministers of this house of God, it shall not be lawful to impose toil, tribute, or custom, upon them."

And the idea behind the separation of powers came from Jeremiah 17:9: "The heart is deceitful above all things, and desperately wicked: who can know it?" The idea being that if people can be evil, then rulers can also be evil. And if that is true then evil rulers should be hampered or restrained by distributing power among different bodies.

All the above information goes to prove beyond a shadow of a doubt that this nation was founded by Christians and Christianity was the very foundation of the Constitution and government. For further investigation into the questions of the Christian underpinnings of our form of government, please view the video titled, *America's Godly Heritage* by David Barton.

Never before in the history of mankind have documents such as the Constitution and the Declaration of Independence been produced. The closest thing to it seems to be the Magna Charta, but despite the fact that it is a noble document attesting to the sovereignty of the people over the crown, it pales in comparison with the depth, scope and inspiration of the Constitution.

We will probably have to make the choice to defend the Constitution with force of arms at a future date. In order for us to do that, as Joseph Smith prophesied, we need to know what it is, what it contains, why it is so unique and what steps we can take to defend it. By learning about it, we may then extrapolate from it the principles by which the Constitution operates, so as to be able to identify constitutionally sound principles and laws when we encounter them in the real world, and forsake principles that are unsound. I think that is especially important for us in these last days.

For although the vast majority of Americans are enamored with the Constitution, as well they should be, most do not understand that the reason the Constitution has been so wildly successful is that it operates on two basic principles: 1. **The people** are sovereign in a society, not the state, and 2. Liberty is an inalienable right **that comes from God**, not the state. Those noble men, the founding fathers, understood these two principles intimately and produced a document to ensure that those two principles were incorporated into the Constitution.

It is precisely because they used those two principles into the Constitution that the United States of America has become the world power that it is. But that is not the most beautiful aspect of America. By and large, America, historically, was also the moral force for good throughout the world. It is by elevating the individual instead of the state that has given the U.S.A. its moral power. And as long as the laws of the nation continue to proclaim the liberty of the individual, and the leaders continue to uphold the principles of liberty embodied in the Constitution, America will flourish.

In addition to the aforementioned virtues of liberty and the sovereignty of the people, the Constitution of the United States have been blessed of God, and the lands of North and South America is a land of promise. His guiding hand helped shape the Constitution, and the Americas have been choice lands in the eyes of God since the beginning of time. The scriptures that prove that are numerous. Here are a few:

And now, we can behold the decrees of God concerning this land, that it is a land of promise; and whatsoever nation shall possess it shall serve God, or they shall be swept off when the fulness of his wrath shall come upon them. And the fulness of his wrath cometh upon them when they are ripened in iniquity.

For behold, this is a land which is choice above all other lands; wherefore he that doth possess it shall serve God or shall be swept off; for it is the everlasting decree of God. And it is not until the fulness of iniquity among the children of the land, that they are swept off.

And this cometh unto you, O ye Gentiles, that ye may know the decrees of God—that ye may repent and not continue in your iniquities until the fulness come, that ye may not bring down the fulness of the wrath of God upon you as the inhabitants of the land have hitherto done.

Behold, this is a choice land, and whatsoever nation shall possess it shall be free from bondage, and from captivity, and from all other nations under heaven, if they will but serve the God of the land, who is Jesus Christ, who hath been manifested by the things which we have written. (Ether 2:9-12; Also, 2Ne. 1:8,9)

These scriptures attest to the fact that the Lord has designated the Americas as choice lands and those that inherit these lands to worship Jesus Christ. If so, then God would never let any nation subjugate them. They would be free forever. And we can see the literal fulfillment of that prophecy. North and South America have no kings or emperors. Each country practices self-determination. That self-determination, of course, is being destroyed by those who want to establish a one-world government. And they are succeeding insofar as they influence the inhabitants of the Americas to leave behind the worship of God and Jesus Christ. And the more America stops worshiping Christ, the more they will succeed. That is why the destruction of religion, especially Christianity, is high on the conspirators agenda.

Now, how can we defend the Constitution if we don't know the difference between a constitutional principle versus an unconstitutional principle? They emerge in laws all the time. Let's let Elder Ezra Taft Benson answer that question.

Third: The powers of the people granted to the three branches of government were specifically limited. Originally, the Constitution permitted few powers to the federal government, these chiefly being the powers concerning "war, peace, negotiation and foreign commerce." All other powers were "reserved to the states respectively, or to the people." (Federalist papers, Number 45, by James Madison and Amendment 10.)

In other words, the Founders further provided for the limitation of power by decentralizing government to the state and local levels. This principle of decentralization constitutes one of the fundamental principles of our system of government. The intent of the framers was to preserve maximum "home rule"—to keep the power closest to the people. This was recognized as the only way in which the principles of self-government could operate effectively.

The Framers, from their own experience, knew that government could become a means of legalized plunder. Therefore, they specifically limited government's role to protective functions. Nowhere can you find in the Constitution the right granted to the federal government to redistribute wealth through taxation and to coerce people into participation in social welfare schemes.

Today, the federal government has assumed an unbridled power to achieve social ends. The chief weapon being used is "transfer payments," where the federal government collects through its tax system from its producers and transfers these funds to another group. Payments are made in the form of social welfare benefits such as Social Security, aid to Dependent Children, Medicaid, Housing Subsidies, Food Stamps, to name a few...

There is one simple test for the constitutionality of a principle: Do I as an individual have the right to use force on my neighbor to accomplish this purpose? If I do, then I may delegate that power to my government to exercise it in my behalf. If I do not have that right, I may not delegate it...

Valley Central Area Special Interest
Lecture Series
Harvard Ward, Salt Lake City, Utah
Sept. 8, 1977

Also, please take into consideration the following words by Elder Benson:

> Americans have always been committed to taking care of the poor, aged, and unemployed. We've done this on the basis of Judaic-Christian beliefs and humanitarian principles. It has been fundamental to our way of life that charity **must** be voluntary if it is to be charity.
>
> **Compulsive benevolence is not charity.** (i.e., forceful taxation for the purpose of redistributing wealth.) Today's socialists—who call themselves egalitarians—are using the federal government to redistribute wealth in our society, not as a matter of voluntary charity, but as a matter of right. One HEW official said: "In this country, welfare is no longer charity, it is a right. More and more Americans feel that their government owes them something." (U.S. News and World Report, April 21, 1975, p. 49.) President Grover Cleveland said it—and we believe it—"Though the people support the government, the government should not support the people."...society condones a dole, which demoralizes man and weakens his God-given initiative and character, can we?
>
> A VISION AND A HOPE FOR THE YOUTH OF ZION
> Address to Brigham Young University Devotional Assembly
> Tuesday, April 12, 1977

It is good to go over once more the one basic principle by which we may tell if a principle, law or philosophy is constitutional or not. Supposedly, the people are sovereign. If that is so, then the people may delegate some of their God given rights to the government to use. That is legitimate. But how can Joe Blow delegate to the government the right to forcefully take money from one man and give it to another when Joe himself doesn't have that right? It just doesn't follow.

We, as a nation, have followed the government's lead for far too long, in letting them promise the world and slowly letting them usurp control over us. Think for a minute. Has poverty gone down since the government began promoting social welfare schemes? Did the lot of the elderly improve when the government introduced Social Security? Does crime diminish when they pass more anti-crime laws? Government today holds enormous power over us. Is our lot better now, or worse for their intervention?

I think most would have to admit that things are either the same, or worse since government started to take over the social aspects of our lives in the twentieth century. But no matter whether an individual governmental program has been beneficial or not, one aspect of governmental intervention in social services needs to be noted.

That is, our government has definitely increased its power over our lives with every social service law passed. And that is the elusive touch-stone of knowledge here. It does not matter what the government promises to do for us, just as long as whatever it is, is accompanied by a loss of personal freedom. In other words, the government will never pass laws that result in greater freedom, responsibility or indepen-dence of the individual. Most government social programs are designed, by their nature, to bring the individual into subservience and make them more, not less, dependent on government. This was never envisioned by the founders, it is usurpation.

It is acknowledged that this information is hard to accept for most Americans. That is because we have been brainwashed, gradually, by the media to think favorably about government social service programs. Please do not be deceived by "new" legislation "designed" to help out in one social area or another. Accepting handouts from the government, no matter how well intentioned those handouts are, is gradual, eventual slavery. May God help us to be more discerning of the covert attempts by our misguided government to enslave us and of the secret combination that, at this moment, engulfs the world is my prayer. God bless this land to all who believe in freedom.

235

Appendix A

Here is the full text of Nic Outterside's original article for the Sunday Herald in Scotland:

The world's most powerful secret society is to meet in Portugal next week on the eve of the European election to carry forward its plans for a globalised world government.

Top of their agenda is a strategy to allow the UN to directly tax global electronic commerce to further internal reforms and strengthen its world-wide power base.

There are also proposals for the replacement of NATO forces in Kosovo with a "European Army."

The time has come to expose their agenda and awaken, political leaders to their threat.

Bilderberg, one of the most secret organizations in the world, comprising politicians, top industrialists and financial leaders, will meet on Thursday at a heavily guarded holiday complex at Sintra in the Estoril region of Portugal, the Sunday Herald has discovered.

Their high-powered conference takes place at a crucial time, just days before the European Union has spent years lobbying hard for a single European currency. Their wider agenda is to create a "one world" government.

The 120 Bilderberg delegates, under the Chairmanship of former NATO Secretary General Lord Peter Carrington and led by US Billionaire David Rockefeller and media magnate Conrad Black will meet to discuss a range of global issues.

According to a Bilderberg source, top of this year's "massive agenda" is a plan to tax global E-commerce with a slice going directly to the United Nations. This strategy will strengthen the current reforms of the UN and "assist the process of the world governance."

Other topics at this year's meeting include:

* addressing the deepening crisis in Kosovo, the "dismemberment of Yugoslavia" and the replacement of NATO with a European Army.

* the Asian economic crisis and plans to create an Asian economic and political block under the leadership of Japan.

* preparations for a Middle East peace settlement and the creation of a Palestinian state.

* the creation of an American Economic Union—a follow-up meeting has been timetabled for early next year in Quebec. This, claims the Bilderberg source, will be the first step to "full hemispheric union."

* the US stock market speculative bubble. An abrupt collapse could have devastating world-wide consequences.

* the development of a new "transatlantic marketplace" — stage two in the Bilderbergers' plans to begin incrementally knitting together the three global regional blocks into one global trading, monetary and political union.

* the extension of the EMU to Eastern Europe, and the early entry of Britain into this second common European currency system.

The Observer, editor-in-chief and political commentator, Will Hutton, who attended the 1997 conference said: "The Bilderberg conference is one of the key meetings of the year. The consensus established there is the backdrop against which policy is made world-wide.

"It is, in essence, a collection of people who are either up-coming or former top politicians and the cream of the world's business leaders—the conference is a well-argued talk fest," he said.

Hutton believes that the Bilderberg conference along with Davos [World Economic Forum] and IMF meetings provides the "common-sense background against which G7 takes its position."

He said the issue of 'globalization' would almost certainly top this year's Bilderberg agenda.

"Following the US-led screw-up in Kosovo we need better social protection and more military common-sense if the globalization aspired to by Bilderberg is to continue," he said.

The Bilderberg conference is credited with selecting and nurturing political talent. Tony Blair first attended in 1993 when he was a junior opposition spokesman and Bill Clinton attended the 1991 meeting in Baden-Baden, Germany before he announced that he was running for President.

The Bilderbergs control the central banks, such as the Federal Reserve in the US, and are therefore in a position to determine discount rates, money supply levels, the price of gold and which countries should receive loans.

Just as NATO has bound Europe and North America together militarily, so the Bilderbergers appear to have bound together American and European strategic and economic interests.

But their meetings and discussions are bound in the strictest secrecy.

According to the official Bilderberg line, the publicity black-out surrounding their meetings: "makes discussion more intimate and candid." There are no massive indiscretions, but exchanges can be quite heated. "Bilderberg is just a flexible and informal international leadership forum in which different viewpoints can be expressed and mutual understanding enhanced."

Critics claim the secrecy enables "this shadow world government" to plot their agenda which is then foisted upon the political movers and shakers of the western world.

"Their power and influence must not be underestimated," said Bilderberg watcher and Scottish TV producer Sara Brown.

"These men live and work in the shadows and they don't want it any other way."

Bilderberg meetings are only held when and where the hosts can provide the highest levels of security for their guests. Last year Mail on Sunday reporter, Campbell Thomas, was arrested and held for eight hours by Strathclyde police for daring to ask a hotel chambermaid about the Bilderberg conference being held at the Turnberry Hotel.

According to US journalist and Bilderberg specialist, Jim Tucker, all intruders to Bilderberg conferences are manhandled, cuffed and jailed, and if they resist arrest or attempt to flee, they will be shot.

After 45 years on annual secret get-togethers, the Bilderbergs are now facing some penetrating observation and questioning about their activities. Former BBC reporter, Tony Gosling, has spent the last two years campaigning for greater disclosure of the Bilderbergers' activities.

Along with Tucker and Canadian, John Whitley, he has compiled a massive dossier on their membership, organizational structure and political agendas.

He believes it is no coincidence that this year's conference falls on the eve of the European elections and G7 and G8 summits.

"With this roll-call of the richest and most powerful men in the world it is quite clear that their determination is to control the outcome of other political forums," he said.

"And when you consider the inclusion of senior representatives from the IMF and all the major central banks that power can be used and abused at will to control global decision making.

"It is all done in secret and is completely unaccountable," he added.

Washington reporter, Tucker, who has followed the activities of the Bilderbergs for more than fifteen years, says: "They want you to believe they are simply improving international relations. But they are controlling the world and making decisions that affect all of us with absolutely no democratic control on what they do."

Leading Tory Euro skeptic and Ludlow MP, Christopher Gill has led a personal crusade to expose the workings of the Bilderberg group.

"I believe there are some very powerful forces at work and their intension appears to be to undermine and destroy the nation state," he said.

"It is all the more sinister that when I ask questions about their activities I run into sand and don't get answers.

"Their agenda seems to be to promote world government. It is a difficult enough job fighting against a European super state but how, as an individual, one can counteract the activities of a group which seems determined to create one-world government is a major task of our times.

"I believe the only course is to try to convince one or other of the main political parties and their leaders to recognize the enormity of this threat to our democratic rights and to fight to defend them."

Gill has been supported in his quest to "out the Bilderbergs" by fellow Tory, Nicholas Winterton, MP.

Winterton has tabled numerous parliament questions asking government ministers for assessments of the power and influence of the Bilderbergs on world trade. Each time he has received either blank or "holding replies."

However, Euro skeptic and close political ally, Theresa Gorman, is less conspiratorial, claiming Bilderberg is little more than a rich club for superannuated freeMasons."

"These conferences are just a gigantic boondoggle," she said.

"I don't think any group like this can mould the world to one set of ideals — I think their importance is completely overplayed."

Last night Scottish academics also doubted the real power wielded by the Bilderberg conferences.

Anton Muscatelli, economics professor at the University of Glasgow said: "An off-the-record forum makes sense for this type of gathering. The last thing companies want is to be seen to have opinions that are politically loaded. Powerful companies are anyway going to have powerful influence."

Muscatelli said he was skeptical about the Bilderberg group's proposals for a global tax on E-commerce.

"Unless you ensured that every country went along with this, it would be extremely difficult to police. It really would require world collaboration."

"It seems a trifle ambitious," said David Bell, professor of economics at Stirling University. "I just don't see how you could make it workable."

Two pro-European British Tories who have attended Bilderberg conferences in the past were both "out of the country for the next week" when the Sunday Herald tried to contact them.

A spokeswoman for former Chancellor Ken Clarke—a UK representative on Bilderberg, who attended their 1993 and 1998 conferences — said he would return a telephone call to the Sunday Herald.

When told it was to discuss Bilderberg, the spokeswoman said Mr. Clarke was unavailable.

Sir Malcolm Rifkind—who attended Bilderberg in 1996—was similarly unavailable and "out of the country."

Scottish Conservative leader David McLetchie refused to discuss the issue of the Bilderberg conference.

NOTE: The Caesar Park Pengha Hotel and conference suites to be used by Bilderberg in Sintra lie adjacent to a huge leisure complex owned by British property millionaires John and Douglas Hall—the owners of Newcastle United FC.

And here is the story that was re-written by his editor without his permission:

The most mysterious—and possibly the most powerful—organization in the world will meet later this week in a resort in Portugal, which has been emptied of holiday-makers, to debate the great issues facing mankind.

The delegates attending the Bilderberg conference in Sintra, on the Estoril coast, will reportedly be protected by Portuguese army and police—with helicopters—while they discuss the shape of the next millennium.

Every year the international media competes to be the first to reveal the location and agenda of the conference, which brings together politicians—up-and-coming as well as established—business leaders, financiers, royalty and intellectuals.

Some people believe Bilderberg is a sinister conspiracy, a super-freemasonry which has planned such momentous events as the ascension of Margaret Thatcher—while others say it is just an international chat-fest. It is only interesting, they say, because the organizers are so absurdly secretive and because they manage to invite too many influential guests.

This year's conference, however, is given an added piquancy because it comes days before the European Parliament elections and G7 and G8 summits. Given that many of the 120 delegates will be major participants in these events, it might well shape them.

The winner of the Bilderberg scoop this year was a Portuguese newspaper, The News, which boasts that it is the country's largest-circulation English-language newspaper. It has published the location and the detailed agenda of the conference—although it admits with laudable candor that it was actually given this information by a publication called Spotlight, based in Washington, which believes Bilderberg is sinister and dangerous.

The News claimed, rather breathlessly, that the conference would open with "a review of the progress being made in the formation of an Asian bloc under the leadership of Japan. Free trade, a single currency and a political union similar to the European Union is planned for the region."

Then delegates would turn to "the installation of an American Union, similar to the EU, with a quick review of the scheduled splintering of Canada."

Next, continued The News, would be Kosovo: "They will discuss the formation of a greater Albanian state following 'trusteeship' of an 'independent' Kosovo, the dismemberment of Yugoslavia (by the return of its northern province, which has 350,000 ethnic Hungarians, to Hungary) as part of a general re-drawing of borders in the region (calculated to continue regional instability and conflict), and the reconstruction worth billions of dollars of the destroyed regional infrastructure at western taxpayers' expense."

Another item, the paper said, would be the "ultimate replacement of NATO with a Western European Union army, probably sooner than later due to the bad press NATO has endured over this current campaign."

It continued: "Efforts will be made to speed up the transformation of the Western European Union into a credible European military force initially relying on American back-up. This will complete American military disengagement from Western Europe and leave US forces available for wider global policing, if necessary, with WEU backup in return."

The News also claimed that delegates would debate a grand scheme of "global taxation" to finance the UN, though it is vague about the details of this extraordinary idea.

According to The News: "Bilderberg will pay hundreds of thousands of dollars to reimburse the Portuguese government for deploying military forces to guard their privacy and for helicopters to seek out intruders. Bilderberg delegates, comprising some of the world's most powerful decision-makers, will be here to discuss highly classified issues which are not supposed to be disclosed to the public by the press before or after the meeting.

"The News contacted the Caesar Park Penha Longa resort in Sintra to verify the information that the secret meeting will be held [there]. The only confirmation we received was that an organization 'wishing for the utmost privace' would be in Sintra and that the hotel was fully and exclusively booked by this organization from June 2 to June 7."

The newspaper continued: "Bilderberg meetings are only held when and where the hosts can provide the highest levels of security for their guests. All Bilderberg participants, their staff members and resort employees will wear photo identification tags. They will have separate colours to identify the wearer as participant, staff member or employee. A computer chip 'fingerprint' will assure the identity of the card's wearer."

The conference, which takes place annually, has been chaired for the past ten years by Lord Peter Carrington, the former British Foreign Secretary and Secretary General of NATO.

The Bilderbergers are credited with selecting and nurturing political talent. Tony Blair first attended when he was a junior opposition spokesman, and Bill Clinton attended the 1991 meeting in Baden-Baden, Germany, before announcing that he was running for US President.

The attendance register always includes high-powered men such as

Henry Kissinger; James Wolfensohn, President of the World Bank; David Rockefeller, the billionaire Chairman of the Chase Manhattan Bank; William Perry, the US Secretary of Defense; Martin Taylor, Chief Executive of Barclays Bank; Jean Chretien, the Prime Minister of Canada; Stanley Fischer, managing director of the IMF; and several royal heads of state.

Former guests are divided over the conference's importance. The Observer's editor-in-chief and political commentator Will Hutton, who attended in 1997, said: "The Bilderberg conference is one of the key meetings of the year. The consensus established there is the backdrop against which policy is made worldwide.

"It is in essence a collection of people who are either upcoming or are former world business leaders, and the conference is a well-argued talk fest," he added. He said the issue of "globalization" would almost certainly top this year's Bilderberg agenda.

"Following the US-led fiasco in Kosovo, we need better social protection and more military common sense if the globalization aspired to by Bilderberg is to continue," he said.

But some journalists believe that it does more than provide an opportunity to debate policy and swap ideas. Tony Grosling, a former BBC reporter, has spent the last two years campaigning for greater disclosure of the Bilderbergs' activities.

"With this roll call of the richest and most powerful men in the world, it is quite clear that their determination is to control the outcome of other ostensibly political forums," he said. "And when you consider the inclusion of senior representatives from the IMF and all the major central banks, that power can be used and abused at will to control any global political decision-making.

"It is all done in secret and is completely unaccountable," he added.

Leading Tory Eurosceptic and Ludlow MP, Christopher Gill is also suspicious. "I do not for one moment discount the possibility of there being some very powerful forces at work and that their intention is to undermine and destroy the nation state," he said.

Gill has been supported in his quest to "out the Bilderbergers" by fellow Tory MP, Nicholas Winterton, who has tabled numerous parliamentary questions asking for assessments of the power and influence they have on world trade. Each time he has received either "blank" or "holding" replies.

But others dismiss these fears as conspiracy nonsense. Anton Muscatelli, an economics professor at the University of Glasgow, said: "An off-the-record forum makes sense for this type of gathering. The last thing large companies want is to be seen to have opinions that are politically loaded."

He added: "Powerful companies are going to have powerful influence anyway." Conrad Black, the media magnate and a permanent Bilderberg member, was also dismissive. He has said in the past that secrecy ensures "intimacy and candor."

But although Bilderbergers might scoff at the conspiracy theorists, they only have themselves to blame for attracting such hostility. For example, at last year's Bilderberg meeting at the Turnberry Hotel in Ayrshire, the second time they had gathered in Scotland, they turned the 132-room, five-star hotel into a fortress.

The hotel was patrolled by police sniffer dogs, every vehicle was searched and armed police were stationed around the grounds. Meanwhile, journalists were told that the agenda, guest list and indeed even the menu were "confidential."

Appendix B

Here is an unusually candid speech by a former mayor of New York City.

The New York Times, March 27, 1922, prints New York City mayor John Hylan's speech stating:

The real menace of our republic is this invisible government which like a giant octopus sprawls its slimy length over city, state and nation. Like the octopus of real life, it operates under cover of a self-created screen. It seizes in its long and powerful tentacles our executive officers, our legislative bodies, our schools, our courts, our newspapers, and every agency created for the public protection. It squirms in the jaws of darkness and thus is the better able to clutch the reins of government, secure enactment of the legislation favorable to corrupt business, violate the law of impunity, smother the press and reach into the courts. To depart from mere generalizations, let me say at the head of this octopus are the Rockefeller—Standard Oil interests and a small group of powerful banking houses generally referred to as the international bankers. The little coterie of powerful international bankers virtually run the United States government for their own selfish purposes. They practically control both political parties, write political platforms, make catspaws of party leaders, use the leading men in private organizations, and resort to every device to place in nomination for high public office only such candidates as will be amendable to the dictates of corrupt big business. They connive at centralization of government on the theory that a small group of handpicked, privately controlled individuals in power can be more easily handled than a larger group among whom there will most likely be men sincerely interested in public welfare. These international bankers and Rockefeller—Standard Oil interests control the majority of newspapers and magazines in this country. They use the columns of these papers to club into submission or drive out of office public officials who refuse to do the bidding of the powerful corrupt cliques which compose the invisible government.

Secret Records Revealed, op cit, (226—227)

Appendix C

When the thirteen colonies were still a part of England, Professor Alexander Tyler wrote about the fall of Athenian (democracy) over two thousand years previous to that time:

A democracy cannot exist as a permanent form of government. It can only exist until the voters discover that they can vote themselves money from the public treasury. From that moment on the majority always votes for the candidates promising the most money from the public treasury, with the result that a democracy always collapses over loose fiscal policy followed by a dictatorship.

The average age of the world's great civilizations has been two hundred years. These nations have progressed through the following sequence: from bondage to spiritual faith, from spiritual faith to great courage, from courage to liberty, from liberty to abundance, from abundance to selfishness, from selfishness to complacency, from complacency to apathy, from apathy to dependency, from dependency back to bondage.

Alexander Tyler